Evil Scotland

RON HALLIDAY

THE AUTHOR

RON HALLIDAY IS Scotland's best-known writer on the supernatural and has been investigating all aspects of psychic phenomena for over twenty years. He is the author of four books on the paranormal including the best selling *UFO Scotland*, *A-Z of Paranormal Scotland* and *Scotland's X-Files*. Halliday regularly contributes to television and radio programmes not only in the United Kingdom but also across the world. He has appeared in many television and radio documentaries and his work has been serialised in national newspapers. He was for four years the author of the popular 'X Files' column in the *Evening Times*. Married with three children, Ron works in university administration.

Evil Scotland

RON HALLIDAY

Fort Publishing Ltd

First published in 2003 by Fort Publishing Ltd, Old Belmont House,
12 Robsland Avenue, Ayr, KA7 2RW

Typeset by S. Fairgrieve (0131–658–1763)

Printed by Bell and Bain Ltd, Glasgow

ISBN 0-9544461-4-3

CONTENTS

PREFACE   ix

1. WE ARE NOT ALONE!   1

2. CLOSE ENCOUNTERS: SCOTS, UFOS AND ALIEN
    ABDUCTIONS   19

3. SCOTLAND'S MOTHMAN AND OTHER
    PHANTOM BEASTS   40

4. BLOOD LUST   59

5. THE UNDEAD   79

6. MISSING: PRESUMED DEAD   97

7. THE DEVIL'S SPAWN   117

8. A LAND OF MYSTERY   133

9. THEY COULD HAVE BEEN SERIAL KILLERS!   151

10. DEADLIER THAN THE MALE: FOUR MURDERS
    THAT SHOCKED SCOTLAND   172

11. THE GAY SLASHER   189

12. THE FIERY CROSS: SCOTS AND THE KU KLUX KLAN   204

13. MURDER OR ACCIDENT? THE STRANGE DEATH
    OF THE DUKE OF KENT   220

PREFACE

A LAND OF mystery. That is how Scotland can be summed up and has been known since time immemorial. Where else in the world would you find such a bizarre collection of paranormal events from unidentified flying objects to loch monsters? In the twenty-first century the village of Bonnybridge in central Scotland is the reputed UFO capital of the world. And there is no better known monster of the deep than that of Loch Ness, which attracts investigators from across the world and was first encountered, and recorded, nearly 1,500 years ago. But that's only the beginning. Mysterious disappearances. Ritual murder. Phantom cats. Poltergeists. Mystic societies with roots deep in the Scottish establishment. Unexplained deaths. Is it true as some claim that Scotland is a window into another dimension? And that our land is an open door to visitors from other worlds? Whatever the truth, there are witnesses to some bizarre sights. Goblins. Dragons. Mothman. Alien entities. Fairies. Pan. Vampires. Just what is going in Scotland? And why do the authorities seem simply to ignore all those weird events? Are they a part of the cover-up? Are they terrified to admit these things are happening in case we, the public, start to panic? Or are they just as puzzled as the rest of us, but simply not willing to admit it?

It is said that ignorance is bliss, but that does not apply to those who have experienced the inexplicable and search for answers. To be abducted by aliens is difficult enough to make sense of, but then to have your experience ignored makes understanding the events that much more difficult. Witnesses simply want answers to the incidents they have been involved in.

In other cases, the truth has been covered-up or at the very least distorted either deliberately or through an inability to appreciate that the paranormal, or those who believe in the power of the supernatural, don't necessarily advertise the fact. The person who believes in the power of magic or in the mystical side of life may be closer than you think. As recent events have shown, people will kill to satisfy their belief in the power of ritual magic. The authorities simply fail to appreciate that the same can happen in Scotland. Evil does not have to have a supernatural link as the activities of some members of the human race all too clearly reveals. Nor does it have to be random. Murder can be carried out because certain individuals believe that they have a higher purpose to follow. Evil, deliberate or accidental, can take many forms as readers of this book will discover.

No book could be written without the willingness of those who have experienced events at first hand coming forward to tell their story. I would thank all those who I have interviewed or discussed particular events with over the years including Andrew Harvie, Tom McGovern, Fiona Martin, Mark Fraser, Hannah Fraser, Gary Wood, Mandy Maxwell, James Maxwell, Malcolm Robinson, Ian Shanes, James Welsh, Karen, Susan, Martin, Mike Johnson, Dr James Baird, William McRoberts, Margaret White, Mary Cuthbertson, Hamish Smith, Bob Taylor, Robert Lee, Liz, Amanda and Robert, Richard Adams, Dougie Bain, Katrina McNab and Steven Holt. I would also like to thank my wife Evelyn for her comments and suggestion on the text, her research, and trekking round Scotland with me to visit various sites! I would particularly like to thank James McCarroll of Fort Publishing for encouraging the writing of this book and for his many constructive suggestions on the content.

ONE

We are not alone!

'**GHOSTS WILL NEVER** harm you.' Most psychics hold to that belief. But people who have encountered these phantoms often tell a different story. Each of us may have a guardian angel but where, then, do poltergeists come from? For every person who has been saved by spirit intervention there is another that has been through a frightening ordeal. In the Braehead district of Irvine, a family was so traumatised in 1997 by events in their house that they ended up abandoning it in the early hours. Margaret White, aged 40, complained, 'We found ourselves walking the streets at two and three in the morning because we cannot sleep there. One of my neighbours put us up for a few nights because the kids refused to be in the house. My wee girl wakes up in the night screaming because she thinks there is some kind of evil spirit beside her. It is torturing our minds.'

Oddly, the house on a council estate was not on old one, but strange events appeared to have begun almost as soon as the first occupants stepped over the threshold. Disturbances had been reported over a period of eighteen years. Margaret and her family had been in the house for less than three months, but had already seen enough to convince them of the house's reputation. Phantoms kept appearing in different rooms. One was an old man, but the other looked like a young girl. There was no evidence that either had died on the premises. So where had they come from? And why were they so determined to upset Margaret and her family? For they went through a traumatic period of poltergeist activity. Doors would be continually slammed shut for no reason. A rocking horse in the children's room started moving all by itself. Voices would be heard within the bedroom during the night calling out names. Household electrical equipment switched itself on and off. Margaret and her visitors felt invisible fingers running through their hair. This was often followed by the noise of hands clapping and running feet almost as if the spirit had a solid body. But when the family saw the ghost-like presences they appeared almost transparent. Mary Cuthbertson, who lived in the house for several years, confirmed that the building was haunted. She reported: 'A number of times I saw the wee girl pulling the hair of my husband while he sat in the chair. She was definitely there although she was sort of transparent like an X-ray'. A ghost-like figure that seems more like a projection than a solid person but whose touch can be felt. An old man and a young girl, who appear to have no connection with the property, but who seem determined to cause upset to the people living there. Is the world of the ghost more complex than we believe? Are we simply dealing with phantoms of the dead or is there something altogether more sinister going on?

Why does poltergeist activity suddenly flare up in a house? Brian Mackenzie from Motherwell found himself plagued by a bizarre eruption of weird incidents after he moved into a new home. According to Brian:

Not long after we arrived strange things started to happen. Personal items like toiletries and ornaments went missing and never returned. After that three library books disappeared from the kitchen table. Sometime during the night footsteps could be heard going upstairs when I knew there was nobody else in the house. Another morning as I walked into the living room a small six-inch envelope shot off the table and landed flat on the floor. It then stood up and started whirling round like a spinning top. This went on for nearly thirty seconds. It then suddenly stopped and the envelope fell flat on the floor. I checked all the doors and windows and found them fully closed so it wasn't the wind.

For Brian this was an isolated incident, but some places seem to attract poltergeist activity. The village of Sauchie, lying just outside the town of Alloa within sight of the Ochil hills, has been the focus for several outbursts, cases that show that poltergeist incidents can be connected both to an individual and to a building. During the autumn of 1960 11-year-old Virginia went to stay with her elder brother and his wife in Sauchie. After going to bed on Tuesday 22 November she was disturbed by a thumping noise that sounded like a ball bouncing. She went downstairs to complain but the noise followed her into the living room. The next day several witnesses saw the sideboard spontaneously move several inches from the wall and then return to its original position. A local minister who was called in went to see Virginia as she lay awake in bed. As he spoke to her, violent knocking erupted from the headboard. A linen chest in the room rose off the floor and floated for several feet before returning to its point of departure. It was noticed that when Virginia fell asleep the disturbances stopped. There could be little doubt that in some way the incidents were linked to Virginia because they also occurred in school, and were witnessed by her teacher and several classmates. Desk lids rose by themselves when Virginia walked by. But strangest of all the teacher's cane was lifted into the air till it stood on one end, while the desk on which it was lying rotated through ninety degrees.

The energy generated by a girl approaching adolescence seems somehow to spark poltergeist activity. But in other instances it may either be the building itself, or the ground that it stands on, that allows something weird to come through. During a six-month period from the autumn of 1986 a terraced house in the same village was the scene of a frightening sequence of poltergeist incidents. The house, built in 1937, was occupied at the time by Mrs

Christine Park and her 18-year-old daughter Danielle. Christine's first odd experience came when she stood on a particular stair and suffered strange sensations including feeling dizzy. A few days later, and regularly afterwards, the sound of heavy footsteps echoed from the loft space above the house even though there could not possibly have been anyone there.

Christine repeatedly heard a swishing noise around the kitchen table with no obvious source for the sound. Most of these incidents seemed to occur when Danielle was at home. Her bedroom was always the coldest room in the house even in summer. One evening Danielle's boyfriend heard her calling his name from the upstairs bedroom. But when he went to her room there was no one there. In fact, she was lying asleep downstairs. Was a poltergeist mimicking Danielle's voice? If so it wasn't an isolated incident. Christine's mother claimed that she had heard the sound of her elder son Robert's voice shouting to her, even though she knew that he was not at home. Then Christine's mother, Mary, who was staying the night and had decided to get up early and make some tea, saw Christine walk into the kitchen wearing a flowered nightgown. Mary asked her if she'd like a cup. To her surprise, Christine made no reply but simply turned round and walked out again. When Mary asked her later that day why she hadn't replied Christine had no idea what she was talking about. She claimed that not only had she not gone downstairs, but also that she did not own a dressing gown like the one described by her mother. So just who had Mary seen? Could a poltergeist have been taking on the shape of another person?

Significantly, the family pet, a collie named Tessa, had refused from the moment they had moved in to go into Robert's bedroom. But one day Christine heard barking coming from the room. When she rushed upstairs she found Tessa inside with the door firmly closed behind her. Deep scratches scarred the wooden panelling below the handle, evidence of Tessa's frantic attempts to escape. She was clearly terrified. On the uncarpeted floor could be seen drops of blood which, it was later confirmed, had not come from Tessa. Robert was puzzled by the blood and had no idea how it got there. But it was the growling noises which came from a cupboard in Christine's bedroom that finally pushed the family over the edge. With nerves as taut as a guitar string they abandoned their bedrooms and set up camp downstairs.

Christine's house was in the middle of a block of three and, unusually, all three homes were affected by the outbreak. Next door, Elspeth Moir's television set began to switch itself on and off. The colour and sound buttons would operate as if they had a mind of their own. Elspeth also glimpsed a face that appeared in the glass door of a stereo unit. She did not recognise the reflection and there was only Elspeth and her son, Andrew, in the room at the time. Had she caught sight of a ghost? She couldn't be sure, but Andrew, though only 9 years old, seemed to have a partial solution to the mystery. He told his mother that for several weeks he had been woken in the middle of the night by a man and woman. The woman was holding a baby in her arms. The baby looked solid though he could see right through the couple. The woman kept asking Andrew his name and told him, 'don't be frightened of us'. She also told him that 'we don't like the dog next door. We shut it in that room so it wouldn't bite us or the baby.'

Incidents like those experienced by the Park and Moir families suggest that entities from other worlds can somehow interact with our own. But it doesn't explain why there was such a strong presence in the house, and one so determined to make contact. Christine and her family found the events too troubling and moved out. Eventually, the spirits seemed to quieten down too. Or had they simply moved elsewhere?

Less than a quarter of a mile away, and some thirteen years later, Mandy and James Maxwell were suffering sleepless night because of strange incidents plaguing their terraced house. It started soon after they moved in when they heard a rustling noise from a carrier bag by the side of the bed. When they saw it move they guessed that there must be a mouse inside, so James grabbed the bag and took it downstairs. But when he opened it, the bag was empty. Shortly thereafter, unexplained banging noises erupted. They were loud enough to give the impression that some invisible person was hitting the walls with a hammer. Worse followed, as James described: 'We heard the sound of a baby crying and a voice whispering in the hall cupboard. Another time I couldn't get the kitchen door open even though I tried it with all my weight against it.' Both James and Mandy would feel a presence in the kitchen and bedroom as if someone was standing next to them. But when they looked around the room was empty. Then there was the night, Mandy recalled, when 'the doors in the bedroom cupboard suddenly flew open for no reason and then kept opening and shutting all by themselves. My husband nailed them shut, but we decided to move into the front bedroom. She added, 'It's horrible being frightened in your own house.' A strange smell hung around the back room. The smell of death? A weird figure had been seen in the house. Mandy described it as 'a big dark figure. It looks like a man but I can't see any feet. It's strange and looks like it's made of water. We've seen it in the hall and at the top of the stairs.'

*

Poltergeist incidents do often seem to go hand in hand with sightings of weird phantoms. In 1989 odd incidents started to happen at the 'Outer Limits' disco in the Tollcross district of Edinburgh. The dance hall operated on two levels. The Bermuda on the ground floor and the Barbados suite upstairs. The halls were connected by two staircases, one for use by the public and a separate concealed staircase for staff. The Barbados suite seemed to be a target of poltergeist interest. Early-morning cleaning staff were terrified when the vacuum cleaner they took out started to glide across the floor even though it wasn't plugged in. It seemed as if an invisible hand was guiding it. As it moved around, disco lights on a gantry directly overhead flashed on and off for several seconds. At other times, a strange smell of burning would sweep through the suite and, as quickly as it had come, evaporate. Doors continually opened and shut all by themselves. Bottles and glasses stacked on the bar shelves would be discovered the following morning lying on the floor, often smashed to pieces.

Though it bore the brunt, incidents were by no means confined to the Barbados suite. Scratching noises and the high-pitched sounds of a woman's screams echoed though the empty building when locking-up time came. In the lower dance hall, the Bermuda, cleaner Hettie Graham experienced a distinct squeeze of her shoulder when there was no one else there. It was in the same hall that several members of staff having a tea break had noticed a shadowy phantom, dressed in black, hovering at an open door, a door that led to the back stairway used by staff. They even caught the phantom's reflection in the mirrors that decorated the walls. Staff were so frightened by the encounter that they refused to work on their own or to stay late. As is so often the case there was no dramatic end to the haunting. After a while the activity seemed to die down though never wholly ceased.

As events at the Outer Limits disco illustrate there appears to be no pattern to poltergeist activity. It can happen anywhere. In the Dreadnought Hotel in Callander guests who have slept in one particular bedroom on the first floor have reported an identical experience. Lying in bed they have the sensation of someone sitting down on the covers beside them. They can feel one side of the mattress sinking down. This happens in what used to be known as the 'Black Room'. It was here that a former owner is said to have thrown his pregnant mistress from the window to her death. In another room along the same corridor a child's face appears on a bedroom wall accompanied by the sounds of crying. A well still stands in the basement of the hotel, where tradition has it that a toddler was drowned during the last century. Could this be the source of the disturbance?

Psychics often take the view that the presence of ghosts can be linked to personal tragedy or suffering. This could explain events that began in Stirling in the 1980s and continued into the nineties. A restaurant in the town had been opened on the site of an old gaol. In fact many of the former cells dating from the eighteenth century were being used as store rooms. Through them had passed a legion of murderers on their way to the gallows. Could the spirits of these doomed men still be attached to the building where they met their fate? There were many witnesses to the events including Ann Coyle, the manageress at the time. Some of them were at the level of childish tricks. Forks and knives laid out by the staff the night before would be found in the morning knocked to the floor or rearranged in odd formations on the guests' tables. The bell above the entrance would ring of its own accord. Lights and electrical appliances would be switched on and off. Ghostly figures were seen and staff were reluctant to go into the storerooms alone because they sensed a hostile presence. Several staff claimed to have seen a grey-coated monk walk down the path to the restaurant although he never came through the door. One medium who visited the restaurant saw a young woman shackled to the walls of the cell. Imagination? When the owner had the wall renovated he discovered shackles and chains hidden beneath later brickwork. So had the psychic seen into the past or were the spirits of long-dead men and women still wandering the building?

Maybe to understand the frightening power of the ghost we should rethink what these phantoms of the night are really like. Ghosts can sometimes appear solid. More like real people than spirits from another age. And they don't just appear when the sun goes down. In the 1990s Dr James Baird, from Edinburgh, was on holiday in Plockton in Wester Ross with his wife and two young daughters. He had planned to go sailing, but though the weather had been generally warm, on this particular day it poured. Dr Baird cancelled the yachting trip and decided to take the family to Eilean Donan castle for lunch. As they headed out in their car along the single-track road with the rain lashing against the windscreen they caught sight of a small figure huddling at the side of the road. The elderly woman, wearing a green coat with hood, was clearly getting soaked from the constant downpour. Mrs Baird suggested that they could run her along the road, at the same time wondering what she could be doing alone, in the middle of nowhere with no house in sight. Would she like a lift? She accepted the family's offer after being told that they were headed for Eilean Donan. In the back the two daughters moved over to make space for their new arrival. A strange atmosphere seemed to envelop the car, as Dr Baird described: 'There was complete silence. No one spoke. But just about a mile further on our passenger suddenly announced, "You can drop me here." I looked around hoping to see the outline of a cottage but there was only wet heather on all sides. Reluctantly I stopped the car. Our passenger stepped out, turned and said, "This is fine here. Thank you very much", and closed the door.'

Dr Baird drove off in an eerie silence, broken only when his 10-year-old daughter, in a voice tense with emotion, said, 'that lady who was driving with us was very strange. Her coat was bone dry when she sat beside us and the seat was not even damp when she got out.' Baird immediately glanced in his mirror, but there was not a soul in sight. He then turned the car round and drove back to the spot where he had dropped the woman off. She was nowhere to be seen. A fact that puzzled the family because there was no obvious place she could have gone to. No building or tree where she could be sheltering from the rain or be hidden from view. She seemed to have completely vanished. Inquiries that day by Dr Baird revealed that a lady called 'Annie' had lived at the spot where his passenger got out. However, she had been dead for ten years.

The next day the family returned to the spot and found the evidence that confirmed what a local informant had told them. The rough foundations, hidden beneath long grass, of a long-demolished cottage. It had been 'Annie's' former home.

Dr Baird's encounter is not an isolated incident. In 1996, Bob Hambleton-Jones, a pilot, was standing in the foyer of Glasgow Airport when he saw a familiar face approach him. It was an old colleague, Robert Macleod, who he hadn't seen for a while. Bob shouted over to him, said a few words, noting that his friend of nine years' standing seemed a bit distracted. After chatting for a couple of minutes Robert suddenly announced, 'I must go now'. Bob bent down to pick up his luggage and when he turned back, Robert had disappeared. Bob thought nothing more of the encounter till the foll-owing day when he opened the morning paper and was stunned to read Robert Macleod's obituary. He had died several days before. When Bob ran into him at Glasgow Airport, Robert was long dead. But to Bob he had appeared as solid and real as any of his fellow air-travellers.

If these really were ghosts Bob Hambleton-Jones and Dr Baird met up with then it seems odd that they were continuing with their normal routines. Had they simply gone into another dimension without realising what had happened to them? Perhaps this could explain other events in central Scotland in the 1990s.

Music teacher Mike Johnson lived in an eighteenth-century mill cottage near the town of Clackmannan not far from Stirling. He described the events, which continue to puzzle him:

> There were several incidents including temperature changes. One time I went to open the living room door, but when I pushed the door it felt like someone was pushing back. I just couldn't get it open. In the end I went through the back window and found to my amazement that the door opened normally. You could push it with your pinkie. I have heard strange footsteps. I was lying downstairs in my bed when I heard the sound of someone walking on the floor above me. I knew there couldn't be anyone there as I was alone in the house. I was definitely awake at the time. I wasn't dreaming. Many of the incidents seem to be associated with that room I once used as a bedroom. There's a funny smell in the room even though it's been decorated. It's never changed. There's also a weird stain on the ceiling which I could never get rid of. Another time late at night I heard footsteps on the gravel drive and thought it was an intruder. I phoned the police and they arrived very quickly with sniffer dogs, but couldn't find anything. The police looked at me very strangely, but I'd definitely heard something.

In a display cabinet in his window stands a small leather boot. Mike explained:

> I found the boot lying in the back garden not long after I moved in, in 1991. It looked strange so it was sent to a museum. They confirmed that it was the boot of an 8-year-old girl dating from the 1880s. A visitor who was a medium said she saw the spirits of several people including a woman wearing a black blouse with long sleeves and a plain skirt. She also saw two men arguing and fighting and one was knocked to the floor. There were two children present, a boy and a girl. The boot could have belonged to the girl as the incident the medium saw happened in the same era as the boot dates from. Maybe it was a traumatic event and that's why the lass's spirit is still here. Some time after I discovered the boot I was given a photo which shows this cottage and in the window is a

strange-looking girl. She has fair hair which seems to be in pleats. It could be the spirit of the girl linked to this cottage.

Mike Johnson's experience involved a pattern of incidents, but often a ghostly encounter can be no more, or less, than a single unexplained event. Moira Robertson, from the Garthdee district of Aberdeen, experienced a bizarre incident in 1998:

> I don't know what time of night it was. I was sleeping in the spare bedroom. All I remember is opening my eyes, but because it was dark not seeing anything right away. I was hovering about two feet above the bed. I tried to shout but nothing would come out at first. I heard whispering-type voices and buzzing-type noises. I saw dark shapes around me. Then noises started to come out of my throat like a record or tape winding up, sort of slow motion. I tried to shout for help because I heard my partner in the bathroom. I was suddenly on the bed and could shout his name. He never saw anything or heard anything. I wonder if I had come-to too quickly before I was supposed to?

But could a ghost even start a car? In June 2002 shoppers in the car park of Safeway's superstore at Lerwick in Shetland were astonished when a driverless car suddenly roared into life. It shot out of its bay, drove on to the payment and only came to a halt when it hit another vehicle. Investigators called to the scene claimed that an 'electrical fire' under the bonnet caused a 'power surge' which somehow started the engine. The car had been left in gear so set off on its own, an explanation that raises more questions than answers. As one witness said at the time, 'I couldn't believe my eyes. I've never seen anything like it in my life.' There was no evidence that the area was an active haunt, but poltergeist incidents happen at any time and in all different types of location.

Even those more versed in the ways of the paranormal don't necessarily have the answers, as they would be the first to admit. Mark Fraser, an experienced ghost investigator, had his own unnerving experience. He had moved north to enrol on a college course at Aberdeen, and saw a cottage for rent near the Banffshire village of Keith and, with his wife Hannah, moved in. They hardly had time to settle down before they realised their mistake. Mark's wife saw blood seeping through the cottage walls. There was constant rapping on the windows and the sounds of doors being slammed. Voices could be heard, although Mark knew that no one else could possibly be there. The couple were overwhelmed by a constant feeling of oppression. One day Mark had a cup of coffee thrown at him by an invisible presence. The dogs the couple kept as pets were petrified of the place, and animals are always a good barometer of an evil presence. Mark had had enough and decided to leave. He later learned that a murder had taken place in the cottage and black magic practised in the area. There seems little doubt that attempting to contact entities from other worlds can bring unintended and unwanted results for those who arrive later on the scene.

But sometimes entities turn up for no obvious reason. In a Victorian tenement in Main Street, Falkirk a poltergeist got completely out of hand. Lisa, a single woman in her thirties, suffered a catalogue of strange experiences that culminated in a terrifying incident. It started one evening with a glowing light rolling over the carpet and a thick mist drifting through the flat. Brilliant-coloured balls appeared out of nowhere, hung in the air then simply vanished, an overture for what turned into a full-scale manifestation. Ornaments were moved around the flat by an invisible hand. One night Lisa awoke to find a hooded figure kneeling at the foot of the bed. What could be the explanation for these strange events? Lisa heard rumours that the bathroom, which had changed little through the years, had been the scene of the drowning of a 2-year-old child by a former occupant. A psychic brought in to investigate the events saw a vision of child's body lying in a pool of water beside Lisa's bed. He had deliberately not been told of the alleged murders linked to the flat, which made his evidence all the more compelling. One day Lisa discovered red stains which looked like blood on the handle of the living-room door. The whole episode came to a bizarre climax. She was woken late one night by a bright light shining from the wall at the foot of her bed. As she focused her eyes she noticed that the wall was lit up as if someone was projecting a film on it. Then she noticed a movement. Across the 'screen' danced a figure which she described as looking like a ballerina. Stunned and confused she got out of bed. She saw that the ballet dancer was now being chased by a strange entity. It was a frightening moment, but what followed was quite terrifying. Writing from an unseen hand started to appear. She saw the words 'You are' forming on the wallpaper in child-like hand-writing and decided not to hang around. She rushed out of the room and out of the house.

Lisa had been in her flat for some time before incidents got underway. But often the appearance of a new owner seems to spark off poltergeist activity. Gill, a bank employee, had been thrilled to buy her first home, a smart flat in a converted mill on the outskirts of Tillicoutry. In a short while the excitement turned to panic. Events began with incidents that Gill at first put down to her imagination. A dark shadow walked by and passed through the wall next to her as she knelt down to put on a music tape. Ornaments sitting on the mantelpiece in the morning would be found lying in the middle of the kitchen floor when she returned from work. In the bathroom, gel and toothpaste were smeared across the walls as if a prankster was playing silly tricks. But events reached a crescendo that no one could have found amusing. As Gill lay in bed one night she was disturbed by the noise of someone running around the room. There was no carpet on the floor so the sound was quite distinctive. Gill was so frightened that she didn't even dare look and hid beneath the covers through the entire night, only moving from the bed when dawn broke and the sounds of running stopped. Gill called in a spirit medium. The psychic told Gill that the disturbance was being caused by the spirit of a child who had died some years before in tragic circumstances. The toddler had fallen down a well that used to stand in the old mill grounds and had drowned before he could be rescued.

But not everyone's experience of a ghost's presence is unpleasant. Minette Anderson from Irvine had no fear of the child spirit that seemed attracted to her back garden. In winter tiny footprints would appear in the snow-covered grass, marks that would start and end almost as if a child had materialised from nowhere and disappeared halfway across the green. Curiously, Minette had lived in the house for thirty-four years before the first footprints appeared in 1996. There was no obvious explanation for their sudden arrival, but Minette had no doubt as to what she was seeing:

> You couldn't mistake the footprints. They were deep but very tiny. I would guess a child of about 3 years of age. They always point in a straight line. And there are always eight of them. They've never appeared during daylight, only when it's dark and snowing. I can't say there was any special reason why the footprints started appearing, but I feel it is a child which has adopted me. I wouldn't like to see my little friend go.

Minette was delighted by the appearance of her invisible friend, but why then are other people's experiences so traumatic?

*

In Johnshaven, a small fishing village south of Aberdeen, poltergeist activity reached bizarre heights. Ann was living with her children and mother in an end-terrace house overlooking the sea shore. This was no old decaying building with a history, but a relatively new home with all mod cons. Even so the family, who took over the tenancy during the 1990s, found themselves plagued by a series of events – incidents that contradict the views of those who believe that everything which happens in this world must have a rational explanation if we only look hard enough.

Events started about a month after Ann moved in. Until then she had been living in a tenement in Aberdeen. A move to less crowded pastures with fresh air and room for the children to play seemed like a good move. But that's not how it turned out. The first disturbances took place at night in Ann's own bedroom. She was woken by the sound of footsteps crossing the bedroom floor and the sensation that someone had jumped on to the bed. From the hall came the sound of children playing. She crept out to look but there was no one there. On another occasion, when Ann was sleeping with daughter Ruth, she heard padding noises on the stairs like a dog making its way up the steps. She was too nervous to get up to take a look. Then she heard the animal shake itself dry, followed by footsteps coming down the landing and a child's voice. Then both phantom dog and child disappeared back downstairs.

At around the same time objects started to go missing only to turn up several days later. It was if someone was playing mischievous tricks. Electrical appliances went haywire, behaving as if they had a mind of their own. The fire alarm started going on and off though a check showed no fault. And the cooker started doing the same though there was no obvious supply problem. More ominously, perhaps, doors slammed shut and somehow managed to lock all by themselves. One night Ann's eldest daughter was pushed off the bed and scratched by an invisible assailant. Ann realised the situation was getting out of control and causing the children genuine distress. Then a small girl Ann didn't recognise ran downstairs, crossed the living room and slowly vanished before her eyes. Although she appeared to be little more than a child Ann felt the atmosphere in the house change just as the girl arrived. The spirit lass gave off an aura of anger and nastiness. To Anne, the very air felt thick and wicked with an overpowering sense of gloom.

One Saturday in June, Ann took the short trip from her home to the local shop. She was out of the house for less than fifteen minutes. When she returned she discovered the kitchen worktops covered in maggots. Ann was shocked but managed to gather herself together and clean up the unwelcome visitors. Then the horror of the situation hit her. Where had the creatures come from? There seemed to be no logical explanation for their sudden appearance. It was as if they had emerged out of thin air. But why would anyone, even entities from another world, wish to torment someone in this way?

The house seems to have been 'activated' after Ann used a Ouija board. According to Scotland's top psychic, Ray Tod, by using the board Ann had drawn the spirits towards her. If these were indeed spirits of the dead, whether they meant to or not, they put Ann through real fear. One night while Ann was sleeping in her bedroom, a long narrow room, she woke up to the sound of voices though she knew that no one else was there. A black mist seemed to descend over her which she described as feeling 'like a blanket'. At the same time a blast of cold wind shot through the room. Through the wall which separated her from the children's bedroom, Ann heard the sounds of laughter and playing. But through the sound of childish talk came the distinct tones of an adult voice. Alarmed, Ann walked quickly through only to find the children had jumped into bed. They admitted that they had been playing. In fact they complained to Ann that they couldn't get to sleep because of people who kept appearing in their bedroom and making them take part in games. They told Ann that as soon as they heard her coming the 'visitors' disappeared again.

But it wasn't just Ann's family who had disturbing experiences in the house. Fifteen-year-old Lily was babysitting for Ann, and passing the time by watching television in the front room. She glanced out of the living room, and saw what appeared to be a mist rolling towards the house. The mist came straight through the window, hung in the air for a short while then started rotating. As it turned, it thickened and darkened until it looked like a small cloud. Watching in terror from the living room doorway Lily could make out shapes inside the mist. Black, solid-looking images of people. Somehow Lily managed to grab the phone and made a hysterical call to Ann. But by the time Ann arrived the mist had disappeared. Lily, however, had no doubt that what she had witnessed had really happened and was not a figment of her imagination. It was too weird to invent. After what she herself had experienced, Ann was in no mood to doubt Lily's story.

Had these phantoms deliberately set out to upset the household? Or was it pure chance that separate worlds clashed? And if so why did it happen in a house in Johnshaven? There are more obvious places where you would imagine these encounters would be likely to occur.

You'd expect to find ghosts in a graveyard, but, in fact, poltergeist activity is rarely linked to cemeteries no matter how old. There are exceptions, however. Edinburgh's Greyfriars Kirk, in the heart of the most ancient part of the city, has been a focus for the strangest burst of activity. A burial ground for centuries, the sloping area of land that runs between George IV Bridge and the Grassmarket is a compacted mass of decaying gravestones. But it also seems to have attracted invisible forces which resent the presence of the casual visitor. In the spring of 1999 visitors to the cemetery reported that they had been attacked by phantoms they couldn't see, but which were solid to touch. Several claimed to have been knocked to the ground. One, a college lecturer, felt a hand press over her mouth. The following day bruises she couldn't explain appeared on her cheek and neck. By November of that year there had been so many reported incidents that a minister, the Revd Colin Grant, held an exorcism. As he went through the ritual, a shadowy figure was seen moving at the church window. There could be no certainty that this 'presence' had any connection with the events in the graveyard, but after the night's ritual was completed the level of poltergeist activity did fall from its earlier frantic levels. It has not, however, entirely stopped.

Hotels, pubs, homes and graveyards. Ghosts seem to visit them all. But even the unlikely setting of a museum can be a focus for paranormal events. In 1998 Bill Mutch, at that time a security guard at Glasgow's Museum of Transport, reported a wide range of bizarre activity in the building. It centred on the museum's prize exhibit, the recreation of a 1930s city street complete with shops, cinema and underground railway station. Bill claimed:

> Things happen here all the time. I've been on duty late at night and heard footsteps echoing down the road as if someone was running hard. Another time I was at the far end when the sounds of a man limping went by. His leg was being dragged along the ground. I've also seen a tall dark shadow go into the model toyshop. I have felt someone tapping my shoulder and heard the sounds of kids screaming beside the old steam trains. I don't know if any accident was connected with the engines. There's also been the sighting of a headless female figure in the old cinema they recreated.

At the end of the street is a mural painted on the wall and Bill believed that this was the source of powerful energy. It had a direct physical effect on him, even to the extent of making him feel dizzy. There are some who argue that an unknown energy source explains ghost and poltergeist activity, that somehow other entities are activated through this energy. If this is true it means that ghosts could appear at any time in anyone's backyard. And though the phantoms that wandered through the Museum of Transport seemed harmless enough that was not Lee Hamilton's experience.

In the Ayrshire town of Stevenston, Lee Hamilton and her son were terrified by incidents linked to an old man who had once lived in the house. Lee claimed that, one evening in November 1999, as she was watching television, she 'went all numb. I felt as if there was something around me and I kept getting these strange feelings. I kept feeling as if someone was walking past me.' Her son Mark had no doubt as to who was causing it and told his mother that there was a strange man in the house. Lee wasn't sure whether or not to believe him, but the incidents continued to occur. Lee explained: 'One night I was convinced that someone had kicked my bed as I lay in it, but there was no one else but me and my two young sons in the house.' Mark once again tried to convince Lee that the strange man in the house was the cause of the problem. Events finally came to a head when Lee woke in the early hours of a Friday morning unable to move or talk. She described 'feeling terrified. It felt as if there was someone else in the room.' Lee had reached the end of her tether and phoned her mother. She contacted the police who escorted Lee and her children to her mum's house. Lee was determined that she would never go back to her own home.

So what is the 'real' ghost? The one that hardly notices your presence or the one that torments you day and night? It often seems that if you go looking for entities from the 'other side' they will respond, though not necessarily in a way you would like. John Anderson from Larkhall wrote of the time that he 'dabbled with a Ouija board and brought into the house a ghost who was hostile'. The spirit 'appeared as a woman who spoke to me. She kept telling me that she was going to kill me.' That didn't happen, but John's experience should serve as a warning that we should be wary of tampering with dimensions that even now we don't fully understand.

TWO

Close encounters: Scots, UFOs and alien abductions

FOR OVER FIFTY years people across Scotland have been reporting sightings of strange flying objects. Many of these have been close-up encounters with disc-shaped craft which witnesses are convinced did not originate from this earth. So are we being visited by alien beings from other worlds? And could this even be happening with the connivance of the military and government authorities? Has there been an organised conspiracy to cover up the reality of an alien presence from the Scottish people?

The evidence that something unexplained is going on seems incontrovertible. Take the case of Gary Wood and Colin Wright who went through a strange ordeal on the night of 17 August 1992. The evening started innocently enough, as Gary Wood recalled:

> The receiver on my satellite dish blew and I rang my friend Ian Phillips out at Tarbrax village to see if he could help. Another friend, Colin Wright, arrived just as I was getting ready to go. We

set off around 10 p.m. As we drove along the A70 in West Lothian we came to a sharp bend in the road. Suddenly, Colin pointed to something overhead. The object was floating twenty feet above the road. It was black in colour, shiny and about thirty-five to forty feet across. It looked metallic. It wasn't making a noise but on seeing it I got really frightened. The thought went through my head, 'If I stop this car something will run up and grab me'. I really felt as if my life was being threatened. I just wanted to get away. I accelerated under the object and I could see things hanging from it. A shimmering light came down, the exact width of the road. And then I wasn't in the car. I was thinking, 'Where's the car? Where's Colin?' I could see only blackness and really thought I was dead. Then I was back in the car on the wrong side of the road with Colin screaming. 'Did you see it?'

Wood remembers driving at speeds of over ninety miles per hour to Ian Phillips's house and hammering on his door. Then came the next shock. It was now 12.45 a.m. A journey which should have taken forty-five minutes at most had inexplicably lasted three times as long.

For weeks after, Gary suffered nightmares. One morning he found himself nearly a mile from his house, half dressed and dazed. Puzzled and worried, he tried to make sense of his encounter and why time was missing from his life. The problem was how to recover the memory of this lost time. Gary decided to undergo hypnotic regression, hoping to discover what had happened between seeing the UFO and landing back in the car.

He went through several hours of hypnosis and though a bizarre tale emerged, Wood could now at least fill in the gaps:

I felt I was in my car and it was like being electrocuted, as if my muscles were being pulled in on me. I saw three wee men coming towards the car. Then there was a taller entity, six to seven feet, translucent like a grey-white colour. It came close to me and said, 'I've got a life like yours but different.' What it was trying to tell me was, 'look, I'm not a monster'. There was also a brown-coloured being with a heart-shaped head and folds of skin, about four feet in height. It looked ancient.

The entities also appear to have put Gary through some kind of medical examination. 'I saw two objects go away from my chest. At the same time the entities were looking at my left leg. I couldn't move at all during this time. There was an object right inside my ear making a humming noise.'

During his ordeal, Wood lost sight of his friend, Colin Wright, but he did see someone else: 'There was a naked female on the ground, in her early twenties with blonde hair. She was trying to cover herself up. She was very distressed. Her eyes were red with crying.' That woman, if she does have a conscious memory of the incident, has never come forward. But if Gary was experiencing a genuine event she must have come from somewhere and, one would guess, from an area close to where he encountered the shimmering object. Gary found the sight of this woman in her distressed state disturbing, but what happened next must have been truly frightening: 'There was a hole in the ground full of gel-like paste. There was something moving in it and then this thin grey creature rose out of it.'

So are alien beings from other worlds really interfering with our lives? Visiting people at will to carry out bizarre experiments? From all over Scotland there is mounting evidence, however hard the authorities may try to deny it, that something strange is happening.

Susan, who lives close to the town of Burntisland on the Fife coast, can testify to that. She remembers quite clearly the bizarre series of events which disrupted her life. And how it all began one afternoon in December 1997 while she was alone with her baby son in the back room of their bungalow. She explained:

> All of a sudden I was overcome by the strangest sensation. I felt that I was no longer inside the house but had been transported to another place. I felt that there were people or entities of some kind surrounding me although for some reason I could not see them. Whoever or whatever they were there was no doubt of their interest in me because I could feel them poking at me around the area of my genitals. I tried to push my hands down to see if my trousers had been opened, but I couldn't move my arms. I began to feel panicky and started flailing about. But the pushing on my genitals didn't stop. It was very sore and uncomfortable. Then I

had a falling sensation and I was back in the chair. Bobby was where I had left him sleeping on the settee. My tongue felt swollen in my mouth and I felt disorientated. I glanced at my watch which was still on my left wrist and was shocked to discover that two hours had passed since I had sat down. It felt like just two minutes.

Of course, the authorities can hide behind the claim that 'nothing really happened, they just imagined it' and carry on as if the whole phenomenon is of no interest. But why, if that really is their view, have the military scrambled jets to investigate unidentified objects? And what do they do with the information they gather? In April 1995 a commercial pilot, Iain Ray, brought his cargo into Edinburgh Airport right on time at 1 a.m. It had been a trouble-free flight, but as Ray taxied off the runway he became aware that British Airways security staff were in a state of high alert. It appeared that air traffic control had tracked an unidentified object on radar, which then hovered close to the airport. Visual sightings from ground witnesses confirmed the presence of the UFO. Curiously, however, a cargo plane coming in to land, asked to take a look, could not detect the object. It was a baffling incident, one that clearly had the authorities concerned. A week later when Iain returned to the airport and asked around trying to learn whether the mystery object had been identified, he was met by a wall of silence. Air traffic denied that there had been any 'unidentified object' and claimed to know nothing about it, which was all rather strange because when Iain spoke to colleagues a rather different tale emerged. When the UFO failed to respond to attempts at contact, three Tornadoes were scrambled from RAF Kinloss to intercept the UFO, which appeared as a bright light about two or three thousand feet above the ground. As the aircraft approached, the object shot straight up in a vertical climb and disappeared at fantastic speed. Efforts by investigators to extract further information from the military authorities and any of the bodies involved resulted in complete silence or, as in the case of the Ministry of Defence, denial that anything odd had happened.

So much is cloaked in a veil of secrecy on these islands. Even when information leaks out it seems to disappear into a black hole. The military are adept at concealing almost anything bizarre, as events in the Outer Hebrides show. At 4.10 p.m. on 26 October 1996 several witnesses on the island of Lewis were startled by a massive explosion in the sky a few miles west of the coast over the sea. The mystery begins almost immediately. Both the local coast-guard and RAF Kinloss, the RAF's main anti-submarine base and home to the Nimrod aircraft, later claimed that no one had reported the incident till almost an hour later, at 5 p.m. This explained the apparent delay in their response to what, on the surface, appeared a serious event. First reports suggested that a large metallic object had crashed into the sea. One witness claimed to have seen an orange ball in the sky with a solid object beside it in the seconds before the explosion occurred.

Incredibly, two hours passed before an air search was launched and it was not till 10.35 p.m. – six hours after the first sightings – that an emergency alert was broadcast to ships in the area. As might be guessed, in spite of the witnesses, the authorities claimed that, in fact, nothing had happened. 'Fortress Scotland's' multi-million pounds' worth of surveillance equipment had detected no unexplained object in the sky, apparently. In fact, the military went into publicity over-drive to dismiss the event. They couldn't conceal, however, the massive array of ships and aircraft that appeared off Lewis on Monday 4 November, just a week after the mystery UFO incident. The authorities had an explanation for this gathering of military might; it was a long planned NATO exercise and its appearance in the area was simply a coincidence. This may well have been true, but it could also have been a convenient cover for a thorough search of the area. Burying UFO activity through ridicule, stalling and disinformation has been the pattern for over half a century.

As far back as the 1950s strange flying objects were being encountered by the military. On 21 March 1956 three Sea-Hawk aircraft from 738 Squadron on a training flight from HMS *Fulmar* approached the coast at Lossiemouth at a height of 15,000 feet. One of the crew, Sub-Lieutenant G. W. N. Coates, was filming with a hand-held camera. The visibility was excellent but neither Coates nor any of the aircrew on the planes noticed anything out of the ordinary. It was a different matter once they had a chance to look at the prints. According to Coates, 'When my film was developed and projected on to the screen, there was what appeared to be a perfect example of a flying saucer, moving on the port side'. Unfortunately, there is no description of what Coates meant by a 'perfect flying saucer' though given the reports of the time he probably filmed a silver or white disc shape. Needless to say, nothing ever emerged from the report of this incident and the film itself has been 'lost'.

If the authorities are willing to ignore the evidence of their own employees then it is little wonder that sightings of UFOs by members of the public receive no obvious attention. Former Glasgow policeman Ben Goodwin who had his own UFO encounter told me that the police regularly saw unexplained objects in the sky, but would not report them as they didn't want to jeopardise their careers. But when it comes to reports of alien encounters it is hard to understand why there is such a lack of interest from government agencies. One might expect there would be a real determination to get to the bottom of it, especially where there are several witnesses to an incident.

On 23 September 1996 two friends, Jean and Lyn, drove from their village home in Fife to a local shop to buy a jar of coffee taking with them Lyn's 10-year-old son Peter. They set off around 7.30 p.m. and though the light was fading it was a clear evening with good visibility. It was Lyn, occupying the front passenger-seat, who first spotted the bright oval-shaped light low down in the sky. She watched it for a few seconds, wondering what it could be, then turned away. When she glanced back the single light had turned into two circles of light. Lyn was now intrigued, as the object did not appear to be moving and so, she was sure, couldn't be a plane and seemed too big to be a helicopter.

She drew Jean's attention to the light and both agreed that it was a bit of a puzzle. Jean, who was driving, slowed the car to a walking pace so they could get a better view. The object was now to their left and seemed to be hovering behind a farmhouse whose silhouette was visible against the gentle glow. Beams of light seemed to be travelling from the sky to the ground. Suddenly, the field below the UFO was lit up like a firework display, the intensity of the light turning night into day all around them.

The explosion of light ended as dramatically as it had begun. The object, which had remained stationary for so long, now started to move and as it did so Jean and Lyn noticed its triangular shape and the dome on its uppermost section. The UFO then moved away swiftly, while at the same time rotating slowly, to display small red dots of light. Puzzled, Jean and Lyn nevertheless continued their drive to the local shop. Jean bought a jar of coffee and they set off on the return journey. But on the way back they were again confronted by a strange object as they passed the site of their original encounter. The time was by now around 8.20 p.m. Ahead, travelling at speed, moved a group of red lights which seemed to form a shape of some kind. The 'shape' then turned suddenly and headed directly for them. A whole battery of lights switched on for an instant, and was just as abruptly extinguished. And then, as suddenly as it had arrived, the object disappeared into the night. Lyn noticed that three cars were travelling behind them though there was no indication that any of their occupants had seen the mysterious object.

Having returned home the witnesses decided after further discussion to revisit the area of the incident. They were both nervous and intrigued, not to mention anxious to resolve an incident which they could not explain. So, at 9.45 p.m. they drove back, and as they approached the spot where they had witnessed the strange objects their attention was caught by a blue glow which was visible just above a wooded area. A star-shaped object could be seen pulsating and emitting coloured streaks of light – alternately red, blue and green – in rapid sequence. Lyn described them as being like torch beams, narrow at the base and widening as they reached upwards. Intriguing, even intimidating, but no one could have been prepared for what happened next.

Moving among the trees were several small entities, and whatever they may have been, they were definitely not human. Above them towered a tall stick-like individual, its height estimated at around seven feet. The strange being seemed to be in charge of its smaller companions. Understandably frightened by the strange encounter, Jean and Lyn turned the car round and drove home.

Although their nerves were jangling Lyn and Jean were still

intrigued by the strange turn of events. So, having calmed down in the familiar surroundings of their home, they decided to return and take a closer look. As they reached the place where they had last seen the UFO, the blue light was still glowing but with the binoculars they had brought it was possible to get a much better view. They could see a shimmering ball that appeared to be emitting heat and energy of some kind. It looked amber in colour with an irregular surface and dark patches. One of these darker patches, situated near the base, could be identified as an opening. The craft didn't appear to be resting on the ground, but was hovering or possibly held up by thin supports. It appeared to be rotating and tilting rhythmically.

To the right of the object but definitely on the ground, lay a circular disc, coloured dark red but possibly reflecting the colour of the ball-shaped craft. All around groups of small creatures were transporting boxes, and objects shaped like tubes, from the shelter of the wood towards the craft. Lyn described these beings as having 'very big, dark eyes and with heads too big for their bodies. They didn't appear to have mouths.' The taller 'supervisor' was still visible and, say the witnesses, they could make out his brown skin and narrow eyes.

The incident had a terrifying ending, and was described by Jean. 'Suddenly dozens of bubble-like things came out of the woods and flew across the field towards us. Then they were all around us, about four feet away, motionless. They were all alike. We could see through them and each one had one of these small creatures inside. They had big black eyes and big heads.'

Later, weeks after the incident was over, Lyn began to have dreams about being taken into the craft which suggests that abduction may have been a part of the scenario. The witnesses, though, had no conscious memory of this having taken place.

It may be significant that this was not the first reported abduction from this part of the country. In 1976 Karen, 10 years old, was living with her family in a farm cottage close to the Fife village of Meigle. She was recovering from mumps and so decided not to accompany her brother and sister on a fruit-picking trip. Instead she took a walk through a nearby wood, an area she had often visited. Karen set off around 9.30 a.m. and arrived at the wood about half an hour later just before ten o' clock. During the walk to the wood she watched a bright rainbow-coloured light in the sky though it may have had no connection with what happened a short while later.

Once in the wood Karen followed a well-worn path till she came to a clearing she often played in. This time, however, it was quite different. So frighteningly different that Karen would have turned and run if she had been given the chance. Ahead of her, staring in her direction, was a group of small 'beings', four in all. And, faced by this strange gathering, she found herself unable to move. She was, she explained, 'frozen to the spot', as if held in an invisible vice.

Even as she watched the entities began moving towards her and, as they drew closer, Karen could see that not only their eyes but also, more remarkably, their skin, was coloured blue. They were small, smaller even than 10-year-old Karen, probably not even reaching her shoulder.

And then she felt hands touching her, cold and slimy. An enormous light appeared from nowhere and the next thing that Karen can remember is lying on a big circular table which had the appearance of hard metal, but felt soft, almost as if it had been moulded to the contours of her body. Entities surrounded her, reassuring her everything was all right. Not a word though was spoken. Communication was made through thoughts which came into her mind. These beings looked human, but she also caught sight of taller entities whose bodies were incredibly thin, like stick insects. She believes that the small entities she first encountered may have been working for these taller aliens.

The place she was in was dark, but she remembers a light shining from somewhere. Drops were put into her eyes which paralysed them for a while. Clearly some form of examination was underway as Karen recalls a 'contraption like a machine', covering her from head to toe and going into her mouth. It may have examined her nostrils as well.

Eventually, Karen was put back at the spot where her mysterious journey had begun. Dazed and shaken she headed for home. When she walked in she received another shock. Karen was sure she had been in the woods only a short while. It couldn't be later than lunch time. In fact it was 6 p.m., way past the usual time for her evening meal. It had been over eight hours since she had waved goodbye and set off with her picnic. Her frantic parents had been on the point of calling the police.

For two years Karen avoided the woods, but in 1978 she experienced a second encounter. The night before the incident Karen had a vivid dream in which she went back to the scene of the first incident and found the small figures waiting for her. At the picnic site she was once again 'taken up' by strange entities. She could feel their little hands touching her legs, lifting her as if she was being guided somewhere. She remembers lying on a table and experiencing an agonising pain centred on her forehead.

Back home she suffered a headache and high fever and was violently sick during the night. A doctor visited and she remembers him saying that her glands were inflamed. She told no one of these events and kept her secret for twenty years. But by 1995, with a small child to look after and having moved to Paisley, memories of the events of the 1970s began to resurface. Karen was particularly worried that her daughter might be a target for the entities that had abducted her all those years before. Her fears increased after a strange experience which occurred during some late-night studying in the back room of her Paisley flat which doubled as her daughter's bedroom. She remembers seeing a bright light coming in through the window and, in the light, she caught sight of a dog-faced entity. When she came to an hour had passed. The coffee she had been drinking had gone cold. Karen had no conscious memory of being abducted, but was afraid that it might have happened.

She also became worried that in 1976 she may have been given an implant. An X-ray revealed an unknown metal object lying just below the surface of the skin in the roof of her mouth. Doctors were puzzled by the object and told Karen that the only way to find out what it was would be to operate. A procedure which Karen, understandably, was reluctant to undergo. Admittedly, Karen did not report her encounters to the authorities, but such reluctance is understandable. The government's attitude hardly inspires confidence among those who have been through an experience to report an incident.

*

So why with, at the very least, a substantial bedrock of evidence that unknown craft and strange entities are present in Scotland, is the Scottish government so indifferent to the UFO enigma? On the face of it, it seems worthy of investigation. Could it be that they have a hidden motive for ignoring it? Are they trying to hide something? Like the fact that they are involved in developing alien technology. Of course, we could only be a bit player in a game involving the US superpower and the UK. But Scotland has been a centre for many kinds of military installations, was an important location during the Cold War and continues to play an important role in European defence. The US and the UK have a long history of military involvement in Scotland and have had plenty of time to establish secret bases and hidden areas with places where super-advanced technology could be stored and tested. In the 1980s defence expert Malcolm Spaven documented over two hundred military installations across Scotland, in his aptly named book *Fortress Scotland*. And these were all sites the military found it impossible to conceal. There may well be secret bases that are well hidden. Even where installations are visible it does not mean that we know exactly what is going on there. But even publicly available information can produce a startling picture. Up to the 1990s Machrihanish on the Mull of Kintyre was a complex and key base with a runway almost two miles long, one of the biggest in western Europe. Millions were spent on building a massive array of hangars, weapon stores and units described as 'accommodation'. Its importance can be judged from the fact that it was used as a store for nuclear depth-bombs and that it served as a training base for the US Navy's Special Warfare Unit 2, the famously glamourised SEALS. In 1983 Spaven wrote: 'Machrihanish's nuclear facilities, diversity of based units, and grossly under-utilised capabilities make it one of the most important bases to watch for military expansion'.

The collapse of the Soviet Union and the ensuing peace dividend changed all that. But could the facilities available at Machrihanish, to take only one of the many bases situated throughout Scotland, have been used for other purposes? To test alien technology? That has been the rumour since the 1990s, but with no definite proof. Claims that Machrihanish contained vast underground hangars have been denied by informants who worked on the base. They claim that the nature of the terrain makes it impossible to dig down to any great extent. Another former worker told me that he had never seen anything 'strange' on the base, though he had witnessed silver disc-shaped objects flying close to Machrihanish. He is sure, however, that they did not land there. Given the resources of the military, legal sanctions and the depth of secrecy operating, breaking into the circle of potential concealment is never going to be easy. And there may be nothing to learn.

But that does not take away from the fact that something inexplicable is going on across Scotland. People encountering strange flying-craft at close quarters. Individuals experiencing alien contact. If the military claims not to be interested its lack of curiosity has to be questioned, and its senior personnel either know more than they are willing to say or are remarkably complacent. After all, they have billions of pounds worth of equipment at their disposal that fails to notice, track or identify objects penetrating our air space.

Take the Loch Nevis sighting. In June 1997 microlight pilot Hamish Smith was flying across Loch Nevis in the West Highlands when he spotted a strange object beneath the water. It caught his attention immediately as he had been across the area many times so it was familiar territory to him. And there was a second witness. Michael Hudson, a priest, was Hamish's passenger that day. They had been photographing remote churches and other landmarks when they caught sight of the USO (unidentified submersible object).They managed to take a snap and when he landed Hamish made a drawing. Hamish told a reporter that, 'He had never seen anything like it. It was not a shoal of fish and the entrance to the loch is only eight metres deep so it could not have been a submarine.' Hamish's photo, however, does show a solid object and his hand drawing a keel-shaped craft. So what could it have been and where did it come from? No one seemed to know or care. Although the police and coastguards were alerted they took several days to arrive, behaviour that does seem odd as, at the very least, they could have been dealing with an upturned vessel with people in it. This is far from the usual attitude of the police and coastguards. But when they did turn up they found nothing. So where had the object gone? Echo-sounding equipment detected an 'anomaly', which is curious, but not proof that anything had been there. Loch Nevis is connected to the sea and this would allow a small vessel to manoeuvre in and out. The object Hamish observed would have been too big, he judged, to do that. And, anyway, it was a submerged vessel. So had it come from the sky and flown beneath the water as many witnesses to UFOs have reported? The lack of interest from the authorities approaches the inexplicable when it is realised that Loch Nevis is less than thirty miles from the Kyle of Lochalsh, and is home to the British Underwater and Test Centre, the main trials' range for torpedoes and other undersea-warfare equipment. But why should they care about an unidentified submerged vessel in Loch Nevis?

Or why should the authorities care about a UFO encounter that leads to a police investigation? In 1979 forestry worker Bob Taylor encountered a hovering object in woods close to the town of Livingston. Bob, who was inspecting trees in the area, came to a clearing in the woods around 11 a.m. on 9 November 1979. He was brought to an abrupt halt as directly ahead of him was a disc-shaped craft hovering a few feet above the ground. It looked solid, but at some parts Bob could see through it to the trees behind. As he stared in amazement two spiky, ball-shaped objects dropped from the craft and rolled towards him with a plopping sound. They grabbed hold of his trousers around the thighs and at this same moment Bob was affected by an overpowering smell. He passed out and was unconscious for around twenty minutes. What, if anything, happened during this 'missing time' is not known. But when Bob came to the object had disappeared. Bob was feeling groggy, could not get his lorry started, but managed to stagger the mile back to his home. Though in a state of shock he managed to tell his wife what had happened. She contacted his employers who in turn informed the police. A criminal investigation followed because it was believed that Bob might have been attacked. The woods were a known haunt of beer-drinking youths. Bob, however, stuck solidly to his story. He was convinced he had encountered a UFO. In spite of a thorough police investigation no one was ever linked to an attack on Bob. The search wound down and the case remains 'open'.

There is no evidence that Bob was abducted or even of a living alien presence. But could the UFO Bob encountered have been some kind of remotely controlled device? Possibly. Bob judged the object to be around twenty feet across and without much depth. This would be on the small side if it was carrying a live cargo but not impossible if, as some argue, it originated from a larger vehicle. Several bigger UFOs had been sighted in the area at around this time covering a period of several days. It has been suggested that this could have been a remotely controlled vehicle produced by our own technology. But if it was translucent in parts, so that Bob could see through it, then what kind of technology was developed? Certainly, nothing that has been made known to the public because terrestrial science seems an impossibly long distance from being able to achieve such an advance. Unless our scientists have been given help from an unknown source.

Other incidents suggest that something really bizarre is going on that may even involve weird experiments. On the evening of 12 October 1999 a witness walking his dog in a field next to Deans High School on the outskirts of Livingston caught sight of something moving in the distance across open ground. He guessed, at first, that this was a fellow dog owner as it was a well-known spot for a stroll. However, as the figure moved closer he noticed that its face, hands and feet were glowing a luminous yellow. The witnesses' dogs started barking at the figure. Then one, clearly frightened, bolted. The witness, however, stood his ground and still uncertain about what he was experiencing called out, 'Can I help you?' The figure appeared to turn its head, but there was no spoken response. At this point the witness, growing increasingly concerned, decided to leave.

It's not the first time that 'glowing figures' have been reported in the area. In 1988 a family travelling by car through West Lothian found themselves being chased by a glowing entity. The figure, humanoid in appearance, emerged from woods, known locally as Knock Forrest, then pursued them down the road at speeds of over sixty miles an hour. The being was over six feet tall, bulky in appearance and seemed to be scowling. A truly disturbing encounter for the four people involved. But what could this figure possibly be? A phantom from another dimension? An alien? Or, to enter, almost, the arena of science fiction, the product of some top-secret experiment? Or is there no connection whatever between the 1979 Taylor encounter and these equally strange events?

One linking factor, though, is the air of menace that was present in all three incidents. The authorities give out the message that the UFO phenomenon is nothing to be alarmed about. But certain incidents suggest that these soothing words may be deliberately intended to mislead.

During the 1990s Robert Lee repeatedly saw UFOs in the area around the village of Kinbuck where he lived. He was convinced that he even knew exactly where they had their base as he had on several occasions seen the white discs take off from the surrounding hills. He had even watched them change colour so that they blended with the terrain and became almost invisible. One day, walking in the hills, he heard the roar of a huge aircraft. As a former military man he recognised the plane was out of the ordinary though he didn't catch sight of it. What he did see, however, was three silver discs rise from the hills in the distance and head in the direction of the aircraft's 'wake'. That same day a Hercules aircraft, one of a group of three, crashed in mysterious circumstances near Blair Atholl. Described as a 'low-altitude stall' in the official accident report published in May 1993, Robert Lee wondered why no mention was made of the silver discs he had seen following the plane. Especially as it emerged that the Hercules's flight path would have brought it over the general area where Robert was walking that day.

Puzzling to Robert Lee, but not to Bill Donovan who is convinced he has the answer. Even if, as he also thinks, no one will ever believe him.

Bill is not sure whether he has ever been abducted, but is convinced of the reality of the alien threat. It all began when Bill was a mate with the North Sea fishing fleet. Early one summer's morning in 1969 Bill stood alone on deck when he spotted an object that seemed out of place. Too big to be a plane, and above rather than on the water, so obviously not another trawler, it seemed to defy explanation. Grabbing binoculars, Bill took a closer look, amazed at what he saw. A disc-shaped object hovering just above the water line which looked like the traditional flying saucer although a humped curvature on top and below gave it an unusual oyster-like appearance. Around the middle gleamed a bright-red band.

Bill yelled to his shipmates, but as they arrived on the scene the object raced skywards and disappeared. Several, however, agreed that they had caught a glimpse of the disc before it vanished. Bill even overheard the skipper order that a note be made in the ship's log. That encounter became a pivotal episode in Bill's life. The memory of the event began to take over his mind so that he could think of nothing else. He began to experience terrible nightmares that continued during his waking moments. No part of the day was free from the persistent vision of an enormous spaceship and its occupants, and of being held by aliens, against his will, inside the craft. Was it just a weird dream? Or was he really being abducted by these entities that were playing with his mind and destroying his hold on reality? Bizarre secrets were imparted to him. The aliens claimed that thousands of their kind were living openly on the earth. They looked almost identical to humans and melted easily into our culture. Several of these individuals had been assigned to watch over Bill, and they would make sure that he never stepped out of line. Significantly, in view of later events, Bill was warned not to discuss his experience with anyone. Not even his wife.

By now the pressure on Bill had reached breaking point. He found the experiences so disturbing, and his inability to talk about them so frustrating, that he cracked under the pressure. A doctor referred him to a psychiatrist and he was pronounced mentally ill. A period of recuperation followed. Put on medication and returned to the world, Bill moved to Glasgow and managed to find a job.

Working in a restaurant, friendships developed with his coll-eagues. Eventually, Bill felt relaxed enough to confide in a work-mate his UFO experience and the way it had profoundly changed his life. The man listened sympathetically and though he made it clear that he found it hard to accept the story at face value, the mere fact of telling it lifted a weight from Bill's shoulders. Having thanked the chef for listening, Bill turned to place a tray of meat in the deep freeze when he noticed one of the waiters eyeing him curiously. Bill gave himself a mental kick for speaking so openly. He wished he'd made sure no one had been around to listen. He comforted himself, however, with the thought that the man would never take such an unlikely tale seriously. Gradually, as the day passed, the incident faded from his mind.

It was to return later with a jolt. That night as he returned home two men grabbed him as he entered the stairway to his flat. 'They looked just ordinary', explained Bill, 'but what they said wasn't ordinary.' They openly threatened him, and told him that this time they would only warn him. But should he dare to open his mouth in public again they would come back and deal with him in a more direct manner. The men then left. The incident scared Bill badly. Not only because he had been threatened, but also because the whole incident appeared so strange he was terrified that he had imagined it. Was his mind going, he asked himself? Deep down, however, he was sure that the event, weird though it was, had been real. And, for Bill, the proof came shortly after.

He returned to work the following morning and was immediately sacked. Trays of meat which he was sure he had locked in the freezer had been found lying in the storeroom. As a casual worker Bill was dispensable so he found himself out on the street. It seemed to him like a deliberate act of sabotage. He had no doubt who was responsible. Aliens masquerading as humans. To anyone who asks 'Bill, why would aliens be interested in you?' Bill replies, 'I have no idea. All I know is that they are. They tell me to keep quiet. To say nothing to anyone. Anywhere I try to work they get rid of me. Maybe I've seen something they don't want me to talk about. I know I'm not normal, but that's because of my experience with the aliens. I'm not lying. There are aliens on this earth. The government knows it, but isn't saying.'

It might be argued that Bill was letting his imagination get the better of him. But he is not alone in experiencing direct interference from the authorities. And Scotland has experienced more than its share of mind-stretching incidents. In fact events occur which border on the bizarre and would lead most of us to wonder where reality ends and fantasy begins. No more so than three friends living on a farm cottage overlooking the town of North Berwick.

Their experiences began with sightings of unidentified objects moving across the skies of East Lothian and over the Firth of Forth. But events rapidly escalated. Around October 2001, the three housemates – Robert, Amanda and Liz – experienced a series of strange visits. As Amanda explained:

> One Sunday I was sitting in the lounge when these three guys came to the door. One was about six feet tall, very grey looking, with a pointed chin, white shirt and black shoes. He looked at me and didn't say a word. The other one was small and tanned. I know it sounds weird, but he was dressed in a black suit. He told me he had to speak to Liz. He was very insistent. I went to get her while they waited at the porch. Then one of them sort of slipped into my bedroom. His body seemed to turn to a jelly-like form and he just kind of oozed through the gap between the open door into my bedroom. He stood there looking out the window. Then they just left. Since then I haven't dared sleep there and I decided to move into the spare room.

This was the first event in a bizarre pattern which coincided with increased UFO activity. Amanda actually witnessed several objects land in a field beside the cottage. From one 'craft' two entities emerged and approached the house. They looked remarkably humanoid. One clearly male and one female. Amanda described her as: '25 to 27 years old. She was wearing a dark-blue top and navy-blue trousers. The chap was smaller than her and had blonde hair'. She then asked the female entity why UFOs continually flew around Torness, the nuclear power station situated a few miles away. She was told that they were protecting the site, but from who or what they didn't explain. Amanda even offered them a drink which the female accepted. They then left. Amanda admits: 'I thought I was dreaming but when I woke up the next day the cups were there which proved these things were happening. I know it was real. I stood at the window and saw the UFO. I could see the red light flashing.'

There were more strange incidents. Liz went to the door and was confronted by two well-groomed strangers; again, one was male and one was female:

> They were in best dress-uniforms. The head guy was in his fifties with silver hair. I wasn't afraid of them and felt there was no need to be fearful. The man told me, 'It's nothing for you to worry about'. One was taller than the other. They were olive skinned. They asked if they could come in. The woman asked, 'is it all right if I search in the kitchen?' I don't know what on earth they were looking for.

These individuals never stayed for long nor explained where they had come from or the purpose of their visit. But they had the unsettling ability to appear actually inside the house out of nowhere. A silver-haired man who appeared to be looking for something was seen in the hall. Later Liz encountered a man sitting in the deck chair in the conservatory who told her, 'I am just here to make sure you are all right.' Were these beings trying to protect them from some unspecified danger?

Is it possible to make any sense of these events? One curious fact was that Robert couldn't see the entities that appeared to Liz and Amanda though he did claim to see people watching them from the bushes which surrounded the cottage. However, of the three it was Robert who claimed to be psychic. As he explained, 'There's a person who's dead who I can see and smell sometimes. I also have out-of-body experiences. I can withstand their influence because I know about them. Maybe Amanda and Liz can't because they're not so aware of them. They don't come from other planets but other places.'

Amanda added, 'I've no idea what's going on or even if these incidents are connected, but they keep happening. One morning I woke up and had a pain at the back of my neck and was sore elsewhere. I've no conscious recollection of anything happening to me.'

Events became so intimidating that the police were contacted. Liz explained what happened next. 'The police didn't find anything. They felt we were being a bit frantic and stupid. We wonder if the

Special Branch are keeping an eye on us because we've seen too much.' There was no doubting that the witnesses were genuinely concerned, as Robert commented: 'I stopped videoing the UFOs because I felt we were inviting trouble. We were being frightened off for the best of reasons.'

By now everyone was at the end of their tether. The final straw was the appearance of a man with silver hair outside the house. He was accompanied by smaller entities hiding in the bushes. The beings ordered Robert to destroy the video tapes. Robert took the warning seriously and burnt them. After that all the bizarre visits they had experienced suddenly stopped. Was it all in the mind? The police seemed to think so after they had visited the cottage several times and found nothing. But Robert had set up a camera and was able to show the police a strange figure in a white shirt caught on tape as he strode through the garden beside the cottage. The police were taken aback. As one of the officers remarked, 'But we were there and there was no one to be seen.' Could it have been an entity from another world?

At the very least there is independent confirmation that unidentified objects were active in the area and had been for some time. The report came from Richard Adams, a retired senior NCO photographer in the Australian Air Force, who had 'spent a lifetime around all types of aircraft and in all types of weather'. In 2000 he, and his partner Pat, spotted 'a bright light or reflection . . . at what appeared to be 1,000–2,000 feet over the shoreline, somewhere between the Bass Rock and Torness.' Adams guessed at first that it might be a helicopter, but quickly changed his mind when the object shot off at high speed, covering a distance of fifteen to twenty miles in an astonishing five seconds. Richard described his amazement: 'the thing came shooting back the way it had come, with the same apparent altitude and incredible speed . . . at least 15,000 miles per hour. Clearly, impossible, but we saw it.'

So what do these accounts suggest? At the very least that something strange is happening in Scotland. That our air space is being invaded by objects that cannot be identified. That our citizens are experiencing contact with entities that are not from this planet. Isn't it strange that in these circumstances the authorities give the appearance of complete indifference? A letter from the author to the late Donald Dewar's office, when he became the first minister of Scotland following devolution, brought no response. Strange when it is remembered that Dewar had a key role in locating Scotland's new parliament on one of the most mystical spots in the country. A location that has led the press to label it the 'paranormal parliament'. Attempts by Bonnybridge councillor Billy Buchanan to get the government to open up, including an appeal on BBC television, have got nowhere. So much for the new Scottish democracy. Of course, some people have suggested that there are good reasons for the lack of interest. The Scottish authorities are well aware of the UFO presence. In fact, they are co-operating with alien entities to produce advanced technology. The evidence is hardly strong enough to support that view. But given the obsession of both government and the military with secrecy it would be surprising if they allowed any evidence to slip out. So UFO sightings and abductions will continue while those in authority continue to look the other way and hope to convince us that such 'unbelievable' things simply don't happen.

THREE

Scotland's Mothman and other phantom beasts

WHY ARE STRANGE beasts roaming the hills and venturing into the cities of Scotland? Where do they come from and what is their purpose? If indeed they have one. The number of sightings of unidentified 'phantom cats' alone runs into thousands. But to those determined on their capture these puma-like creatures remain elusive beasts. And phantom cats are only one in a range of weird entities that appear determined to make Scotland their home.

Reports of an unknown creature that haunts the mountain ranges are less numerous though equally puzzling. Is it possible that in Scotland we have a yeti-like beast more usually associated with the distant Himalayas? Ben MacDhui in the Cairngorms is Scotland's second highest mountain. It is also the possible home of Scotland's answer to the yeti, the 'Big Grey Man'. Reports of a mysterious entity prowling the slopes of Ben MacDhui were brought to public attention in the 1920s though sightings had occurred well before then. In fact, Professor Norman Collie, who was the first to speak openly of these events, encountered the creature in 1891, but waited thirty years to reveal what he knew. Collie, a well-known mountaineer, and veteran of climbs in the Alps and Himalayas, was making a solo ascent of the mountain. He reached the summit just as a thick mist descended. Collie decided that having reached the top he might as well turn round and go back down. As he made the descent he heard loud crunching in the snow behind him. He assumed it was a fellow climber though was surprised that he had not noticed him on the way up. But as the footsteps continued Collie realised that the strides being made were enormous. Several times the length of a human's. Overcome with fear, he rushed down the hillside, staggering blindly among the boulders till he reached the safety of the nearest forest. Collie didn't catch sight of an entity of any description, but was convinced that he had been followed by a flesh-and-blood creature.

Many years after Collie's encounter another mountaineer, Peter Densham, told of a similar experience on the summit: 'I had the sudden impression someone was near me . . . I stood up and was conscious of a crunching noise from the direction of the cairn on my left. I was overcome by a feeling of apprehension and found myself running at an incredible pace.' Like Collie before him, Densham experienced an overwhelming desire to leave the mountain and reach lower ground as quickly as possible.

However, an encounter reported by one mountaineer, who concealed his identity to avoid publicity, is more detailed and specific. According to his account, he saw:

> About twenty yards away a great brown creature swaggering down the hill . . . [it] had an air of insolent strength about it . . . it rolled slightly from side to side, taking huge measured steps. It looked as though it was covered with shortish, brown hair. Its head was disproportionately large, its neck very thick and powerful. It did not resemble an ape. Its hairy arms though long were not unduly so, its carriage was extremely erect.

Wendy Wood, a well-known political activist, and another visitor to the mountain, had no doubt there were strange things going on. She later wrote of her encounter describing how she heard a loud voice right beside her, speaking what she thought was Gaelic though she could not make out the sounds properly. She also had the sensation experienced by Collie and Densham that someone, or something, was following her.

These occurrences are by no means confined to Ben MacDhui, but there has been a far greater concentration of incidents linked to the mountain. Many other sightings have occurred within a twenty-mile radius, well within the range of a human-like creature using Ben MacDhui as its base. Physical evidence of the creature's presence has also, allegedly, been found. In 1952 James Rennie claimed to have discovered a mysterious set of tracks close to the village of Cromdale. These 'were running across a stretch of snow-covered moorland, each print nineteen inches long by about fourteen inches wide.' There was a seven foot gap between each stride with the tracks following a more or less straight line. Snow, of course, doesn't lie here as it does in the Himalayas, so perhaps all we can expect to find are tracks in the mud although these don't last for any length of time in our damp climate. The truth is that we are not geared up to search for the creature. A yeti in Scotland seems to defy commonsense. However, there are vast expanses of the country that are rarely visited and almost never after dark. And the Highlands cover an area of thousands of square miles. We know that flesh-and-blood pumas have hidden in far more densely populated parts of the country and never been caught. So why not a creature with more cunning and intelligence, but one that simply wants to avoid direct contact with man? An ape-like being, a remnant of an ancient race, identical to the yeti of Tibet.

But while the survival of a relic from the distant past may explain these strange encounters in the Highlands what can we make of an entity that almost defies rational experience? Mothman has been usually associated with the United States, but a sighting of a similar creature has been reported in Scotland. This entity is described as half-man-half-bird. Its legs and torso are human-like, but in place of arms it has wings and feathers. The parallel with an angel is obvious, but the being doesn't seem to radiate goodness and has a sinister air. However, it may be wrong to jump to conclusions. Scotland's only known encounter with the creature took place in October 1992 in Edinburgh. The witness, a woman, woke up in the early hours of the morning and caught sight of an intense white light clearly visible through the window. She got out of bed to take a closer look and her attention was drawn to a tree at the foot of the garden. Crouching on a thick branch was a creature which, at first glance, she took to be a giant bird as big as a man. But as she took a longer look she became aware that apart from its huge size there were other strange aspects. Its body appeared to be a mixture of human and bird-type features. It had wings on its back, but a human chest and limbs. The entity did not seem to be aware of her presence and made no attempt to confront her.

There have been no other reported sightings and very few strange flying-entities reported of any kind. In 1998 a witness travelling through Glencoe late at night reported seeing what he described as 'a large black bird-creature in the sky. It was about eight feet across and resembled a pterodactyl.' There is a vague similarity to Mothman although there are also differences that indicate that we are not dealing here with an identical being. But it does seem odd that we have two different types of airborne entities which are distinct. The Glencoe witness has suggested that what he saw might be a skree, a mythical creature of doom. It is claimed that just such a creature was seen at the site of one of Scotland's most notorious disasters, the triple train-crash at Gretna in 1915, which killed over two hundred people. But Mothman, the skree and the Glencoe flying beast may well be different entities. It seems more likely that, as on the ground, the skies above are filled with beings of all kinds. They are just harder to spot.

*

Compared to Mothman, phantom black cats may appear an almost normal phenomenon, but in many ways they are the most bizarre of all. They are the most reported yet the most elusive of all the strange beasts roaming our land. There have been hundreds of sightings of mysterious black cats in Scotland, over an area stretching from Ayrshire to Sutherland. Although the press has labelled these strange beasts black – or phantom – pumas many of the animals sighted have fawn coats, often described as similar in colour to a Labrador. They are usually reported as being slightly larger than an Alsatian dog, but distinctly cat shaped. Sightings occur typically in the open countryside, but the closest encounter took place on the edge of a built-up area. The witness was oil worker William McRoberts. The date of the sighting was 27 December 1992. Mr McRoberts reported:

> I was driving my family along the A726 which runs alongside the perimeter of Glasgow Airport. The car in front was going slowly, then suddenly came to a complete halt. I drew up behind. Almost immediately after, I was astonished to see a puma plodding along by the side of my car. It was about the size of an Alsatian dog but more muscular. It was a definite fawn colour. It pounced over the fence the way a cat does. It didn't look at the car or appear to be disturbed by our presence which surprised me.

Much further north, near to the town of Keith, farmers who for several years had been losing livestock, blamed these mysterious disappearances on a cheetah-like animal they claim occasionally to have glimpsed. It looked like a cat, but was the size of a dog and had prominent triangular-shaped ears. It seemed like a simple case of misidentification until, one January morning in 2000, police constable Alan Milton was driving through the countryside around Keith when he spotted a strange animal. He reported:

> I saw this beast at the side of the road. When it saw me driving towards it, the animal ran across the road and into the forest. It was beige with a curly bushy tail and cat-like triangular ears. It was the size of a dog, but there was no way it was a dog. It had a very long dipped back like a cheetah. It's probably some sort of cat that somebody's let go into the wild. We have had reports of wild cats being involved where sheep have been killed. A large animal has been suspected, but we can never tell what did it.

Further evidence that a bizarre beast was on the prowl in the Grampian area came nearly two years later. Doris Moore, who lived near the village of Insch in Aberdeenshire, was walking along the street outside her home in January 2002 when the encounter took place. Retired farmer Wilfred Simpson, a neighbour, was following behind the victim and saw the creature. He claimed, 'I heard her scream and thought she had fallen. I saw a black beast disappear round the corner of the stables. She told me she had been bitten by the animal and there was some blood on the front of her legs and her trousers had been ripped. She also had three puncture wounds to her thigh.' Mr Simpson described the animal as about the size of a Labrador dog, but with a long thin body and the motion of a cat.

But most sightings don't involve any form of threat or physical contact. In February 1986 in Glen Bernera, almost directly opposite the island of Skye, Charlie Greenless, a forestry worker, was checking bags of fertiliser that had been dumped in preparation for spreading from a helicopter. At about midday Charlie, having completed his inspection, clambered back into his van. It was at this point that he spotted a strange animal. The creature sat on its haunches no more than twenty yards away, nestling in the heather. It was light fawn, similar in colour to a Labrador. Its face, ears and whiskers though were distinctly cat-like, but it was much larger than any feline. The size, in fact, of a deerhound. After a couple of minutes of sitting quite still the animal suddenly rose and bounded across the road to disappear into the dark shadows of the pine forest. Later, Charlie learned that there had been several sightings over a number of years of the same, or a very similar, creature. It had even wandered into a domestic garden. On another occasion, a deer had been found killed and partly eaten, with the skin rolled back off the flesh, as pumas typically do.

Former Army Outward Bound instructor Tom McGovern is convinced that we are dealing with a flesh-and-blood beast. He has encountered several black cats in the area around his home in Braco, Perthshire. He explained:

> I was at the bottom of my garden resting. A black cat came down the river bank at the water's edge. It was moving very quickly and appeared to be hunting. Its legs seemed to be short but it was

crouching as it moved so I couldn't judge its true height. Its coat was medium length and very thick but dull looking, not glossy. It simply ignored my friends and I who were standing watching.

In West Lothian and East Kilbride sightings of the creatures have been so numerous that 'cat hunters' have been out to track the phantom beasts in their lairs. Brian Wood has been scouring the Bathgate Hills after several sightings of a black, puma-like animal. The creature has even been spotted padding through the streets of local towns and villages. Further west in East Kilbride Jimmy McVeigh has been on the trail of black cats since he caught sight of one back in the 1970s.

Some of the most positive sightings of a big cat, or cats, occurred in the town of Ardrossan in December 2002. One night, near the end of a month in which several local people had already reported seeing a puma-like cat, many residents were wakened by chilling and unearthly cries. They seemed to be coming from a patch of wasteland near the railway line. They were certainly not being made by a human being, nor did they sound like canine noises. Police were called to investigate and, to their horror, saw an animal about three feet tall with a dark coat and a long black tail. It was, the officers were convinced, a puma, but as they cautiously approached the beast it disappeared into undergrowth. One local woman, who did not wish to be named, said: 'My daughter heard the screams . . . and at first thought it was a dog. Then it became louder and stronger and she realised it wasn't a dog and she got quite worried. It is quite frightening to know there is a wild animal prowling the area.' According to Phil Crosby of the Scottish Big Cats Team it was the real thing: 'The description fits that of a puma. The screeching noises could mean that it is searching for a mate.' Although it was suggested by some that the sighting was actually of 'Beauty', a Great Dane that lives in the area, the fact that police took the view that it was a puma is highly significant.

Dumfries and Galloway is another hotspot and, in the summer of 2003, there was a number of sightings in the area. Several people saw an animal, variously described as a lynx, puma or panther, in a variety of locations including Thornhill and Sanquhar. And a deputy headmaster, Bob McGoran, reported seeing a big cat resembling a North American lynx at Johnstonebridge near the M74 motorway. Dumfries and Galloway police took the sightings seriously and issued a 'steer-clear' warning to members of the public keen to see these exotic creatures at closer quarters.

For years the standard explanation was that the appearance of these animals coincided with the passing of the Dangerous Animals Act in 1975.This piece of legislation stopped individuals having as pets truly 'wild' animals like lions or tigers. To avoid prosecution, and the cost of disposing of these beasts, owners rid themselves of their unwanted 'pets' by setting them free in isolated places.

On the surface it seems an unlikely response given the risks that such a freed animal might pose to innocent passers-by, but it is clearly not impossible. But even if true, would this account for the hundreds of sightings in Scotland and elsewhere in Britain? There have been dozens of sightings in Cornwall alone, and the 'Beast of Bodmin Moor' has figured in many a tabloid headline. And as these reports have been coming in for almost thirty years, can it reasonably be suggested that this same group of freed 'cats' is still going strong? And why, after so many sightings, mangled sheep and alleged photographs, has the physical evidence that a puma-type beast has been involved been limited to one dead specimen? And the mystery deepens when we go back in time and find identical incidents taking place. As long ago as 1927 Inverness-shire was hit by a wave of unexplained attacks on domestic animals. Sheep and goats were the main victims. The savaging of animals continued for months then stopped as suddenly as it had begun. Which was also the case with a series of bizarre attacks on sheep on the west side of the Pentland Hills near Edinburgh in the 1930s. On this occasion no one even caught a glimpse of the creature which must have been responsible for the incidents. So are we really dealing with live beasts? Or could they be phantoms from another world? If so then how do we explain the dead livestock which even farmers believe to be their prey? But let's not forget Scotland has an ancient belief in the *taghairm*, a giant spirit cat that would appear from nowhere and feed on the flesh of any living being including humans.

*

Frequent though reported sightings of phantom pumas undoubtedly are, Scotland has earned the greatest reputation as the home of loch monsters. Sightings have been concentrated on Loch Ness but, in fact, these creatures have been reported in locations across Scotland. Though they are usually held to be placid beasts there are incidents which should warn us that they are not always as friendly as is believed.

On 16 August 1969 William Simpson and Duncan McDonnell were cruising Loch Morar in their motorboat. Suddenly they became aware of a loud splashing noise directly behind them. McDonnell looked up and saw an object in the water heading at speed towards the boat, moving through the disturbance left by their wake. He later claimed that 'it took only a matter of seconds to catch up on us'. The object hit the craft side-on. McDonnell had no doubt that the collision was intentional. He was also sure that they had been struck by a large animal of some kind and, although the impact had brought the beast to a halt, he was worried that it might try and swim beneath the boat and capsize them. Simpson had joined his crewmate on deck, having rushed from below when he heard the commotion. He immediately caught sight of the creature which he judged about twenty-five to thirty feet long, its three humps standing clear of the water. The skin had a rough appearance and looked dirty brown in colour. A snake-like head could be seen above the waves. Simpson took his shotgun and fired in the direction of the animal which rapidly disappeared below the surface.

Speaking after the incident Duncan McDonnell claimed:

> When we came off the boat we were both in a state of shock. I did not think that experts would want to examine the broken oar for possible skin samples. I had no intention, in fact, of telling anyone about it. I do not know if the oar will still be there. It could have been washed from the shore into the loch. I cannot really say if the monster bit a piece off the oar or if it was splintered when we tried to keep the beast away from the boat.

Largely forgotten now, Loch Lomond was once the focus of monster sightings. In September 1972 James Dickson from Glasgow spotted a 'gleaming black object with two humps' travelling at speed across the water. He reported:

> The parts that showed were about a foot across although it could have been broader underwater. The two humps were spread over about thirteen feet or more and the thing moved with great speed and grace. It seemed to hover about the same spot for some time and then veered direct left before disappearing. There was no suggestion of it being a ripple in the water. The object was definitely a creature and big enough to overturn a small boat.

Mr Dickson was not alone in his intriguing sighting. Ex-coxswain Lionel Saysell, a man with twenty-three years experience in the Navy, commented, 'It was certainly like nothing I have seen in all my years at sea. It made a ripple rather like a bow wave and seemed to travel some distance before disappearing.' Mr Saysell wondered if it might be a water disturbance of some kind. But John Craig, another witness, was quite certain he had seen 'a huge creature appearing some distance from the shore. It was definitely a creature, very long and moving very fast. I saw two humps. We all watched breathlessly till it disappeared.'

Around the time of these sightings a swimmer in the loch was attacked by an unidentified creature. The victim was 20-year-old Geoffrey Taylor from Huddersfield who was planning to cover the whole length of the loch to raise funds for charity. Taylor fought to remove the creature, which had wrapped itself around his leg. According to Jack Donald, who was steering the launch accompanying Taylor, the swimmer 'finally threw it away from him but twice it attacked him'. The fact that Taylor managed to beat off the attack suggests that maybe he had not encountered a 'monster' of the size reported at Lochs Morar or Ness or even seen earlier in Loch Lomond. But, in fact, Taylor's experience fits in well with the earliest origins of the loch-monster legend. The first reported incident involved St Columba and the creature of Loch Ness, which had been attacking people fishing or swimming in its waters. There's no evidence of the gigantic size more recently associated with these beasts though the one Columba confronted was clearly powerful enough to savage a grown man. Perhaps there are different types of loch creatures and the one encountered by the saint had more in common with the Loch Lomond variety than other kinds. Whatever the reality, loch monsters remain elusive creatures.

Is it likely that a flesh-and-blood beast as large as that reported in the lochs could exist yet never be caught? There are strange parallels with another creature that was once very much part of the Scottish scene. Dragons are viewed as mythical beasts but incidents from Scotland's past suggest that these might have been real living animals. The idea that a creature like the dragon walked the earth and even survived into relatively recent times seems hard to believe. But just because there are no dragons around today can we be so sure that such animals did not exist in the recent past? In its day the Linton dragon was as famous as the Loch Ness monster. It inhabited a cave at a spot still known as Worm's hole, close to the village of Linton in the Borders. A Norman carving of the dragon over the door of Linton Kirk shows a knight on horseback with his lance confronting the beast, suggesting that this was no fictional event but a genuine encounter. According to tradition, it was killed by a colleague of King William the Lion, George De Sommerville, who brought back the dragon's tongue to prove that he had finished the animal.

Although several hundred miles separate Linton from Sutherland a very similar dragon story can be found here. It too is generally dated to the Middle Ages although its origins may be much older. The slayer of the creature was a local man, Hector Gunn. The hill where the creature hid itself was known as Worm Hill (*Cnoc na Cnoimh* in Gaelic). There are many places with worm in their name; 'Worm Law' occurs in the Pentlands, all sites where it was believed dragons had their lair. The extensive distribution of the place name, and accounts of killing the beast, suggest that whatever it was, a type of animal we now call a dragon did exist. And was a dangerous creature.

It has been suggested that dragons may have been the last relic of a dying breed of dinosaurs, and there may be a case for this. Several hundred years ago Scotland's landscape was much wilder. Wolves survived till the 1740s and it may be that other more ancient creatures inhabited the forests that at one time stretched in an impenetrable mass all the way from the Scottish borders to Edinburgh and beyond. So could these have been the remnants of the last of the dinosaurs? And could they have been related to the monsters of the lochs? Dragons were known to live around the water's edge. So could the present day loch creatures be descendants of the fire-breathing dragons that terrorised our ancestors?

No dragons have been reported within living memory, but is sighting an animal like this any easier to imagine than confronting a goblin? Encounters with such a creature are rarely reported. It is astonishing, therefore, to learn that as recently as the 1980s a man out with his dog was confronted by what he could only describe as a 'goblin'. Martin had been given a springer spaniel for his fortieth birthday, which he intended to train as a working dog. He chose as the training ground a site just outside East Kilbride, an open area of ground surrounded by shrub, moor and heather. One evening, however, his normal training routine turned into a bizarre encounter. Martin recalled:

> The dog had gone into the scrub woodland to my right and started chasing what I took to be a rabbit or hare. The dog was barking as it ran in a wide circle. I could see something in front of the dog. But I was surprised to see as I watched that there was something red on whatever it was he was chasing. A dark blood-red. I thought maybe it was an injured animal, but it was going at some speed. The dog could never quite catch up with it and chased it round four or five times. They covered quite a bit of ground. The animal was moving closer to me by now and I realised that it was completely red. That was obviously puzzling. I whistled the dog over to me. But instead of the dog the creature he'd been chasing came over. I think it could have been the sound of the whistle that attracted it. I don't know where the dog went to at this time. He just fell quiet all of a sudden.

Martin then experienced a unique and direct encounter:

> The creature came towards me through the heather. As it approached I could see that it was an owl shape. It had a rounded

head on a very thick set neck. But the head was sunk into its shoulders. My mind was trying to tell me it must be an owl, but I knew it wasn't. It had square shoulders like a person. And as it got within fifteen yards of me I thought 'it's made of leather'. It wasn't smooth. It was partly wrinkled like a diver's suit when it comes out of the water. It didn't have any arms or legs that I could see and just seemed to be gliding along. It didn't seem to be making any sound. There was no noise of it brushing against the heather as it passed by. It just glided up towards me. I remember, however, that it was bobbing up and down when it was being chased by the dog. It moved as if it was bent forward. But when it came up to me it was definitely standing upright. It had square shoulders like a person not falling away like a bird's. It just seemed to be a body with a head and looked like something that had been skinned or plucked. It was about twenty to twenty-two inches in height. It wasn't skinny. It looked sturdy, in fact. It was a little fat thing. And ugly. There were wrinkles on its face. No nose or mouth. It had a large head compared to the body. It looked completely solid, not like a phantom or ghost.

In keeping with the rather fearsome reputation of these entities the creature showed no fear, as Martin explained:

It came within six feet of where I was standing and looked up at me. Two blue eyes just appeared out of nowhere on its face. The eyes were almond shaped, but up and down and not sideways like a human's. There were no eyebrows or lashes. And the thought went through my head 'it's a goblin!' I'd seen something that shouldn't be here. Then it turned side on and went off through the heather into the shrubland. In the direction of a nearby farm. It went off fast. I headed for the car and at that point the dog turned up. So I left the area right away. I wasn't frightened, but I was concerned.

Curiously, and though Martin was certainly not aware of it, the creature's appearance was in keeping with descriptions of a similar entity encountered across many centuries. According to tradition a goblin could be recognised because it wore a close-fitting suit that looked as if it was made of smooth black leather. A remarkable echo of Martin's account, which suggests that the weird entity he encountered was no figment of the imagination.

*

But these creatures are only one type of a whole race of strange beings. Entities that seem to inhabit a strange borderland world where fantasy, imagination and reality collide. But to some people, those with the power to see, these creatures we call 'fairies' are a diverse but ever-present race.

To our ancestors fairies were the alien entities of their day. A strange clan of beings whose land seemed to exist alongside our own yet lie in another, hidden place. But to appreciate the power and threat of the fairy race, we should forget the picture-book portrayal of these creatures. They can come in all shapes and sizes. They are often human-like in appearance although smaller in height and possessed of supernatural powers. They have the ability, shared by ghosts and aliens, to walk through solid walls and appear inside a house as if by magic. Time has no meaning in their dreamlike world so though you might be there for twenty human years it would seem as if no time at all had passed. Fairies also liked to steal babies and put another in its place. Just as modern-day abductees claim that aliens have taken babies from their wombs and put hybrids, half human and half something else, to take their place, to be brought up, unsuspecting, as part of our race.

But it would be a mistake to think of these entities in the past tense. They are still met with today, but many of these encounters are ignored or unreported because to even suggest that you might believe in these entities exposes individuals to ridicule. Psychic Ian Shanes reported seeing several of these creatures around Loch Morar in the 1990s. They were of various types. Elf-like creatures about eighteen inches tall. Entities with human heads and lizard-like tails. Another area was under the control of the elves that were using the streams that ran through it as transport canals. Their homes were, as in tradition, beneath two small humps which rose up from the surrounding flat land. In 1976 small entities with blue skins confronted a girl in a wood near Meigle in Fife and took her aboard some kind of craft. Are aliens and fairies connected in some bizarre way that we can't even begin to imagine?

Mystic Robert Crombie claimed to have encountered several of these beings in Edinburgh's Royal Botanic Gardens during the 1960s. Here wandering among the plants and shrubs were centaurs, half human, half horse as well as the more traditional elves and pixies. Crombie saw them all as friendly entities who were pleased to talk to him though surprised that he had the ability to see them. Crombie, however, was an unworldly character who seemed willing to take every bizarre creature he came across at its word. He even felt at ease following an encounter with the very 'demon king' of myth. Could Pan, part human, part goat, worshipped by the ancient Greeks, and regarded as the real Devil by Christianity, actually exist? And have stalked the streets of Edinburgh in the 1960s? Robert Crombie had no doubts. Walking in the ancient heart of the capital down the Mound towards Princes Street, Crombie was suddenly aware of a strange creature beside him. The being spoke to him, asking if he recognised who he was: 'Look at my cloven hooves, my shaggy legs and the horns on my forehead.' But he was not the Devil, claimed the creature, but the ancient god of old, Pan. Some months later on a trip to Iona, Crombie again encountered the strange entity. Though why an ancient pagan god should choose to appear on an island seen as a bastion of Christianity remains a mystery. Crombie, however, felt the being was no threat and became its willing tool, never doubting its sincerity. Whatever its true intentions it may, even today, be prowling the highways and byways of Scotland, approaching those it believes hold no ill will towards it, enticing them to become a friend.

But if bizarre creatures roam the land, or use the airways, is it any surprise that strange entities should inhabit the waters around our coasts? What was it that, almost unnoticed, was destroying animals around the shores of Scotland in the 1990s? Could it have been some half-man-half-fish beast which we, perhaps, too quickly assume belongs simply to myth? And could these creatures even be responsible for mysterious attacks on animals grazing on farmland close to the coast? Then there are the countless sudden unexplained disappearances of divers and swimmers. Accidents of nature or surprise attacks by an unidentified sea creature?

It might be wrong to think of those entities we call merpeople as a figment of long-lost myth, as a strange collection of these creatures held by the Royal Museum of Scotland shows. And as recently as August 1949 several mermen were seen by a number of witnesses near Craigmore in the parish of Kinlochbervie. And into the 1900s the area round Cape Wrath on Scotland's northern coast was known as 'the Land of Mermaids'. A witness at the turn of the century claimed to have seen 'a real mermaid' with 'reddish-yellow and curly hair and greenish-blue eyes'. He added 'she never moved . . . as she reclined amid the noise of the surf with her fish-like tail dangling over the side of the rock.' A peaceful scene to be sure, and an air of romance hangs over humanity's encounter with this strange race. But other incidents are more disturbing and suggest that these creatures have a less pleasant side.

A man about to jump into the sea at Inverbervie near Aberdeen to rescue a drowning girl was forcibly held back. Keeping a firm grip on his arm, his friend warned him that the woman was not human. She was one of the merpeople and that if he approached her she would drag him under the water. Just at that moment laughter drifted from the sea to mingle with the gathering gloom. The incident may have been exaggerated in the telling, but it does reveal one frequently ignored fact. The merpeople had a reputation for taking people to their death, and it could be that human flesh formed part of their diet. In Orkney the merpeople, known as the Fin Folk, were believed to be a race of beings that could live on the land or in the water though the seas were their natural home. Most of the time they remained submerged and travelling on land required some adjustment to their natural way of moving and breathing. So could an intelligent, fish-like entity survive and hide in submerged caves or shallow water close to land, undetected? It may be that such a group of beings have been driven, through fear of humanity, to live among the many islands that surround the Scottish mainland.

In the 1980s there were mysterious and savage attacks on seals around Orkney and Shetland. From the partly devoured bodies discarded on the rocks there was no doubt they had been attacked by a predator that must have emerged from the sea. Then in the 1990s seal pups, in the same area, disappeared at an astonishing rate. Unidentified animals were feeding on young seals even threatening the survival of the whole population. Scientists were baffled. One explained, 'The drop in numbers is such a dramatic change from the normal picture that we are certainly concerned. Even in the recent virus plague which killed thousands of seals the number of abandoned pups remained steady.' But no explanation for the dramatic killing spree was ever found.

A spate of mysterious whale deaths also puzzled scientists. As the Aberdeen newspaper, *The Press and Journal*, noted, there had been 'mounting concern' over the number of sperm whales washed up on the coastline. All bar one had died in Scottish waters. According to an expert 'the first was washed ashore on the Moray Firth. Soon after five were found at Mull, followed by a pair at Ulva and a further four in the Uists. . . . . There have been as many sperm whales stranded in the past six months as were found in the period from 1913.' Even the local dolphin population was affected. A news report on 28 July 1990 drew public attention to the odd series of events. It ran, 'It could be some time before the results of an investigation into the death of a bottle-nosed dolphin in the Moray Firth are available. The dolphin was found on a beach at Nairn. A post-mortem examination of the dolphin was ordered following growing concern about the increasing numbers of mammals being washed up on Highland coasts.' So who or what was attacking animal life in the area? Was it an unknown predator? And could the unexplained attacks on our sea life be connected to the supposedly 'mythical' merpeople?

There are strange pieces of evidence which together may lead to a bizarre conclusion. One dates from 1161 when fishermen, sailing close to the coast, caught in their nets a 'monster'. Except that this 'monster' looked almost human with a bald head and beard. He had a strange diet. The only food he would eat was raw fish. The creature seemed quite able to live on land though one day he managed to escape from the castle where he was being held and was last seen diving into the sea heading, presumably, to wherever he had come from. The other piece of the jigsaw can be seen in the coat of arms of the Earls of Atholl. On one side stands a 'wild man', bearded and half naked. Above him sits a mermaid. The 'wild man' represents a real entity that was found roaming the Atholl estates some time in the sixteenth century. He too appears to have been an eater of raw meat. And could the mermaid at his shoulder have been his consort? Whatever truth lies behind this strange coat of arms, it certainly suggests that in recent historical times the 'wild man' and 'people of the sea' were seen as being closely connected and, maybe, of one and the same race. The merpeople, or people of the sea, were not limited to a life in the water and could adapt to life on land. This could explain the many accounts of merpeople marrying into the human race. And maybe they are still out there.

The seas and oceans remain the great unexplored wilderness of the world. No one knows what we will discover at great depths beneath the waves, though of all the phenomena that have lasted into recent times, the existence of the merfolk may be the hardest to prove. It is surely an assumption, however, that a creature with a human body and fish's tail simply could not have existed. The world is full of strange-looking animals and many with bizarre features, like the half-bird-half-reptile pterodactyl, are 'known' to have inhabited the earth. And though no one has seen a pterodactyl there are many witnesses to the merfolk. But, on the other hand, maybe these creatures don't really exist in our world at all.

If not, then where do these entities in all their bizarre forms originate? A clue can, perhaps, be found in the experience of Fiona Martin. In 1998 Fiona was being driven past a radio transmitter in the north of Scotland when she saw something suspended in mid-air above the enclosed buildings. She snapped a quick photo, but could hardly have been prepared for what she saw when the film was developed. The picture showed a distinct dog-headed creature floating beside the radio mast. It looked like the ancient Egyptian god, Anubis, which though usually portrayed today as jackal headed was also drawn by the Egyptians with a dog's head. Does

Fiona's sighting confirm what psychics have claimed – that currents of energy bring through entities from other worlds? And could the type of energy we are creating with our modern technology, from nuclear-power plants to mobile-telephone masts, be providing ever more paths for weird creatures from other dimensions to enter into our world? Maybe these beings are using our earth as some kind of playground, darting in and out as the mood takes, or as a mystic gate opens and closes. Some, perhaps, enter by accident and find themselves trapped. Others may come deliberately with no good purpose in mind. Whatever the answer one fact is clear. There are creatures appearing in every part of Scotland that simply defy rational explanation.

FOUR

Blood lust

THE VICTIM'S FATHER knew before anyone else that something strange had happened. Two thousand miles away, in his Rome apartment, Professor Fornario woke with a start. A voice in his head was speaking clearly but calmly. It told him that an accident had happened to his daughter Nora, who he hadn't seen for some time. She was living in London, deeply involved with spiritual and occult circles. Fornario did not know whether to believe the telepathic message he had received. Although Italy was a hotbed of occult groups, and considerable controversy had been created over the activity of visiting mediums, Professor Fornario was not himself a believer. But the voice that woke him that night told the truth. A tragic accident had befallen his daughter in the early hours of a November morning. She had been found dead on the remote island of Iona, naked apart from the cloak beneath her shoulders and a silver chain around her neck. By her side lay a knife used in ritual magic. The site of her death was the mysterious fairy mound, a spot that already had a reputation for causing the disappearance of unwary locals.

Nora's father never visited Iona so probably went to his death unaware of the full circumstances of his daughter's tragic end. But he is not alone. Seventy years on the death, some say murder, of Nora Fornario remains an unsolved puzzle. A mystery that the authorities of the day never attempted properly to unravel.

It's hard to think of Iona as an occult centre. More a bastion of Christianity. It is certainly today, as it has been for the last thousand years, a centre of pilgrimage for the devoted. A focus for the devout believer. So what drove a novice dabbler in the black arts to head for the little island in the summer of that year? Maybe she thought it was a safe haven. Or perhaps she had something else in mind. For one thing is sure. Iona is not quite what it seems.

There are strange tales linked to the island, weird incidents that must have been known to the people of the time. So it is hard to understand why, in the sixth century, St Columba chose it as the site for his mission to convert Scotland to Christianity. Even more curious is Columba's contact with the 'other side'. Here was a man who regularly met strange beings at an ancient fairy mound on the west coast of Iona. At the exact spot where, centuries later, a visitor to the island was to suffer a bizarre fate. One that has mystified students of the paranormal ever since.

When Nora arrived with a companion in tow in August 1929 she seems to have had no clear idea of how long she intended to stay. Unfortunately, the friend who accompanied her has never been identified. A key witness who could probably have shed light on later events. Why she travelled there with Nora and then suddenly left has never been satisfactorily explained. Nora had arranged lodgings with a Mrs Macdonald at a house that lay close to the shore not too far from the ferry landing point. Norah was 33 years of age, the daughter of an Italian-born doctor and a mother from a well-off background. By the time Nora arrived on Iona her mother had been dead for several years and her nearest relative was her professor father in distant Rome. Nora herself appeared to those who met her to be of a rather unsettled nature. She had become fascinated by, and actively involved in, the kaleidoscope of magic societies and occult orders that had their home in the cosmopolitan scene that was London. She seems to have become obsessed with it. This obsession came into the open after she moved to new lodgings at an isolated croft owned by the Cameron family. On an island the size of Iona it may be out of place to describe any place as isolated. In fact, it was only half a mile from the main village site at Port Ronain. But in the darker months, in that windswept landscape, with only the sounds of nature to disturb the rhythm of the evening, a house standing on its own can feel a world away from the everyday life of a big city.

So while Nora had time to sit on the shore writing or contemplating the beauty of nature, there was also time to sit in the lonely isolation of her small bedroom brooding on the nature of the spirit world. And how that might be used by her or against her. According to those who knew her at this time she frequently went on late-night walks. The place she most often headed for was a site with a formidable history: the Fairy Knowe or mound; the *Sithean Mor* in Gaelic. A grassy hillock, lying just south of the spot where Iona's only road ended, at an area of fertile land dominating the middle-western part of the island known as the Machar. The Fairy Knowe was visited as often by Columba as it was later to be by Nora Fornario. It was here that Columba was several times seen to communicate with entities described by his contemporaries as 'angels', whatever, in reality, they may have been.

Nora shared Columba's belief in the power to contact beings from other worlds. She was not short of money and could afford to indulge her occult passion. She had no paid employment, but her family was well enough off to allow her to employ a housekeeper, Mrs Edna Varney. Speaking from Nora's home in Mortlake Road, London Mrs Varney told reporters that Nora was 'a woman of extraordinary character who claimed to cure people by telepathy' and 'went off into trances for several hours'. A self-induced trance state is the classic way of entering the spirit domain, and explains why Nora told the Cameron family at Traighmor that they should not be concerned if her trances lasted as long as a week. But she never did manage that feat. Nora probably did not possess the dedication of mind to master the self-control necessary to interact with the spiritual realm on an equal footing.

But did she go time after time to the fairy mound because she was building up to a key magic ritual? And if so what went wrong that fatal night? We know that she was last seen alive around 10 p.m. on Sunday the seventeenth when she left the Cameron's simple two-storey cottage at Traighmor. Then she simply vanished into the night. And, according to the police, died all alone on the *Sithean Mor*. Detective work allows no room for fables or mysterious entities. Not the kind of evidence that would stand much scrutiny in a court of law. So, suicide, which requires no external hand to accomplish it, or that other verdict loved by the authorities when they have no obvious explanation to hand – accidental death – proved very convenient solutions in Nora Fornario's case.

But did she really die alone? Who was the cloaked man who was reportedly seen near the body? Whoever he was, if he was from this world, he was never caught or interviewed. But it does beg the question of just what was going on. Could Nora have been the victim of some kind of sacrifice? As the report in the *Times* describes it 'the body was found unclothed on the hillside. Round the neck was a silver chain with a cross. Nearby lay a knife which had been used to cut a large cross on the turf.' It certainly suggests that some kind of ritual was being enacted.

However, not everyone is convinced. Calum Cameron, the 12-year-old son of the lady with whom Nora was staying at the time of the events, for one. He claimed in the 1980s that what Nora had with her on the 'Hill of Angels' was no sacred weapon but a simple kitchen knife. Cameron may well be correct, but that does not rule out the possibility that a ritual was being carried out. It is the consecration of the knife beforehand that is the key, the magic procedure that turns an ordinary knife into a supernatural instrument. The type of knife is quite irrelevant. Any kind will do. The key question surely is that, if it was indeed an ordinary kitchen knife, why had she bothered to take it with her in the first place? She must have brought it for a reason. And the answer surely is that it had been consecrated for ritual purposes.

Which brings us to another possibility. Could a second person have been involved? A stranger to the island acquainted with Nora would surely have been noticed. But what if they had kept their association secret? There were many regular visitors to the island connected with the religious community. Could one of them have been secretly assisting Nora carry through whatever she was attempting to do? It remains an outside chance. On the other hand, if a cloaked figure was seen near Nora on that last night, as one witness claimed, he may have been nothing less that an entity from another world. And surely Nora's killer. But if not, and 'simply' a flesh-and-blood person, just what was his role in this strange affair?

And what explains 'blue lights' seen dancing around the fairy mound at about the same time Nora was known to have been there for her final visit? Traditionally, blue lights have been associated with the presence of supernatural beings. Entities maybe demonic maybe angelic who live like humans do in some strange world that borders on our own.

More likely than not Nora was aware of Iona's strange mix of spiritual currents. It is a melting pot of mystic tributaries. But that doesn't solve the puzzle of whether or not she went to Iona simply to bathe in its aura or to use it for some kind of end. The 1920s had been an occult battleground, a period when opposing factions had built on their confrontations from an earlier time. Those who believed in the power of ritual and spells had come together in two key groups: the Order of the Golden Dawn and the Rosicrucians. But even within these groups rivalries erupted and individuals had fallen out with each other. With their ability to conjure up spirits from other worlds the conflict between groups and individuals spilled into other dimensions. But the target remained those who walked the earth. In retrospect, Nora appears a practitioner of the black arts with no special status. If the incident on Iona had not turned her into a celebrity of notoriety we would not remember her as we do other mystics like Aleister Crowley and McGregor Mathers. But though not in the first rank of magicians there was a clear belief that, around the time of her visit to Iona, she had fallen out with someone in the occult underground. And there was the fate of Raoul Loveday to consider. Loveday, a disciple of the notorious Aleister Crowley, died in mysterious circumstances at the Italian Abbey of Cefalu. It was widely believed that he had met his death because he had fallen out with Crowley. An event that no one who believed in the power of ritual magic could afford to ignore.

So was it simply fear or some other reason which took Nora to Iona? According to some accounts Nora believed that in a previous life she had lived on the island. If so she was no doubt aware of Columba's strange decision to bury alive one of his followers, a man known as Oran. When the grave was opened three days later Columba was, apparently, astonished to find that Oran was not dead. He appeared to be almost incoherent but the things he was saying were quite clear if not exactly what his listeners wanted to hear. His words included the strange statement that 'there is no great wonder in death. Nor is Hell what is has been described.' It seems unlikely that Columba would bury one of his followers alive as a sacrifice. So what was going on? It may be that Oran's experience has been mixed up with an ancient ritual practised on the island. A pagan shamanistic experience whereby the practitioner 'travelled to other worlds' and brought back to his people his accounts of these strange journeys.

Could Nora have believed that she was a reincarnation of this Dark Age monk? Nora – a name with such strange echoes of Oran that it does make one wonder if it is pure coincidence – made a remark to her housekeeper of key significance. Mrs Varney reported that Nora had told her that: 'Several times she said she had been to the "far beyond" and had come back to life after spending some time in another world.' Just as Oran appears to have done 1,500 years before.

There are no doubt sceptics who will dismiss the paranormal link and Nora's connection with Oran as pure speculation. But those who reject the role of the supernatural have missed a key factor in Nora's death, one aspect that has not been raised previously. Where was Nora in the time between her disappearance on Sunday and the discovery of her body on Tuesday? Could it be that her body was put in or was going to be put into the ground? Does that explain the mysterious cut marks on the surface of the mound? It is possible though it is hard to believe that Nora could have been placed beneath the ground without the 'grave' being discovered when she was found. On the other hand it has to be admitted that the investigation of her death does not appear to have been a thorough one. The authorities seem to have worked back from the belief that the whole event was a strange accident. So perhaps they didn't look too closely at the Fairy Mound itself. But even if they did, and had discovered nothing out of place, it leaves an even greater puzzle. Where did Nora's body lie from the time she disappeared on Sunday 17 November till its discovery on Tuesday 19 November at 1.30 p.m.? On an island as small as Iona, and as prominent a landmark as the Fairy Hill lying just off one of the few roads, it is hard to believe that no one noticed a naked corpse right through Monday and into midday Tuesday.

But that's not how it was seen at the time. Nora's death certificate was endorsed by the procurator-fiscal for the area. Clearly, Nora had died in unusual circumstances. It might be taken for granted that some basic questions needed to be cleared up. Such as why Nora lay for so long in the open air without being spotted? After all the Fairy Hill is less than half a mile from the house Nora was staying in. It was a site she was known to visit regularly. But if you think that the suspicion of the police was bound to have been aroused you would be wrong. There seems to have been a strange lack of interest. No written report was prepared by the procurator-fiscal for one thing. His signature on the death certificate proves that, far from being concerned over the incident, he accepted the doctor's verdict. There had been nothing bizarre in Nora's death, apparently. She had simply died of exposure, a verdict that, looking back, seems almost impossible to accept. Particularly when we take into account the police's discovery, in Nora's little bedroom, of a whole boxful of what were described as 'strange letters', the contents of which were never revealed. Perhaps we must look to other dimensions for the solution to the unexplained death of a woman who so wanted to contact the spirit world. Maybe Nora Fornario got too close to the 'land beyond' for her own good.

*

But what makes a murder a ritual killing? It must be carried out for a reason other than the perverted pleasure of depriving another human being of life. To those involved in the dark side of magic the act of death has a special significance as it releases, they believe, a form of energy that can be used for other, maybe demonic, purposes. Alternatively, some bodily part or fluid from the victim may be removed to be used later in a ritual of some kind. Was this the motive behind the Bible John killings? These were serial murders from the 1960s that stunned a nation and remain unsolved to this day. A triple batch of deaths that have puzzled a succession of investigators because they seem to have no purpose and stopped abruptly for no apparent reason.

By the time the man who became known as Bible John turned up at Glasgow's Barrowland Ballroom that Saturday in August 1969 he had already killed once. In February 1968 he had been prowling the same dance hall and struck up a conversation with 25-year-old Patricia Docker. Witnesses saw the couple at various times as John walked Patricia back to her home in Langside Place. At some point in the early hours of the following morning, Friday 23 February, John strangled Patricia and left her unclothed body in Carmichael Place just round the corner from where she stayed. She had been having her period and John had deliberately removed the sanitary towel she was wearing. It seemed an odd thing to do, and surprised experienced police officers who had seen more than their fair share of strange behaviour. The police jumped to the conclusion that the killer had been frustrated in his attempts to have intercourse and that his passion had turned to murder. Oddly, in spite of the fact that both John and Patricia had met at a busy venue, no one remembered seeing them. There was a good reason for this. The police believed that Pat had attended the Majestic Ballroom in Hope Street. They spent a fruitless two weeks interviewing patrons at the dance hall before someone tipped them off that she must have met John at the Barrowlands. The place she had actually gone to though not set out for. By the time they discovered their mistake the trail for the killer had gone cold.

Not that John cared. He was prepared to take incredible risks to get what he wanted. Even turning up at a dance hall on a Saturday night was taking a chance. In spite of the heaving crowd, if you were chatting to one of the women, you might easily be remembered by her pal. But John didn't seem to worry too much. He had already chosen one victim from the same dance hall. Now

Jemima, or Mima, McDonald, a single mother of three, was unfortunate enough to be the next. Exactly why or how she got into conversation with John is unknown. But around midnight Mima left the Barrowlands and set off for her tenement address in Mackeith Street. She wasn't alone. She felt safe enough in John's company to allow him to walk her back to her flat.

Several hours later, on the morning of Saturday 17 August, Mima's body was discovered by her sister Margaret in a derelict building only thirty yards from her home. Police quickly noticed similarities with the murder of Patricia Docker some eighteen months before. Both had last been seen alive in the company of a man they had met at the Barrowlands. Both women had been strangled and their handbags had been stolen. They had been having their period and the murderer had carefully removed each woman's sanitary towel. It all seemed more than coincidence.

Witnesses soon came forward claiming to have seen Mima McDonald. They had caught a good view of her companion. He appeared quite a distinctive individual. To the police it seemed that if his picture could be widely displayed, someone, somewhere would be bound to recognise him. It duly appeared with a volley of publicity and a detailed description of 'John'. He was, the public were told: 'Aged 25–35. Six feet to six feet two inches tall. Slim build with a thin pale face. He had reddish fair hair, cut short and brushed back. He was wearing a blue suit of good quality with hand-stitched lapels and a white shirt.'

But John seemed quite unconcerned by this intense media interest in his activities. He carried on as if he was from another world, not even bothering to change the venue at which he selected his victims. There were dozens of dance halls in 1960s Glasgow, but John headed straight back to the Barrowlands for his final killing day.

As he moved through the crowd, he seemed almost indifferent to the picture he presented. According to Jean Langford he stood out from the men who usually turned up. Smartly dressed though he undoubtedly was his clothes had little in common with sixties fashion. She chuckled at his well-tailored brown suit with three buttons, the blue shirt and diagonally striped tie. John's cutaway suede boots caused Jean real amusement and she overheard one of the dancers make a joke about them. Jean had made the trip to the Barrowlands that Thursday with her sister Helen Puttock. They both enjoyed dancing and, though Helen was married, her husband had no objection to her evening out. And so Helen struck up a conversation with John while Jean danced with another man who also gave his name as 'John'. Neither sister's dancing partner claimed to know the other.

Did John have murder on his mind at this stage? Common-sense would indicate that he did not. Not only had he allowed himself to be seen closely by two people he had no intention of killing but also as the two couples left the dance hall John demanded to see the manager. The cigarette machine in the foyer had jammed when Helen tried to buy a packet. According to Jean, John became enraged and complained to the manager and then to the assistant manager. He could hardly fail to notice that he was drawing attention to himself.

But he seemed nonplussed, even unaware of the fact that he would be better remembered because of it all. And even then he didn't steal away into the night, but calmly walked down the road with Jean, Helen and 'John' to the taxi rank where they waited and chatted till a cab was free. Now they were down to three as the other 'John' waved goodbye and headed for a bus. He was never heard from again. Bible John, Helen and Jean clambered into the taxi. Now there was another potential witness. The taxi driver. As it turned out he couldn't remember much about his passengers, but John could hardly have guessed that when he got into his cab. He had, as can be imagined, more important matters on his mind. He was anxious to get Helen on her own so told the cabman to let Jean off first even though she lived further down the road than her sister.

Jean was dropped off at the Kelso Street roundabout, waved goodbye to Helen, and watched the taxi turn back towards Earl Street, Helen's address. A short while later the cab stopped to let John and Helen out. They must have quickly headed for a back court not far from Helen's flat. By one o' clock Helen Puttock was dead and not a soul had heard her cry out.

A man walking his dog in the early hours of that Friday morning found her body. Helen was lying face down in the back court where she had led John. She still had on the ocelot fur coat and black woollen dress she had worn on the previous night's trip to the Barrowlands. But it was clear from the grass on her body and marks on the ground that Helen had made a frantic attempt to escape when John began his attack. Like Patricia and Mima before her she had been strangled and sexually assaulted.

The sisters' journey in the taxi, where Jean had spoken with John, now became of key importance in the murder hunt. The killer had given clues about himself, but how far could they be relied on? It was on this final journey that John made reference to his knowledge of the Bible and was thereafter dubbed by the press 'Bible John'. He quoted passages, although it wasn't necessarily clear from which part of the Old or New Testament they came. There seemed to be a reference to the story of Moses among the bulrushes. But knowledge of that famous incident, often taught in schools, hardly requires a biblical scholar.

It was also during the taxi ride that Jean believed she heard John mutter something about his surname. She didn't quite catch what he said and thought it sounded like Templeton, Sempleton or Emerson. They do have a similar sound, but Jean's memory could well be hazy on the matter because, if John mentioned all three, he was clearly not referring to a surname. Could he have been saying something completely different, something that does have a biblical connection? What he may have actually muttered was not 'Templeton, Sempleton, Emerson', but the 'Temple of Solomon, Jerusalem'. It would also link with John's reference to Moses. It was Moses who led the Jewish people out of slavery in Egypt. He had with him the mystical Ark of the Covenant, a strange box-like structure built under God's direct instruction. The Ark was eventually housed within the Temple of Solomon in Jerusalem. The site of the Temple was regarded even in Western Europe as one where strange, paranormal events could occur. In the twelfth century the first leaders of the mysterious Knights Templar organisation dug into the then ruined Temple and removed various objects they discovered, objects that were believed to have super-natural power. Some of these artefacts, it is claimed, ended up in

Scotland when the Templars fled to this country to escape accusations of devil worship. True or not there can be no doubting that the Templars inspired a whole range of secret societies from the Freemasons to more arcane practitioners of the Black Arts. Even today, there are individuals who believe they possess secret knowledge and that by using certain materials, phrases and rituals they can gain access to hidden worlds denied to most of us. Could Bible John have been one of them?

If so this would explain a key link in the killings. One that marked out the murders with Bible John's stamp. The fact that all three women were having their monthly period at the time John met and then strangled them. Did he know that for Patricia, Mima and Helen this was that time of the month? Or was it pure bad luck for the victims? The police took the view that if John had been allowed by the women a certain amount of sexual intimacy, then the murders would not have occurred. In other words, John, his sexual urges aroused, found that his female companions would not allow him to go any further. His response, the police believed, was either one of sexual disgust or fury. An uncontrollable anger that he took out on the women he had so recently chatted up.

But how could John have guessed when he met them that Patricia, Mima and Helen were having a period? The odds against picking up three women, one after the other, each of whom is in that bodily state would make it a highly unlikely sequence.

However, if John was only attacking women who aroused his loathing he must have picked up several women before and during the period June 1967 to October 1969. Women he had a normal relationship with, but who have never come forward. So what triggered the explosion when he encountered a woman who was having a period? Was it some perverse, twisted desire to force an outlet for the violence contained within him?

Or did he have a more definite purpose in mind? Did Bible John deliberately target women having a period for a sinister, but not sexual, purpose? Menstrual blood, though it may seem difficult to believe, was regarded as possessing magical properties by a wide variety of magic-obsessed cults. It is possible that, far from being frustrated by the fact that his female friends were having a period, John believed his victim's blood flow to have supernatural properties. Could John then have been part of some strange black-magic group, one to which menstrual blood formed a significant ritual object?

Unlikely? In each case the sanitary towel that the victim was using was carefully removed and, in Helen Puttock's case, the final murder, placed beneath the left armpit as if left as a clue. A hint the killer guessed the police would never understand, and an act that does not suggest a man who was disgusted or angered by encountering a woman who was having a period. It would suggest that, far from repulsing him, it was what he had come for. It was this realisation that may have triggered the panic evident in Helen Puttock's desperate attempts to escape. Attempts which strangely went unnoticed even though the murder took place, according to the police, at the back of a close.

Serial killers do not stop because they have found something more 'interesting' to do. They don't suddenly decide to take up darts because they've had enough of murder. They just keep going till they get caught or they die. But serial murder with a purpose is a different story. John stopped because he had got what he wanted. And if he was involved with others, it may be that he had obtained for them what they wanted. However, John could well have been acting on his own. A psychological profile of Bible John indicated that he would be the type of person who would have an active interest in black magic and the occult. It could well be that such an obsession drove him to commit murder with no help from anyone.

But if he was a man driven by obsession why did he slip away so abruptly and so successfully? Because after Helen Puttock's murder he disappeared as though he had never been. The man we remember as Bible John seems to have known that, like a phantom, he could vanish into the night and never be seen again.

So was there a cover up? If so, that would have to involve the police and suggest that officers were involved in occult circles of some kind. That seems highly unlikely. But if there was a plan to target specific women then John could well have had accomplices. Jean Langford remarked on the length of time both her own and

Helen's 'John' spent together in the male toilets as they got ready to go. Clearly, a conversation of some kind was going on. And it was highly convenient that as Bible John was getting into conversation with Helen, the second John was engaging Jean's attention. Then, at the last moment, as they wait at the taxi rank, Jean's partner walks off for a bus, leaving Bible John to travel with the two women, knowing that at some point he and Helen will be left on their own. In fact, Jean's John shares a key fate with Bible John. After 31 October neither is ever seen or heard of again.

31 October. The day on which Helen's body was found. An important day in the occult calendar. The day on which the veil between this world and the next is at its thinnest. It's the best day in the year, black magicians believe, on which to summon up the spirits of the dead. But it could, of course, just be coincidence. As may be the fact that there were three victims. Three is one of the most powerful mystical numbers. And to practitioners of black magic, numbers bring influence especially over entities from other worlds. They are also highly symbolic. So to a twisted mind, to kill three women, and the last on 31 October, would be in occult terms a highly significant act. One that could raise the perpetrator's ability to greater levels in ritual magic. So Bible John's killing spree could have come to an end because he had achieved what he set out to do. And there was simply no need to carry on and run the risk again of being caught.

*

So could there be more unexplained deaths in which the ritual aspect has simply been overlooked? Take the shocking discovery made on the banks of the river Tay in 1971. It is a strange coincidence that postman Ian Henderson took his child for a walk along the shore that morning in May. It must have made the day's events all the more poignant. But the object he saw bobbing gently in the water looked innocent enough at first glance. A broad estuary like the Tay is full of floating debris. There was something odd about this scene though which forced Ian to give it a second, more thoughtful, look. Ian, a 32-year-old postman in the fishing village of Tayport, had set out for the local boating pond, situated on the east common, with his son Neil to spectate at a model-ship race. Rough weather had, however, wrecked any chance of the competition going ahead so Ian took a detour down by the river as consolation. A fateful decision, as it worked out. It fell to him to make the grim discovery. The bundle of clothing lying a few feet from the bank's edge had a horrifying story to reveal. As he turned it over a small face stared up at him. The face of a dead child.

The pathologist who examined the body was fairly confident about the basic facts. The male child was between three and four years old and had met his death by drowning. He was wearing a pyjama-type jersey over a blue shirt. He was just under three feet tall. So a missing child and, everyone assumed, the parents or relatives, friends and neighbours would soon appear to give him a name. After all, this was no newborn baby which could arrive and go without being missed. He was a toddler who could have been on the verge of entering a nursery school. A well-nourished individual with an identity. A child who could probably speak and must have spoken to people. Who did not look as if he had been locked up in a darkened room or hidden from public view. But in spite of massive publicity not a single person came forward to identify the lad. There wasn't even a definite lead to connect him to anyone or any place. He seemed to have come from nowhere. A child without a past whose future had been abruptly cut short.

Various suggestions were mooted to explain why no one had claimed the boy as one of their own. He and his family had met a tragic death in a boating accident, maybe even as far away as the North Sea. The body had been taken by the tide and ended up on the banks of the Tay. The river was wide at the point the lad had been found. Over a mile across. No other cadavers, however, which could be linked to the wee boy ever turned up. No reports of a missing family or of a lost boat. That left suicide or murder. If it was suicide then clearly an adult must have played a part. But if a parent or relative was involved then it increased the chance that someone, somewhere would notice. The fact that no one had noticed suggested not only a crime, but also a conspiracy. A determination to conceal the fact of the child's death. That the unnamed boy had been deliberately killed and his body disposed of somewhere on the banks of the Tay. But if concealment was a key motive why throw the body into a river? Surely a burial in some faraway spot would have been more sensible. Unless the child had died for some unknown purpose.

Meanwhile, with the police inquiry grinding to a halt, the little body was released to be interred in a local graveyard. A grey stone monument, paid for by public subscription, marks the site of the coffin. Freshly laid flowers and battered children's toys put there by parents and their offspring through the years are a poignant reminder of those tragic events. For the little boy has never been identified. And the incident remains an unsolved mystery.

Thirty years later and four hundred miles away Aidan Minter, a 32-year-old businessman, was crossing London's Tower Bridge on the afternoon of 21 September 2001. He was on his way to a meeting, but his attention was caught by a small bundle bobbing in the current below. He assumed it to be simply debris though kept his eyes on the object as it moved downstream. Suddenly the full horror of what he was seeing hit him. There could be no mistaking the severed bones projecting from the darkened load. When the police reached it they discovered a headless torso. It was the body of a 5-year-old boy, of African origin, dressed in orange shorts. Examination revealed that the lad's neck had been cut and the body drained of blood. Days later police frogmen dredged another strange bundle from the Thames: a cotton sheet inside which rested six wax candles. A name had been scratched into each candle. The name, it is believed, of the dead boy. No one, however, came forward to claim or identify him.

Whoever the little boy was there could be no doubting that a bizarre crime had been revealed. One unique even in London's catalogue of horrors. The child, it appeared, had been killed in a black magic rite then dressed in orange and thrown into water as part of the ritual of killing. The police admitted they were dealing with no ordinary crime. A spokesman announced, 'we cannot rule out a ritualistic motive. The candles were found in the Thames thirteen days after the little boy. We believe the two discoveries may be linked.' An expert on witchcraft-related killings confirmed that using the body parts of a young person is a key aspect of ritual murder in South Africa's shanty towns. It is believed to enhance the effectiveness of a black magic spell. Police were also convinced that the orange shorts had been put on the body after death. Orange and red are considered lucky colours in witchcraft killings, so the shorts possessed a ritual significance.

But does a bizarre death in London in the twenty-first century tell us anything about a body found on the banks of the Tay in 1971? There are clear differences. One lad was black, the other was white. The Thames toddler had been brutally mutilated. The body in the Tay was intact. The deaths occurred four hundred miles and thirty years apart. Clearly the people who carried out the acts were not connected. But there are also similarities. Both deaths involved young boys. Both had been dumped into fast-flowing water rather than being hidden. Both were around the same age. Both were wearing clothes when it would have been easy to have removed them and make identification more difficult. And no one has come forward to claim either boy. So what can we learn from the Thames murder? An aspect of the crime that the police, hardly geared up for this kind of murder, cannot be blamed for overlooking in the Tay case: the ritual aspect of the 'unknown child's' death.

The date on which the body was found in the Tay, 23 May, does not have any particular significance. But, according to the experts, the child's body had been in the water for three to six weeks. A period of time that would cover a key date. One of the 'holiest' days of the year in the pre-Christian era: 1 May, Beltane. The end of the winter and the start of summer. A date that long ago was celebrated with fire, festivity and sacrifice. Even human sacrifice. To some it remains a 'holy' day. Could the little lad have been suffocated in some weird pagan ceremony?

And then there's the tab mark on the shirt. It was a make that went under the Achilles label. Pure chance? Police investigation revealed that this particular brand had ceased production. In fact the last batch had come off a factory line in Leeds five years before and could have been up to twelve years old. So why was the child wearing such an out-of-date top? Even in large families to hand down clothing of that vintage seems a bit strange. If it had been worn by other members of the family then, surely, it would have presented a pretty well-used appearance. That it could have been deliberately put on the child as a symbol seems to have escaped the notice of the police. But what could be symbolic of the shirt? The name: Achilles was a hero of the Greek myths. And what is the most famous story linked to Achilles? The fact that he was made invulnerable to human harm by being dipped in a river. It seems hard to believe that this was pure coincidence.

Like the boy discovered in the Thames, the Tay lad was wearing distinctive-coloured clothes. Blue in this case. The colour in Scotland traditionally connected to the supernatural. Fairy folk were believed to have blue skin and to dress in blue. This tradition was particularly strong in Fife along the coast of which the boy's body was found. There was the 'Blue Stone' of Crail, allegedly thrown by the Devil at a local church and a 'Blue Stone' in St Andrews, a meeting place for fairies. Myths to some, but not to those interested in working magic to which colours have a significant part to play in summoning up the powers of darkness or as protection. The pharaohs of ancient Egypt wore blue to ward off evil spirits.

The colour blue also appeared on the pyjama top the boy wore. This piece of clothing was decorated with ovals and rectangles coloured yellow and blue. Yellow, as with blue, is a colour symbolising the Devil. It is an unlucky colour associated with jealousy and treachery. Geometric designs have close links to magic rituals. We think usually of the pentagram, the five-pointed star, drawn on floors and walls as protection against evil. But other figures from the pyramid to the circle, and variations in between, have their own mystic significance.

Chief Superintendent William White, who was directing the inquiry, commented that the police did not 'consider it significant that the body was minus trousers, stockings and shoes – the action of the sea could account for these articles being missing'. This could well have been true, but it is also possible that they were deliberately removed to draw attention to the other clothing the lad had on, particularly as the blue shirt had been deliberately altered in order to fit him.

There are other odd aspects. Not only was the boy wearing a blue 'Achilles' shirt, but it was labelled as a size three. Three is the most sacred number in magic rites. It is a combination of one (male) and two (female) and is seen as the perfect number of the universe. It has a special potency and significance. The number three appears again in a bizarre phone call made to the police a few days after the discovery of the body. The caller, who did not identify himself, said that the boy could be identified through a Donald Paterson who lived at 2 New Hamilton Road, Dumfries. The address and name, according to the police, turned out to be non-existent. The same was true of the phone number the caller gave, Dumfries, 35111. So what was the purpose of so specific a statement? Did the caller intend leaving a clue in the phone number? Three was the number found on the boy's shirt and a most sacred number in magic rites. Five is a key number in magical and religious texts as any reader of the Bible will know. And then there are the three ones. Six is well known as the number of the Devil as in '666' the notorious 'mark of the beast' described in the Bible's 'Book of Revelations'. But the number one also has a long tradition as the Devil's number. The caller gave three ones in a row '111' which is the equivalent of '666'. Was the caller saying to anyone who could understand that the boy had been suffocated or drowned in water because he had literally the Devil in him or as a sacrifice of some kind to ward off or appease the powers of darkness?

But that's not all. Those interested in the workings of magic have for centuries linked numbers to letters. The number one, for example, can be linked to the letter A. Usually several letters are linked to one number so that, for example, the number three is linked to C, L and U. If we take the numbers given by the anonymous caller in the order he gave them we get:

3 = CLU
5= ENW
1= AJS

Which could read 'Clue NWAJS' with the AJS repeated twice more for emphasis. This may have mystical significance or a more precise meaning. The caller must have known that the details would be widely reported in an investigation rapidly running out of leads. It could have been intended as a warning to one person or a group.

Ritual murder may appear far-fetched, an event only portrayed in films or in horror stories. Unfortunately, rare though they may be in real life, they do occur. In January 1971, Olton and Eileen Goring told their seven children that Eileen was dying of cancer. One of them would have to be sacrificed in order that Eileen should live. Sixteen-year-old Keith Goring was strangled and stabbed to death, then stretched out in the shape of a cross in the front garden while other members of the family danced around him. Both parents were tried, found guilty and sent to mental institutions. To an unbalanced mind, a ritual killing may seem a perfectly reasonable way to solve a problem. They may even feel that they are doing it as part of some greater plan.

Could some unbalanced person have thought that the little boy possessed by the Devil and carried out some weird exorcism? Was the ritual carried out on the banks of the Tay? Even in Tayport itself? Maybe they didn't mean to harm him. It could have been meant as a service of protection, but somehow it all went wrong. And the lad drowned. Thirty years have passed, but somewhere, probably locally, there are people who know the answer to the riddle. Individuals who could easily throw light on the fate of that unknown child.

FIVE

The undead

IN THE SUMMER of 1923 two men were roaming the area between Atholl and Braemar in the Scottish Highlands. Poaching is best carried out under the cover of darkness as those involved in the unlawful trapping of game naturally want to avoid drawing the law's attention to their clandestine activities. The two poachers involved, George Reid and Andrew Wilson, were well known to the local police, but because of their expert knowledge of the area felt confident that they would always keep one step ahead of the authorities. On this particular evening Reid and Wilson arrived late on at a bothy at remote Fealaar. Forcing a window they scrambled inside and began a fire to cook a meal. They were miles from anywhere so had no doubts they would be safe from unexpected arrivals. Reid volunteered to go back outside for water and threw a leg over the window sill. He paused for a moment and Wilson, only half watching, assumed that he was about to swing his left leg and drop out. Instead Reid started to scream. Stunned, Wilson could only watch in amazement, till the spell was broken by Reid shouting in rising panic that a creature had got hold of his leg and was sucking blood from it. Wilson ran to his companion and managed to haul him back inside. Reid was in a frantic state, his leg smeared with blood. He told Wilson that he could remember seeing several white winged-creatures hovering in the distance and blue balls of lights which kept moving around. He had not been aware of any creature approaching him as he watched. Wilson cleaned the blood from Reid's leg revealing a series of puncture marks. It was from these wounds that blood had been drawn. After exchanging a few more words, the men agreed that it might be better to stay inside the bothy till light broke. Then when they thought it was safe to do so, they emerged gingerly to inspect the area around their shelter. They could see no tracks of any animal that would explain the attack, even at the spot where splashes of blood from Reid's leg had dripped to the ground. There was no doubt that wounds had been inflicted, but could that incident have a simple explanation? And his imagination then did the rest? Not as far as Reid was concerned. For the rest of his life he was convinced that he had been the victim of some kind of vampire, and avoided the bothy at Fealaar. It might be easy to dismiss Reid's encounter, if it didn't fit a pattern. A tradition of a native creature that most Scots nowadays seem largely unaware of, or, maybe, simply choose to ignore.

Of all the strange entities encountered across Scotland, vampires are the hardest to accept. They seem to belong to the world of myth rather than reality. And vampires are not creatures we usually associate with Scotland. If we think of a connection it is with Slains Castle near Peterhead. It was the sight of this brooding ruin that inspired Irishman Bram Stoker to write *Dracula*. His vision of the immortal being, dependent for his continued existence on human blood, has left an enduring legacy. Yet the idea of the vampire is not new. It is in fact hundreds of years old. And while it is now almost completely tied to Eastern Europe this was not always the case. If we go back several hundred years the belief in vampires was widespread throughout Britain. And there were certain parts of the country where vampires were known to be especially numerous. Scotland had earned a reputation as a hotbed of vampire activity.

Memory of the native vampire has virtually disappeared from Scottish consciousness. So much so that the undead are seen as an alien species. But eyewitness reports from across Scotland over past centuries directly confirm the belief in the existence of such a creature. Other incidents contain a strong vampire thread. A vampire presence that had been overlaid by later interpretations, but beneath which can be detected a belief in the reality of the 'living corpse'; the undead. It might be wondered why vampires disappeared from Scotland when, at one time, there were so many vivid reports of their activities from Berwick to the Highlands. Scotland was a nation being preyed on by the undead.

During a time that Berwick on Tweed was ruled by Scottish kings it was terrorised by a strange creature. A man who had died, but had come back to life again. According to a report of the time 'after he was buried he used to, at night, emerge from his grave and rush up and down the streets of the town. Anyone who met him was terrified and nobody wanted to step outside their house till daybreak when the creature returned to his coffin.' Eventually it was agreed that the situation could not be allowed to continue. A group of people came together and went to the grave. They dug up the body, cut it into bits then burned the whole lot in a furnace. This 'living corpse' had the characteristics of a vampire though there was no evidence that it was feeding on the blood of the living – the traditional hallmark of the undead.

But other contemporary incidents make it clear that a supply of blood was believed to be an essential ingredient in resurrecting the dead. In the Dumfriesshire town of Annan a dead man, even though interred with Christian rites, rose from the grave to torment the town. An eyewitness of the time reported that 'going out from his tomb in the night time he used to wander through the streets and around the houses from the fall of darkness to the rising of the sun'. Two brothers decided to deal with the creature and went to the spot where he was buried. They expected to have to dig deep to reach his body but were surprised to find that he was lying not far from the surface. The corpse was swollen and the face red as if it had been gorging on blood. And, indeed, when they started hacking at the body, fresh blood ran from the wounds, evidence that the vampire had been feeding on the living though it was unclear as to exactly who his victims had been. The body was dismembered and the pieces thrown on a bonfire. The only way to ensure that a vampire would cause no more trouble was completely to destroy its physical body.

An encounter close to the Scottish border with England also suggests that we are dealing with a flesh-and-blood entity and brings us closer to the present era. In the village of Croglin, in the latter part of the nineteenth century, a woman was attacked one night by a strange-looking entity with a brown face and flaming eyes. The creature bit her on the throat, but ran off when she screamed. Some months later it appeared again at her window, and her brother shot the being in the leg. They watched it disappear over the churchyard wall into a family vault. When the vault was opened they found in a coffin a brown, mummified figure with a recent gunshot wound to the leg.

However, the vampire theme has not been confined to the Borders as an incident with vampire overtones, and linked to the town of Forfar, shows. In this case, after her boyfriend died, his fiancée insisted on burying him in a double coffin. A few days later she had the grave opened so that she could be buried alive beside him. She was dressed in white as if a bride at a wedding. Not long after people walking through the woods close to the graveyard claimed to see a white-gowned female hovering among the trees, waving and beckoning to them. It was believed that the young woman had guessed that her boyfriend was a vampire and decided that she had to be reunited with him. Even if this meant allowing him her own blood and becoming herself a vampire in the process.

A bizarre tale from Strathy, though it involves the wife of the local minister, is suggestive of the resurrection of a 'living corpse'. The woman, dead and laid out in the living room, was viewed by many people. She appeared quite lifeless though in death she still managed to look young and attractive. The woman was buried, but local thieves decided to raid the grave and steal the rings she had been interred with. On the same night as the funeral they opened the lair and took off the coffin lid. But as they worked, the corpse started to move. The men ran off. In the account it seems that the woman returned to her husband, covered in blood. She remained alive for many years after and even had children. So what had been the fate of the two thieves who apparently disappeared without trace? The implication is that, in reality, she had feasted on their blood in order to come back to life. Items of value had been buried with her, and openly talked about, in order to encourage thieves to visit the graveside. If known wrongdoers vanished there would be few to worry about their fate.

These reports from across Scotland suggest a widespread tradition of vampire encounters. But Scotland also had a theme more in keeping with the modern view of vampires. These were women who dressed in long, flowing green dresses. Attractive and seductive, they would lure young men to them and sink their sharp teeth into their flesh, sucking the blood of their victims. They were, in reality, old hags, who maintained their youthful looks by consuming the blood of the young people they attacked. They did not usually kill their victims, but left severe wounds around their necks and shoulders, wounds that would not heal though their victims do not appear to have turned into vampires themselves. The women, known as Boabban Sith, could be kept away by the presence of a horse. Could this be a link to the bizarre horse-slashing incidents?

Although attacks on horses have only come to public attention in recent times, these unexplained incidents stretch back many years. There are documented cases from the nineteenth century and it is difficult to believe that they were the first. But why would anyone want to attack a horse? The answer might lie in their magic properties. These animals have long been regarded as sacred beasts especially in pre-Christian pagan society. The horseshoe was commonly used as protection against witchcraft, and is still used as a good-luck token. In the past the blood and body parts of the horse were seen as powerful magic against evil spirits. And though there is a view that horse attacks are linked to black-magic cults, it is just as likely that they may be connected to vampire protection. The ideal objects to ward off vampire attacks in all their varied forms are the blood, mane or sexual organs of a horse.

But bloodsucking vampires might still take a person unawares. They do not necessarily attract attention to themselves, looking no different to the next person. One account of such a creature links us to the heart of the royal family. Glamis Castle had a bizarre reputation and one story tells of the presence of a vampire. A female servant was caught sucking the blood of a visitor and was supposedly bricked up inside a room. There, it was claimed, she was left to die. The suspicion remained, however, that the servant was not the only such creature working in the castle, and that a group of strange entities was involved in bizarre practices, including the drinking of human blood. These activities were allowed to continue because of the privileged positions of those involved, members of a secret cult that included individuals with important positions in Scottish society.

And, incredibly, this could be linked to the activities of the bizarre murderer known as Sawney Bean. He has come down to us as Sawney Bean though his real name was Alexander Bane, which could be translated simply as Alex the killer. However, if 'Sawney Bean' was originally a Gaelic term it might refer to entities that did not belong to this world. Whatever their true origin the tale connected with Bean is a strange one. With his family he is reputed to be responsible for the mysterious disappearance of hundreds of innocent travellers. Bane, however, wasn't killing for profit, but to stay alive. He and his followers were feeding on the bodies of those people unfortunate enough to fall into their clutches. One account describes how a couple was attacked and, while the husband fought back, his wife was dragged from her horse and eaten before his eyes. Even as they stabbed her throat some of Alex's group gathered round, like ravenous vultures, to drink her spurting blood. Bane is described as a cannibal, but given the history of the area could the truth be even more bizarre? Could those involved be a group of the undead, attacking the living in order to maintain their weird existence, halfway between life and death?

The authorities of the time, however, were more concerned with stopping the murders than pinpointing motives. It was believed that the deaths were connected and several suspects from the local area were arrested, convicted and hung. The killing went on, however, and it was clear that the wrong people had been executed. Suspicion eventually centred on Alexander Bane. A group of soldiers searched the cliff that ran for miles along the shore and claimed they had caught the whole Bane family in an enormous cave with pieces of human flesh suspended from the roof of their 'home'.

Alexander Bane was reputedly born in Edinburgh, but moved over to the west coast with his wife where he supposedly set up home in a cave which by tradition is said to have been situated below Bennane Head just south of Girvan in Ayrshire. But why would he choose to live in a cave? Was this because of poverty or were there more sinister motives behind his arrival in the area? The place where Bane moved to had a reputation as a vampire 'centre'. Maybe Alex Bane was aware of these stories. Perhaps he knew of a local cult that practised the drinking of human blood. Aristocrats were engaged in all kind of bizarre rituals at this time, as the activities of the Hell Fire Club in England show. In France the King's closest friends were practicing Satanism. Rumours linked Glamis Castle to bizarre blood-ritual practices. In Fife the activities of the 'Beggars Benison' club were so notorious that its last surviving members destroyed the records of their meetings. Maybe Bane supplied groups like these with human sacrifices. Or maybe his own 'family' were, in reality, people who had joined a strange blood-drinking cult he had started. Several centuries on it is difficult to disentangle the reality behind the fiction but the accounts of Bane's activities are too strong to dismiss as pure fabrication.

*

The Sawney Bean murders took place over 200 years ago. So it has to be wondered why there isn't more recent evidence to confirm the reality of the vampire? Or has the evidence simply been overlooked? Has there been a trend to compartmentalise the vampire or to neglect strange incidents that have vampire overtones yet overlook them because they don't fit our preconceptions of what makes up vampire activity? In the Highlands there was an entity known as the 'blood demon'. It attacked both humans and animals to suck their blood. The poachers Reid and Wilson could have been victims of this feared entity at the Fealaar bothy. But could the presence of the blood demon explain more recent incidents? In August 1976 John Stewart, a farmer from Ballageich Hill near Glasgow, found that overnight five of his geese had been mysteriously killed. Each one had on its body a number of puncture marks about one and a half inches deep, regularly spaced about four to five inches apart, the classic signs of a vampire death. There were no other obvious injuries on the geese. A six-foot-high wire fence surrounding the compound was torn to shreds and, in its kennel, what its owner described as 'a normally vicious Alsatian guard dog', was cowering, apparently terrified. Though there was a police investigation within hours of the events, there was disagreement over who or what had been responsible. The director of Glasgow Zoo, Richard O' Grady, said: 'I have no doubt it was a puma. I believe that it was the same cat that has been in Ayrshire over the past two years.' There is no doubt that a puma-like animal had been reported in the area, but that does not necessarily mean that it can be held responsible for every unexplained animal death. And, of course, the alleged puma was never caught. In this case the deaths seem very un-puma like. The geese were killed almost delicately, not ripped open as might be expected. In fact, the puncture marks were the only wounds and the geese had been left in one piece, not eaten. It is hard to understand why a puma would leave its victim behind as there is no evidence that whatever was responsible was disturbed in its 'work'. And why should an animal which could easily leap a six-foot-high fence, rip it apart? Then there's the Alsatian dog. Why would it be so frightened by the appearance of a puma? Taken overall the 'big cat' explanation doesn't fit, though that does not mean that an unknown entity was responsible. The evidence is tantalising but, as always in these cases, leaves room for various interpretations.

The Ballageich incident is not an isolated event. In Cumbria, just over the border, several sheep had their jugular vein severed with no other injuries. But this took place as long ago as 1810. And a similar incident again involving sheep took place no more recently than 1905. But a more recent incident, from the 1970s,

Close encounters: why are the Scottish authorities covering up alien encounters and abductions? (ch. 2)

Illustration by Michael Esk.

Normally associated with the United States, the sinister Mothman has also been seen in Scotland. (ch. 3)

Illustration by Michael Esk.

Big cats like this puma are roaming the length and breadth of Scotland. (ch.3)

Photograph by Tom Vezo. Courtesy of Nature Picture Library.

This is the most famous photograph of the fabled Loch Ness monster. But other Scottish lochs are thought to have their own monsters. (ch.3)

Courtesy of Hulton Archive/Getty Images.

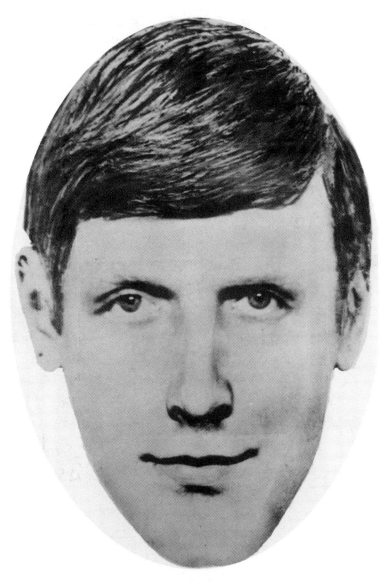

Contrary to received wisdom, was the man known as Bible John a ritual killer who used the blood of his victims for occult purposes? (ch. 4)

Courtesy of Scotsman Publications Ltd.

Rosslyn Chapel, eight miles south of Edinburgh, is one of the world's seven omphalos, or paranormal locations, where this world and other worlds interact. (ch. 8)

Courtesy of Scotsman Publications Ltd

Andrew Cameron of Troon, the double murderer

and one of his victims, Kay Wyllie. (ch. 9)

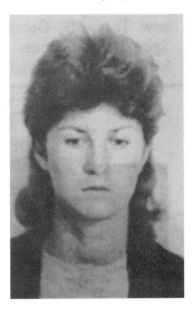

Courtesy of Ayr Advertiser.

IAIN SCOULAR

HIS VICTIMS...

Catherine McChord   **Elizabeth Walton**

Like Andrew Cameron police believed that Iain Scoular of Cambuslang, also a double murderer, could have become a serial killer if he had not been caught. He is seen here with his two victims, Catherine McChord and Elizabeth Walton. (ch. 9)

Max and Sheila Garvie in happier days, at a wedding in 1965. Their bizarre sex life led inexorably to one of the most notorious murders of the twentieth century.

Brian Tevendale, Sheila Garvie's lover and co-accused, at his trial for murder in 1968.

Trudi Birse, the lover of Max Garvie, and a willing participant in his four-in-a-bed sex sessions. She is with her husband, Alfred. (ch. 10)

Courtesy of Scotsman Publications Ltd

Stuart and Nawal Nicol on their wedding day.
Dubbed the Black Widow by the press, Nawal Nicol boasted of having
fifty lovers in a year after her husband's murder in 1994
(she was, however, innocent of any involvement in his murder).

The men who
murdered Stuart Nicol.
Both were said to be
lovers of Nawal Nicol.
On the left is Muir
Middler, and on the
right, Jason Simpson.
(ch. 10)

Pamela Gourlay, who savagely murdered Melanie Sturton in Aberdeen in 1999, being escorted by police officers during her trial. (ch. 10)

Courtesy of Ciaran Donnelly.

GEMMA VALENTI

The devil's spawn and
her offspring: mother-
and-daughter killers
Isabell Carvill and
Gemma Valenti at their
trial in 2003.

Carvill is handcuffed to
Isobel Black, who was
convicted of attempted
murder.

Kenneth Finnie, their
victim, is also pictured.
(ch. 10)

Courtesy of Ciaran Donnelly.

ISABELL CARVILL   ISOBEL BLACK

VICTIM

KENNETH FINNIE

Crafty, devious and brutal, William Beggs had much in common with the notorious serial killer, John Wayne Gacy of Chicago, who was also gay. Thankfully, Beggs was caught before he had the chance to kill again. (ch. 11)

Courtesy of Mirrorpix.

Inspired by the Highland clans, men of Scottish descent founded the Ku Klux Klan in 1865, just after the American Civil War. The Klan's perverted doctrines led inevitably to disgusting crimes like this lynching of two black men in Indiana in the 1920s. (ch. 12)

Courtesy of Hulton Archive/Getty Images.

Who really killed the Queen's uncle, George, Duke of Kent in 1942?
Could it have been the British government? This memorial near
Dunbeath commemorates his memory. (ch. 13)

Author's collection.

might point to a solution while deepening the mystery. In Ayrshire, farm worker William Anderson was astonished one evening to see a glowing figure moving through the nearby fields on all fours. As the creature moved closer to the building, horses tethered in stables started screaming. Even though they couldn't see the figure they could sense its approach. At first Anderson had thought that it must be a large dog. It was the only explanation he could think of. However, he was forced to change his mind. The figure, coming to a fence, made no attempt to leap over it and instead simply floated right through. It then started to change shape, standing on two legs and looking almost human-like. William Anderson decided to make a hasty departure. It is certainly well known that farm animals across Scotland have been attacked and mutilated by mysterious intruders. There is undeniably something odd going on in the countryside, but how much can be tied to vampirism? Of course, we may simply not be aware of the signs. Would anyone recognise evidence of vampirism even if they saw it? Do their activities simply go unnoticed in an age when people have long given up believing that such entities exist?

In a world of science vampires appear utterly out of place. Blood-drinking exploits by mass murderers – most infamously by Peter Kurten, the 'Vampire of Düsseldorf' – are enough to convince people that vampirism is the product of a diseased mind. And anyone who dares hint that it could be a genuine phenomenon is seen as not far behind. It is a view that is hard to disagree with given that there are no known victims, nor, in modern times, have any deaths ever been linked to such a creature.

It is true that across the United Kingdom there has been a series of horrific murders with vampire overtones. In 1949 George Haigh, best known today as the acid-bath murderer, killed several people and disposed of their bodies by dissolving them in tubs of acid. The resulting slush was then simply poured away so that no trace of the bodies remained. Haigh, who liked to claim a connection with the First World War Scottish general of the same name, had failed to cover his tracks. He was the last person seen with Mrs Durand-Deacon, who had mysteriously vanished, and the trail led straight to him. Haigh was arrested and put on trial. In fact,

Haigh was notorious at the time not as the 'acid-bath murderer', but as the 'vampire murderer'. He claimed that he had drunk the blood of his victims after each murder, and that it was this blood lust that had led him to commit crimes, not the hope of financial gain. His claims, however, were not taken seriously. It was suggested that it was a ploy to convince the jury that he was insane. The truth of his blood-drinking urge was never investigated. Haigh was found guilty and hung. The 'vampire' thread to his crimes was forgotten.

The vampire tag resurfaced in more recent cases. In July 2002 a 17-year-old teenager went on trial in Wales for the bizarre murder of 90-year-old widow Mabel Leyshon. It was claimed that the young killer, after stabbing her twenty times, had drained Mabel's blood into a saucepan before drinking it as part of a black-magic ritual. He had then cut out her heart and left it beside her. At the murder scene police found two pokers laid out in a cross and a red candle was balanced on the mantelpiece. The murderer, who could not be named because of his youth, claimed that he had become obsessed with vampires and wanted to become one. Through the ritual ceremony of drinking the blood of a person he had killed, he could achieve this end. The area where he had carried out the attack was, he had told friends, 'perfect' for vampires because it was full of old people who would not be missed. It was clear that the murder had been carried out solely for a ritual purpose, because Mabel Leyshon had not been sexually assaulted and nothing of value had been taken from her home.

In 2000 26-year-old Daniel Ruda and his wife Manuela, 23, took up residence in Scotland. Both were originally from Germany, and had come to this country with a particular purpose in mind. A bizarre one, as the world would eventually learn. However, they made no effort to attract attention to themselves, going about their business in quiet anonymity. In June 2001, satisfied that they had absorbed everything Scotland had to offer, they returned to Germany to practice what they had learnt. That was unfortunate for their friend Frank Hackert. Daniel and Manuela were determined to become vampires and Hackert was their intended victim. The couple had built a strange shrine in the living room of their flat in the town of Bochum in the Ruhr valley. It was here that the couple attacked Hackert with a hammer then laid out his body on an oak coffin before stabbing it sixty-six times, a significant number in occult practice. At their trial both Daniel and Manuela Ruda claimed to have learnt both vampirism and Satanism in Scotland though Manuela had also spent time in London. Understandably, the trial judge took the view that the pair were insane rather than genuinely evil, and they were sent to a secure psychiatric institution.

These events, though horrifying, do not demonstrate the classic vampire phenomenon. The true vampire is a dead person who returns to life through imbibing the blood of the living. Can the living turn themselves into vampires by killing other living beings? Neither George Haigh nor the 17-year-old from Wales claimed to be vampires already. Daniel and Manuela Ruda told police that they were learning to become vampires, not that they were already undead. However, if they were telling the truth, and they made no attempt to deny the murder of Frank Hackert at their trial, they had learnt vampire behaviour in Scotland. Was that from existing vampires, or from others who were imitating the undead?

Throughout history certain groups have believed that drinking human blood can rejuvenate and strengthen the drinker. The Illuminati is a secret group which, it is said, wields huge power across the globe. Its members include some of the most important and powerful people in the world. According to some, the drinking of human blood forms part of their initiation ritual. Writer David Icke has gone one step further, one step too far some believe, and he claims that this secret society is made up of extraterrestrials that need human blood to maintain the human bodies they have taken over.

The suspicion that those who have achieved fame and power are part of a secret cult is nothing new. Several hundred years ago Michael Scott, one of Scotland's greatest mathematicians and thinkers, with contacts in influential circles across Europe, was accused of engaging in vampire activity: drinking human blood to maintain his youth and intellectual vigour.

But that, whether believable or not, does not explain the

strange disappearance of the zombie-type vampire so familiar to our ancestors. The man or woman who is buried as dead then comes back to life. Feeding on blood, but not necessarily in the Scottish experience of the phenomenon, turning victims into vampires. If this was indeed a genuine phenomenon, it is reasonable to wonder why it suddenly came to an end. Of course, there are those who suggest it carried on, that incidents of vampirism have simply been overlooked. The evidence, they argue, is there but is simply being missed. Incidents which have been interpreted in a different light because the undead simply defy belief. And a spate of incidents, if viewed from a different angle, might prove them right. During the eighteenth century bodies were disappearing from graveyards at an alarming rate. Perhaps it had been going on for some time and it was just that people sat up and took notice. Society was becoming more formal and cemetery burial more of a regular event. So when large numbers of bodies went missing from designated burial places it became more obvious than it had in the past. People became so alarmed that guards were employed and towers constructed to protect the dead. But bodies still disappeared. At the time, these incidents were blamed on the 'resurrection men', individuals who were digging up corpses to sell for medical research. And doctors, particularly medical students, found themselves accused of grave robbing. A regular supply of corpses, it was believed, must be needed by the profession for dissection, so who was more likely to be responsible?

There is no doubt that recently buried bodies were being claimed for medical investigation. Even doctors accepted that it was happening. But they denied, even to a committee of the House of Commons, that they were responsible for the vast scale of grave robbing. And they were at a loss to understand why cemeteries across Scotland were being raided to the extent that they were. There was only a limited number of medical schools and, with individuals regularly dying where there was no call to bury them, for they were unclaimed, the number of bodies which required 'salvaging' from a graveyard was not as great as the coffins being pillaged. And there was another mystery. Just how was it possible to remove the bodies from their resting place so neatly even under the eyes of the cemetery guards? In March 1829 in Kirkmichael, Ayrshire twenty-two bodies vanished over a short period of time. Who in this area, far away from the nearest medical schools in Glasgow or Edinburgh, would make use of such a large number of corpses? It was remarked at the time that: 'the means by which it was accomplished was one of the mysteries of their occupation. This was never fathomed by the public and, curiously enough, no accidental circumstances occurred to furnish the solution.' Many bizarre explanations were put forward to explain how the lair was cleared, the coffin opened, the body removed and all returned to such an undisturbed state that it was often days after before it was realised that the grave had been robbed. The evidence that grave robbing was not wholly related to the training of doctors is that even after the use of bodies for dissection was legalised, corpse stealing continued. And continues to this day. The bizarre 'resurrection' of Charlie Chaplin's body in 1978, supposedly as part of a ransom plot, but for motives never fully explained, is only the most notorious example. But there have been many other cases of corpse stealing, including famous figures such as Abraham Lincoln. These incidents are often believed to be a strange attempt to extort money. To the authorities it appears the only possible explanation.

So it is understandable that when, in December 1881, the body of James Lindsay, Earl of Crawford disappeared from its Gothic tomb at Dunnecht House in Aberdeenshire, financial gain was put forward as the motive for the crime. Strangely, though, there had been a considerable gap between the time the body was removed and the realisation that it had gone. From the state of the tomb it was clear that months must have passed. Letters were eventually received demanding money in return for revealing the hiding place of the body. But why had the grave robbers waited till their crime had been discovered before making their demands? It all seemed a bit too pat and there was never any satisfactory explanation. The discovery of Crawford's body in July 1882, covered in blankets, lying in a shallow grave only five hundred yards from Dunnecht House simply deepened the mystery. Just what had happened to his body between the time it was removed and turned up again? It was known that Crawford was deeply interested in archaeology and Egyptology. Could there have been something from his past which explained these strange events? A belief in the power of some to resurrect the dead. That was what was rumoured but, as in most instances of grave robbing, there was no convincing answer as to why, or how, it had happened. Though if the undead have existed, we can be sure they won't have vanished simply because man has reached the moon or the twenty-first century has dawned.

But can we be certain that vampires are only interested in draining our physical blood? Maybe they can also prey on the individual's psychic force, sucking the spiritual energy from their victims. There are many reported cases where invisible assailants behave like psychic vampires. In the 1990s Jennifer Morgan moved to a village just outside the city of Aberdeen. There appeared nothing remarkable about the semi-detached house she rented from the council. Certainly, no one mentioned any strange incidents taking place there before she arrived. But soon after she had settled in Jennifer was subjected to a terrifying ordeal. More frightening because her husband had to work away from home and so she had to face the disturbing events on her own. About a fortnight after she arrived, Jennifer, going to bed around midnight, sensed a presence in the room. She tried to ignore the feeling, telling herself it was all in her imagination. But as she lay down and tried to get to sleep invisible hands gripped her round the throat. She felt she was being choked. Somehow she managed to scramble out of the bed and get downstairs. The presence did not follow her. In fact, the feeling that 'something' was in the house was confined to the main bedroom. But every night after this first encounter whenever Jennifer retired to her bedroom at night, the same thing happened. And always around midnight. The presence became so strong and persistent she had the clear impression that the phantom was trying to take over her body. Even to physically get inside her. The incidents only stopped when, eventually, she moved out of the house.

Psychics disagree about why these incidents occur, even though they are regularly reported. To some it is a form of contact. The only way that spirits who have known us during their lifetime can get in touch is by drawing our attention to their presence. To others it has more sinister overtones. Invisible entities, with no good intentions, using the physical body of the living to drain off spiritual energy for their own purpose.

These suspicions have a long pedigree. In past times it was believed that certain beings, which only appeared at night, could suck the life force from humans and even make a woman pregnant. It was known as an incubus when it appeared as a man, and as a succubus when it was a woman. In reality they were the same entity, which took on the shape of either sex, depending on whether it was drawing energy from a man or woman. To men, it took the form of a beautiful young woman who would have sexual relations with the 'victim'. To a woman, it came as a man. It was believed that a woman could even be impregnated by the incubus. Is this how the undead are created? Through sexual contact between human beings and entities from another world? It is otherwise hard to understand why some people have the potential to come back to life while others languish forever in their coffins.

Although no one today talks of the presence of an incubus or succubus, there are strange encounters which suggest that human energy is being used by some kind of unexplained presence. John Allan, from Glasgow's Drumchapel estate, experienced doors slamming and furniture being moved around by an invisible presence. At night he felt his legs being pulled and a presence hovering over him. Most frightening was the feeling that the invisible entity was actually trying to enter his body, a sensation which has been experienced by a variety of people across Scotland.

Betty Armstrong recalled an encounter which took place when she lived next to a graveyard in Kirkcaldy. She said:

> My daughter was 3 years old and was sleeping in the small bedroom at the back of our downstairs flat. On this particular night she woke up screaming and wouldn't go off to sleep so I decided to pull up the quilt and stay with her as long as necessary. Half an hour later she was sound asleep so I got ready to slip off the bed. But I was unable to move. I felt as if my legs had died. I could not move a muscle. Then I felt as if something was sucking all the energy out of me. A 'thing' was actually crawling up my body. I was

petrified. Eventually it reached my waist. I cried out, 'God help me.' The 'thing' stopped. It seemed to snigger. I prayed out loud and the 'incubus' or whatever it was took off out of the window back to its grave in the churchyard at the bottom of my garden.

The phenomenon of possession and psychic vampires might be one and the same. The body is taken over by an entity but, far from this being an act of random evil, might have a real purpose as far as the entity is concerned. It needs the force present inside the human to prolong its existence. There may be evil intent, but it may also be the instinct to survive. And investigation by dowsers may confirm this. They have detected currents of energy, unknown to science, that run through many houses. It is these, some suggest, that allow the poltergeist and ghosts to appear, and could also explain the manifestation of the psychic vampire. The need to draw on energy, including human energy, could explain many bizarre incidents. It may even account for continued or prolonged bouts of illness. A person's life force being sucked away by an energy vampire. Bizarre thought it may seem, individual experiences can fit into just such a scenario.

One incident involved a young woman, Teri, living in Perth, who kept seeing people invisible to everyone else. These visions were accompanied by acute and distressing physical symptoms. In fact, Teri had the sensation that these unseen entities were trying to take over her body. Recurring pains that had no obvious explanation led to a period abroad at a health clinic. But even specialist doctors could not discover the cause of the severe stomach cramps which were plaguing Teri's life.

Events had started when Teri was 16 and experienced what she described as 'some sort of energy coming over me'. After this incident, things happened around her that could be connected to poltergeist activity, but the significant difference was that Teri constantly felt an invisible presence beside her. And had the experience that 'someone was trying to speak through me'. On another occasion she started to sing songs she had no idea she knew and started to write letters to people she had never heard of. All these events can, of course, be interpreted differently. Many psychics would put it down to an attempt by spirits to contact Teri. And that might appear to be a plausible explanation, but for the events that brought Teri's torment to a sudden end.

An experienced medium brought in to deal with Teri's problems thought it would be safer to take time to resolve the situation and began with a healing session. But events rapidly took over. As the session progressed it became clear that an entity had attached itself to her and, according to the medium, was ' living off her and afraid to leave her'. He put his hands on Teri's head and attempted to draw the spirit from her. The result was dramatic. Teri jumped up, started thrashing her arms and running round the room. This was the physical impact of the entity withdrawing from her body. Teri later explained that she felt as if she had been 'taken over' by a spirit form, though she could not say what it was or why it had been drawn to her.

Teri may have been fortunate that early action was taken to deal with the problem. Psychic vampirism might even, in the last resort, result in death. In January 1977 Mrs Betty Martin from Cowdenbeath in Fife suffered a bizarre death. The 40-year-old believed that she had been possessed by some kind of evil spirit, perhaps even the Devil himself. Her situation terrified her, so much so that she asked a local minister to exorcise her Broad Street home. She even claimed that she had seen the psychic entity which was tormenting her. It had appeared in a chair opposite her, glaring at her with a fixed stare. Mrs Martin found its presence so frightening that she left her home and went to stay with her mother who lived nearby. Soon after she moved she was found dead. It was reported that police entering the house were blessed by the church minister. It may be the case that the flow of energy from a victim becomes so intense that they lose the will to live and fade away. The threat of the psychic vampire may be more real and pervasive than that of the bloodsucking kind.

Those experienced in occult practices suggest that many people are potential vampires or victims of vampires. That in our sleep we create astral bodies which in disturbed people roam across the land, draining energy and maintaining their existence from the life force of other living beings.

But to some the threat of a vampire can be all too real. In 1970 Adam Smith entered a north London cemetery with a crucifix and a pointed stake. His midnight expedition was intended to kill a vampire he believed was active in the area. By some stroke of chance, he was caught in the act and arrested. Attempting to end the existence of the undead is not a crime, but wandering a cemetery at night may be. In court, however, Smith was found not guilty. Certainly, there are those who have no wish that vampire hunting be taken seriously. Because we all know that there are no such things as vampires and it would be disturbing to suggest that there is evidence that, though far from conclusive, certainly leaves room for doubt.

SIX

Missing: presumed dead

WHAT ARE WE to make of those events where people simply disapp-ear into thin air? The scale of missing persons is astonishing. Every day someone somewhere vanishes as if they had never been. Of course, there is no doubt that a number head for the bright lights of the city. Others simply want to change their identity and start a new life. Personal unhappiness can be a powerful spur to breaking with the past and seeking anonymity. But can that explain every mysterious disappearance? Why do so many people seem able to walk out of the front door in the morning then vanish so com-pletely they are never heard of again? Maybe we just don't have the crucial evidence to show that these individuals have simply ceased to exist. But that wasn't the case in July 1990. There is no doubt that something strange happened on what began as a sim-ple pleasure trip for a band of expectant tourists.

On Saturday 14 July 1990 a party of eighty-eight people set out to spend time visiting Orkney's inner islands. The day's events included a landing, in the early evening, on Eynhallow, a tiny isle less than two miles across lying within sight of the Orkney main-land. It was a rare opportunity to visit this isolated spot. There are usually only four such sailings a year. But to those keen on the wilder side of nature it was an attractive destination. The unin-habited island is home to a colony of seals, rare birds and boasts the remains of an ancient Viking settlement. The trip, which had been arranged by the Orkney Heritage Society, went as planned until the group reached Eynhallow. The roll-on, roll-off ferry, spec-ially chartered for the day, returned to the little harbour of Tingwall once its passengers had disembarked. It was only a short distance to its home berth so there was no problem chugging back for the pick-up just a few hours later. Tidal flow restricted the time that visitors could spend on the island. Even two hours was long enough to enjoy the delights of Eynhallow, no matter how enthusiastic, so everyone was in a good mood as they returned to the ship and happy to continue on the next leg. But as the party of visitors tramped back on board after their walk round the island they discovered that two of their number were missing. Crew members had carefully counted eighty-eight people out but only eighty-six had returned.

The rest of the tour was abandoned as an immediate search of the area was launched. It was from Kirkwall that the local lifeboat set out as a rescue plan swung into action. Those with local know-ledge guessed that the missing two might have fallen down the sharp-sided cliffs that marked the boundary of the island. A search of the coastline for the bodies, however, revealed no sign of the couple. At the same time an investigation of the interior by a party of rescuers brought no sighting of the lost pair or of any of their belongings. Around 10 p.m. a decision to call off the search for the day was forced on the party due to tidal conditions, backed by a growing suspicion that the missing couple might never have actually landed on the island. Even at this early stage there was confusion over what had really happened. A police spokesman commented that evening, 'We are trying to find out if the two people who seem to be missing exist. There are not many hiding places on the island.'

The crew of the ferry, which also by a strange coincidence went under the name *Eynhallow*, were sure that they had not made a mistake. And had not, as some were by then thinking, simply miscounted. They had clocked eighty-eight people leaving the ferry and, as only eighty-six had been checked back in, there could only be one solution. Two of the party must still be on the island.

More resources were brought into the search when it resumed on the Sunday. A rescue helicopter criss-crossed the island using the latest heat-seeking equipment, but no sign of life was detected. On the ground below police officers drafted from the mainland carried out a second search of the terrain. But they had no more luck than the first group. No evidence of any missing person was discovered. With no proof that the two were on the island the spotlight turned again to the crew. For the third time they asserted that they had made no mistake. But the police in Kirkwall who were running the search-and-rescue operation were becoming increasingly mystified by the contradictions at the heart of the events. As well as sifting every inch of Eynhallow and its coastline they had spent Sunday the fifteenth tracing Orkney residents who had taken part in the visit to the island. They hoped to discover if anyone who had travelled on the ferry could remember two faces that weren't there on the return leg. Inquiries drew a blank. No one, it seemed, could remember the missing tourists. But with over eighty-eight on board, and many people not known to each other, was this really surprising? No record had been kept of the people who had travelled on the ferry. The headcount had been the key factor in checking that no one had been left behind. As Chief Inspector John Ratter, of Kirkwall's Northern Constabulary, commented:

> We must keep an open mind. We have corroborative statements from the crew members and yet we do not have a missing person – it's a strange one. Perhaps someone miscounted, but how do you know? When people came off the boat they went everywhere. Some of them were tourists. Others were local people. How do you account for them all? If someone is on holiday you might not find if they are missing for weeks.

It was the major flaw hampering the whole investigation. With large numbers on board that day and no list of names how would they ever learn who had disappeared unless a friend, neighbour or relative noticed? And who could tell when that would be?

On 18 July, four days after events on Eynhallow, having contacted everyone local who had joined the excursion, the police widened their appeal. Following this, the number of individuals who could be accounted for rose to eighty-two. That still left at least six unidentified trippers. So, by the end of July, attempts to contact holidaymakers had extended to the continent. At the same time trawlermen were encouraged to look out and report any unexplained items floating in the seas around Orkney.

And then . . . nothing. Interest in the unsolved mystery of the disappearing Eynhallow visitors was overwhelmed by more immediate and dramatic events – the murder by the IRA of Member of Parliament Ian Gow, and the Iraqi invasion of Kuwait. Eynhallow rapidly faded from public awareness as the press turned its attention elsewhere.

So the mystery, if it was a mystery, was left without a solution. But to those who know Eynhallow the events of July 1990 simply formed another chapter in a long tradition. Unknown to most of the visitors that day Eynhallow certainly has a strange reputation. In ancient tradition it was a mystic 'vanishing isle'; a land that could appear and disappear and even change shape. In pagan eyes such a place would be the point of entry into other dimensions where humans could come in contact with the inhabitants of other worlds. At least that is the tradition. But has our modern interpretation of the 'vanishing island' been missing the point? Maybe in ancient legend it was a place where people disappeared rather than the island itself, a kind of mystic halfway house between this dimension and the next. And there is a strange story linked to the island which backs this up. It is about a Viking captain who was chased through the waters of Orkney by a half-crazed rival out for revenge. He gave his manic pursuer the slip by taking his ship into a cave burrowed into the cliffs of Eynhallow. This seemed to surround his vessel with a magic cloak of invisibility. Was there some strange energy force radiating from the island? It is a well-established tradition that cats taken on to

Eynhallow die of a convulsive illness, and that neither mice nor rats can survive on the island. Clearly there is, and has been, something unusual about the Eynhallow aura. Something that turns this pleasant-looking island into an evil location.

Eynhallow was also known as the home of strange beings. The mermen. Entities who reputedly live half in and half out of the sea, but who at certain times of the year can take on human shape. In our modern age the very idea of mermen would raise a bit more than an eyebrow. But perhaps if we revisit tradition with our modern perspective we can open a whole new vista on the Eynhallow mystery, because mermen of times past look uncannily like a very contemporary phenomenon. While the small, grey-skinned entity with the almond-shaped eyes has become in popular imagination most closely linked with alien abductions the truth is that encounters with lizard-like beings have been equally well reported. Indeed, according to those who claim repeated abduction experiences, it is these reptilian lookalikes who are the real masters of the universe. And the mermen of Orkney tradition are a close match to these beings. Particularly when we remember that in some traditions mermen looked wholly human all the year round, but were different from 'earth people' only in that they had their homes deep underground or on the ocean floor. Their supposed fish-like skin was really a protective outer suit made of strange material.

So were the missing visitors abducted by beings from another world? Or did they cross the threshold into another dimension? Either way, it is asking a lot to believe that such weird incidents could happen. But there is no doubt that Eynhallow was in times past seen as one of the mystic centres of Scotland, though that fact has long since faded away. It attracted early Christian missionaries just as Iona did. In fact, it is claimed that St Columba himself visited the island. In Orcadian tradition Eynhallow was the last island to be captured from the mystic race of people who once ruled Orkney – the Finnfolk, who are strange beings with magical powers. So did the two 'tourists' head for the island with a motive quite different to those of their fellow visitors? Psychics have suggested that the strange couple might have gone to Eynhallow for a definite ritual purpose, to make use of the powerful currents of energy coursing through it. But if that was so why did they disappear so quickly? There is really nowhere on that small island where they could have remained hidden for long. And if they had a secret plan why travel there in such a public way?

So was it all just a big mistake? Some Orcadians certainly think so. Andrew Harvie, who was on the ship that day, claimed:

> Nothing out of this world happened that summer's evening. It was all just a simple mistake. There was nothing mysterious. The crew counted them before we left and checked them back on again using a handheld counter clicker. There was confusion over the numbers simply because it was a joint trip with the RSPB. Two young babies who were being held in their parents' arms were counted when we went on and not counted after we came off Eynhallow. The crew reported it probably because they had to. We left for Eynhallow from Tingwall about 7.30. It was a glorious evening. The visit depends on the tide so we knew we'd have to be on our way well before 10 p.m. There's no harbour so we had to land directly on to the beach. When they thought someone was missing we had a quick look around just in case. That was for about ten minutes. The lifeboat was on an exercise in the area and they took a look. But the whole thing was blown out of all proportion. The papers made a lot of noise because they had nothing else to write about at the time.

So was there any mystery? It is hard to believe that it was all a fuss over nothing. If a simple miscount lay at the bottom of it all why haven't we been plagued by a regular series of false alarms from the many day-tripping sea excursions across Scotland? Why Eynhallow alone? But without the conclusive proof that someone did indeed disappear we must, for now, keep an open mind. Unless one day some evidence turns up on the island itself. And that's a long shot.

*

But no such doubts can confuse the circumstances of one of Scotland's most enduring mysteries: the disappearance of three lighthouse keepers from their isolated tower on the Flannan Isles, situated in the Atlantic Ocean some twenty miles off the tip of the Outer Hebrides.

The Flannan Isles lighthouse first beamed into life on 7 December 1899. It was situated on a remote block of rock, Eilean Mor, the largest of the island group, twenty miles off the Butt of Lewis. In an area notorious for shipwrecks, the lighthouse was one of the last to be constructed in a building programme that had been determined to illuminate Scotland's sea lanes since the early nineteenth century. So the Flannan lighthouse shone every day for a year manned by the standard three keepers. Three on duty at any one time, rotating with a relief keeper every two weeks. In December 1900 the keepers on the Flannan Isles were James Ducat, Thomas Marshall and Donald McArthur. Joseph Moore, the fourth member of the team, was having a week's rest in Lewis where he had his home. Ducat was the principal keeper, Marshall his assistant. McArthur was acting as temporary help during the absence of the usual keeper, William Ross, who was on sick leave.

The keepers must have been into a regular routine by the time of the winter storms. A year had passed without any incident of note. But appearances can be deceptive. On 7 December 1900, a year to the day since it opened, the light seemed to disappear. There was, of course, at that time no wireless or even telegraph communication to the Flannan lighthouse. So there could be no instant alarm if any problem sprang up. The fact that the light hadn't, apparently, been seen for days, wasn't reported till the steamer *Archtor* reached the port of Oban. On its way from Philadelphia to Scotland, it had passed by the Flannans on 15 December searching for a glimmer of light from the beacon, but there was only unrelenting blackness. It is not clear though who the captain gave his report to. In any event, it did not make its way to the Northern Lighthouse Board in Edinburgh, who looked after the light. They were to remain in ignorance of the mystery for a few days yet.

As it turned out, the crew of the *Archtor* had not been the first to spot the lack of activity on the island. The Northern Lighthouse Board, as a precaution, had employed Roderick Mackenzie, a gamekeeper from Uig on Lewis to keep an eye on the light. As it happened he had delegated the responsibility to his two sons. They reported that the light was seen by them on 7 December, but not on the eighth, ninth, tenth or eleventh of the month. They claimed to have seen it on the twelfth, but not again till the twenty-sixth when it was relit by the relief crew.

However, the authorities only became aware of these problems after full details of the events of 15 December were made clear. As Robert Muirhead, superintendent for the Northern Lighthouse Board, observed, 'Had the lookout been kept by an ordinary light-house keeper . . . I believe it would have struck the man ashore at an earlier period that something was amiss and, while this would not have prevented the lamentable occurrence taking place, it would have enabled steps to have been taken to have had the light relit at an earlier date.'

It is surprising that Muirhead didn't notice an odd fact in the reporting of the Mackenzie brothers. In the period between 7 December and 26 December they claimed to have observed the light only once. And that was on 12 December, when a vicious storm, according to the official log kept in the lighthouse, was at its height. Marshall described a 'sea lashed to fury. Never seen such a storm. Waves very high. Tearing at Lighthouse.' It is remarkable that in such atrocious conditions the light was visible from Uig, over twenty miles away, when it had not been seen on calmer nights.

However, as Muirhead had noted, it made no difference. Nor had the *Archtor's* report. No action was taken till 20 December, and that simply because the relief ship was due at the lighthouse, in accordance with the usual schedule. As luck would have it, bad weather delayed the arrival till the twenty-sixth, Boxing Day. The *Hesperus* carried Joseph Moore who was taking over from James Ducat, whose turn it was for a rest period. But when the ship arrived at its destination and moored as close as it dared to the landing jetty the stillness on the island seemed to pierce the winter air with an ominous lull. It wasn't everyday a relief ship arrived at the lighthouse. In fact, as can easily be imagined, it was a bit of an event. The arrival of the *Hesperus* would normally have been an occasion for celebration for one member of the lighthouse team. At the very least the crew would have been expected to see a figure waving to them in welcome and preparing the jetty for a landing. But there was no sign of human life whatsoever.

The skipper of the *Hesperus* was a Captain Harvie. On their approach to the landing jetty he had been puzzled by the fact that no preparation had been made for their arrival. None of the usual welcoming signals had been flown. To attract the attention of the keepers Harvie ordered the steam whistle and ship's siren to be sounded. They waited, but there was no response from the lighthouse. Still reluctant to attempt a landing without the presence of the lighthousemen, the crew next fired a rocket. But on the island still nothing moved. There was now no choice, in spite of the risk, but to get someone ashore. Without the assistance of the Flannan keepers, however, it wasn't possible to manoeuvre the ship any closer to land. Harvie ordered a rowing boat to be lowered with relief keeper Joseph Moore aboard. It made for the jetty on the east side of the landing area. Not an easy journey in the rough waters flowing around the island.

Once secured, Moore had to scramble up the one hundred and sixty steps, steep and narrow on the sharp cliff-side, two hundred feet from the sea mark, and make his way across open ground to the lighthouse. The lighthouse consisted of a tower, standing seventy-five feet, and an accommodation block, all surrounded by an enclosing wall. In a letter to the Northern Lighthouse Board, Moore himself wrote of his strange journey of discovery: 'I was the first to land leaving Mr McCormack and his men in the boat till I should return from the lighthouse. I went up and on coming to the entrance gate I found it closed. I made for the entrance door leading to the kitchen and store room, found it also closed, and the door inside that, but the kitchen door itself was open.'

At first glance, everything in the lighthouse seemed in good order. There was no sign of disturbance and the lighthouse beam was ready for operation. The gates and doors were properly shut, and the kitchen table was cleared and clean. There was nothing to suggest that the keepers had left in a hurry.

But it was dawning on Moore that the lighthouse had been free of occupants for some time. The fire in the kitchen on that cold December afternoon was not lit and Moore judged 'not lighted for some days'. And when he discovered all the rooms empty and in particular 'the beds unmade just as they left them in the early morning', he needed no further convincing that everything was not as it should be. He fled the deserted building, noting in passing that the clock had stopped, and carried the news down to McCormack, still sitting in the boat. This time the others were forced to land and the whole group carried out a search of the lighthouse. A search that confirmed Moore's astonishing news. The three keepers had vanished into thin air.

Or so it seemed. But such an event appeared so hard to believe that doubts soon crept in. Could they be hiding or lying injured somewhere on the little island? It struck the group as unlikely given the small size of the place – just over forty acres – but on that Wednesday with darkness falling there was little time to search in safety. The light had to be relit, so Moore and three others were ordered to remain on the island to make sure that the Flannan Isles beacon once again sent out its warning signal.

It couldn't have been an easy night for Joseph Moore and the 'volunteers', Messrs McCormack, Campbell and Lamont. It may have been a relief when a search of Eilean Mor the following morning revealed no clue as to what had happened to the lost lighthouse men. No dead bodies. No mad murderer with a bloody axe hiding among the crags, cranes or ruined buildings.

But mystery itself can be disturbing. And there was plenty to raise doubts over the explanation being touted by Robert Muirhead, superintendent with the Northern Lighthouse Board with responsibility for the Flannan Isles lighthouse. His conclusion, in a report to Board headquarters in Edinburgh, was 'misadventure', the favoured explanation when strange deaths or disappearances occur. Muirhead argued, after 'weighing all the evidence which I could secure', that the three men had 'all gone down to the proximity of the west landing, to secure the box with the mooring ropes etc, and that an unexpectedly large roller had come up on the island, and a large body of water going up higher than they were and coming down on them had swept them away with resistless force.'

It was a solution to the mystery which, though plausible on the surface, carried a note of desperation. It supposed that at the very time, on a sea-calm day, when all three experienced keepers were at a spot well above sea level, at that precise moment, completely unawares, they were struck by an enormous wave. Likely? True, the box halfway up the cliffs, which they might have been attending to, had gone. Support for the huge-roller theory perhaps, though there were other explanations for its disappearance. Strong winds for one. Indeed, one theory, first mooted by Muirhead was that all three men had been blown over the cliffs. He eventually rejected this on the grounds that the direction of the wind meant that the men would have been blown inland rather than off the island. Further indication of feeble detective work as the direction of the wind would make a significant difference if the men were at a spot where the wind direction put them in danger. As to the missing box, it may have vanished, but its contents, the mooring ropes, were lying on rocks below, a fact that hardly suggests they were the victim of a monster wave. The ropes would surely have been washed well out to sea and landed, if at all, at some other part of the cliff shore. Muirhead also recorded, without comment, that a crane at the west landing was completely undamaged which, again, suggests that talk of a giant wave lacks substance.

However, there was no difference of opinion over the timing of events. Everyone was agreed that the tragedy, whatever the cause, had occurred on Saturday 15 December. And it was even possible to narrow it down to within a few hours. After lunch ('dinner' in the words of the time, as it was the main meal of the day) and before the lighthouse lamp was lit. At that time of year, in that latitude, it would have been dark by 3.30 p.m. The lamp would have been lit before then. Dinner would have been taken around 1 p.m. The dinner dishes had all been washed up and the cutlery placed neatly away. The beacon lamp had been cleaned and the wick (the light was paraffin fuelled) trimmed for use. This all shows that preparations were in hand for firing the lamp that evening.

It is possible though that a broader time band has to be considered. Lighthouses were required to keep a written log, but these might be filled in days late. There was obviously no regular check on the matter. Details to be put in the log might be scrawled on a scrap paper, or as on the Flannan lighthouse on a slate, for later copying. The last full entry in this case was for 13 December. It read simply 'Storm continued through night. Wind shifted W. by N. Ducat quiet. McArthur praying.'

In fact, the log of the thirteenth might have been a continuation of the twelfth as a storm had raged for both days. The twelfth read, 'Gale N. by NW. Sea lashed to fury. Never seen such a storm. Waves very high. Tearing at lighthouse. Everything shipshape. James Ducat irritable.' On the same entry, but presumably later, it reads, 'Storm still raging, wind steady. Stormbound. Cannot go out. Ship passing and sounding foghorn. Could see cabin lights. Ducat quiet. Donald McArthur crying.' It seems reasonable to suggest that it was in this terrible weather that the box containing the mooring ropes was lost and other damage sustained. There is no need to argue for a freak wave on the fifteenth.

It was also in this atrocious weather of 12 December that the lookout on Lewis claimed to have seen the Flannan light shining. Enough said!

There was, apparently, no entry for the fourteenth and that for the fifteenth was on a slate. It read simply, 'Noon. Grey daylight. Me, Ducat and McArthur praying. 1 p.m. Storm ended. Sea calm. God is over all.' The *Archtor* had not seen a light when it passed by on the fifteenth, but that report came in after events on the island were publicised. It was accepted because it seemed to fit with the evidence discovered at the lighthouse. It did not correspond to the reports from the appointed observers on Lewis who had, by their own admission, seen nothing since the twelfth (and that doubtful) even with the aid of a powerful telescope. Taken at face value, however, the log entry appears to provide conclusive evidence that all three had been alive up to noon on the fifteenth.

Unless, of course, the reported entries were doctored. The last entry in the official log was dated the thirteenth. It would not have been possible to alter the log without it being obvious that it had been tampered with. So there is a chance that the tragedy actually happened on that day. There was no entry for the fourteenth, it should be remembered, and only a slate chalked record for the fifteenth which could have been scrawled by anyone. But what reason could there be for concealing the date of whatever happened? It suggests collusion or conspiracy. But if so by whom, and why? If one of the keepers killed the other two it would only be possible to escape from the island with the help of a third party. A possible scenario. Lewis was only a boat ride away. But there is one unbridgeable barrier. There is no evidence to suggest a motive for such a drastic action by one of the keepers, apart from rumours of various love triangles. To date they have never risen above the level of rumour.

Probably the answer lies on the island rather than elsewhere. Joseph Moore wrote a rather poignant letter to the Northern Lighthouse Board on 28 December. Just two days after the discovery he was clearly struggling to come to terms with the bizarre turn of events. He was aware of Muirhead's theory that a freak wave could explain the events and, noting that 'nothing appears touched at east landing to show that they were taken from there' adds, 'On the west side it is somewhat different' and then lists the missing box and other damage. But he is clearly far from convinced that a massive wave strike explained it. Moore remarks on the fact that 'Mr Marshall had his seaboots on and oilskins. Mr Ducat also had his seaboots on. He had no oilskins only an old waterproof coat, and that is away.' So, both men had clearly left the building, but for what purpose? Moore adds enigmatically, 'There is only one thing I know that Mr Marshall never wore sea boots, or oilskins, only when in connection with landings.' So did Marshall head down to the landing jetty because he was expecting or was going to meet a landing party of some kind? And what of Donald McArthur? Moore notes, pointedly I believe, that 'Donald McArthur had left his wearing coat behind which shows, as far as I know, that he went out in his shirtsleeves. He never used any other coat on previous occasions, only the one I am referring to'. There's no easy explanation as to why McArthur went out on a December day without a coat. The weather would have been raw, bearable for only a short time. He could not have been heading down to the west landing or straying far from the protection of the lighthouse. He may have rushed out suddenly. But why? And how could his attention have been attracted if his two companions were several hundred feet away down the cliff side?

And there is another odd fact that doesn't chime with the official explanation. Why were all the dinner dishes washed up and everything spick and span, but the beds in an unmade state? Could the men have left their beds in a rush for some reason and never returned? But why then and by whom was the lighthouse carefully 'cleaned up' yet the bed clothes missed and left in an untidy state? No matter what way it is viewed the events do not make up a coherent jigsaw. All that is clear is that at some date after 13 December and probably, though not certainly, on the afternoon of the fifteenth, the three lighthousemen disappeared off the Flannan island.

So what had happened? The island, Eilean Mor, was only forty acres in extent so there's little doubt that if any trace of those men had remained it would have been discovered. Had they been washed into the Atlantic as the authorities suggested? A storm had whipped up the seas for several days before the fifteenth, but the men had sensibly stayed inside the lighthouse during this period as noted in the log. To be hit by a wave all three keepers would have had to have gone down the cliff side to the jetty. But why would they have done that in rough weather? The storm would have been allowed to pass before they headed for the landing bay. However, the evidence of McArthur's coat suggests he was indoors when whatever happened occurred. Not freezing on the cliff side in his shirtsleeves.

It may be that an outsize 'roller' was to blame. Freak waves do happen. But it still doesn't explain the loss of McArthur, who could not have been out in the open. However, if it was not an accident, what is left that is in any way convincing? It was suggested that one keeper killed the other two and then committed suicide. But there was no evidence of a fight. No bloodstains on wall or floor. No implements lying about which could be linked to a struggle. But if natural explanations are put to one side we can rapidly head into free fall. Were they attacked by a mysterious sea monster? There was, it was claimed, oddly glowing seaweed found in the men's quarters. Had it been dragged up from the depths by an unknown creature? It was all speculation and nothing was proved though rumour had it that the authorities had suppressed any evidence which contradicted the giant-wave theory. Maybe they were justified. When men vanish in mysterious circumstances all kinds of explanations creep out of the woodwork. The island was known to be haunted. The ruins of an ancient church were said to be the spot on which spirits of the dead walked. And what of the rock on which the lighthouse stood? Could strange creatures be lurking in underground caves linked to the lighthouse by a secret tunnel? Since UFOs hit the headlines, it has been suggested that the men could have been abducted by alien beings or walked into another dimension to travel endlessly through time.

*

However, even when a body turns up, far from solving a puzzle, it can turn an incident into a complete enigma. On Christmas Eve 1975, 55-year-old Peter Gibbs, former leader of the Scottish Symphony Orchestra, was combining business and pleasure on the island of Mull. He had arrived some days before, on Saturday 20 December, accompanied by 32-year-old university lecturer Mrs Felicity Grainger. Gibbs was the managing director of Gibbs & Rae, a company he had established three years before, and which owned and developed property in the Glasgow area. Gibbs was looking for fresh challenges and had been considering buying on the island. One potential property was the well known Western Isles Hotel situated in Tobermory. He was, however, using as his base for the stay the Glenforsa Hotel located near the village of Salen. Whether by accident or choice he had booked into the only hotel on the island with a landing strip in its grounds.

Shortly after arriving Gibbs, a keen pilot, learnt that there was a single-engine Cessna for hire on the mainland. He contacted the plane's owner, Ian Hamilton. Curiously, Hamilton himself had a bit of a past. He had led the group that lifted the Stone of Destiny in a daring raid on Westminster Abbey back in the 1950s. The men, however, did not know each other and Hamilton had no involvement with Gibbs's activities.

On Tuesday 23 December, Gibbs and Grainger met Hamilton at the airstrip just outside Oban where the Cessna was hangared.

Having checked the plane, impressing Hamilton with his technical knowledge, Gibbs clambered into the cockpit and, accompanied by Grainger, flew the aircraft to the Glenforsa Hotel landing strip. The flight went smoothly. Gibbs must have been confident of both the Cessna and his own flying skills as, the next day, Wednesday 24 December, and again accompanied by Felicity Grainger, he set off at eight-thirty in the morning for Skye. It was a flight of about an hour. Having spent the day looking over property he returned to Mull about 4 p.m. and passed the next few hours relaxing over drinks and dinner in the hotel. What happened next seems, looking back, abrupt and out of character. Events that don't quite chime with the picture that emerges of a man at ease with himself, relaxing though at the same time enjoying the task of sizing up potential investments. Just what got into Peter Gibbs? Some time between eight and nine in the evening, Gibbs suddenly announced his intention to make a night-time flight. The reason he gave, according to Felicity Grainger, was to test the hotel airstrip for an emergency landing. Gibbs did not explain why the matter had assumed an unaccountable urgency, or why it had to be carried out at night on a landing area which had no illumination. The airstrip was basically a flattened grassy area nine hundred yards by thirty. Not exactly an easy spot to locate in the dark even by the most experienced pilot. His attempts to provide alternative lighting seem amateurish, foolhardy and even downright weird. He asked Grainger to put two torches on the ground, a foot apart, pointing towards the Cessna. His intention, apparently, was to use the torchlight as a landing beacon, an arrangement described later by an aviation expert as 'absolutely worthless as a form of indication'. But on that winter evening Peter Gibbs, a former Spitfire ace, appeared oblivious to danger.

Around 9.30 p.m. Gibbs took off, watched by Grainger on the strip, and from the hotel by manager Roger Howitt, Howitt's brother David and their wives. These witnesses later claimed that they had seen the torches being held too far apart for just one person, suggesting that there had been three people on the strip. But Felicity Grainger always denied that there was anyone else other than her and Gibbs present.

Gibbs took off, made a circuit, and disappeared from view behind a clump of trees. The Cessna did not reappear though there was no sound of a crash or flare from an explosion. By 10 p.m., with no further sighting of the aircraft, it was clear that the flight had not gone according to plan. It did not mean a disaster had occurred. Gibbs could have decided against a night landing and headed for a main airport at Glasgow or Prestwick. At 10.30 p.m. Howitt contacted Prestwick air-traffic control, as it is the centre that monitors all flights along the west coast. Local police arrived within the hour and quickly established that no plane had landed at any local airstrip. Gibbs seemed to have vanished into the night.

As dawn descended on what should have been a time of festivity, Christmas Day, rescue teams were already swinging into action. Overhead, helicopters combed the whole breadth of the island, including the coastal shores while, on the ground, an army of volunteers conducted a succession of line searches. Not a trace of the plane or of Peter Gibbs was found. By 29 December the search, running out of places to look, came to a halt. Gibbs's disappearance was a mystery that was not going to be solved quickly.

And a puzzle it remained, until 21 April 1976, four months after the Cessna with Gibbs at the controls was last seen climbing skywards. Local shepherd Donald Mackinnon caught sight of an object balanced on a fallen tree trunk. As he moved closer he recognised with horror that it was a human body. The corpse was lying on its back, its legs lolling in frozen contortion each side of the trunk, the head gently, as if it had been carefully placed, resting on the ground.

Called in by the police David Howitt identified Gibbs by the badly faded clothing on the corpse. As might be expected the body had decomposed, but it could be easily seen that it bore no impact marks or fractures. Later examination revealed another fact that seemed unimportant at the time, but years later would assume a key significance. There was not a trace of salt water on Gibbs's clothes. The police, meanwhile, claimed that the pilot had parachuted from his plane. But this was contradicted by the assistant manager of the Glenforsa Hotel, who reported that Gibbs was not wearing a parachute harness. Strangest of all, however, Gibbs had been found only a mile from the Glenforsa Hotel, in an area that the rescue services had already gone over thoroughly. Donald Mackinnon, who had no axe to grind, claimed that several times he had passed the spot where he eventually found the missing pilot and was adamant that, on these occasions, there had been no body there. As he argued, it was the sort of thing you would have noticed.

So how had Gibbs arrived there? He did not seem to have spent time in the sea, as the absence of salt water on his clothes showed. Even if he had brought the plane down to stalling speed and jumped out he would surely have suffered an injury of some kind, one that would have left a visible mark. But the pathologist had to report that there was not the slightest evidence for any such injury. Anyway, could Gibbs or even the most experienced pilot in the pitch black of a December night, flying over unlit countryside, manage to bring down a plane to a height from which he could eject in safety? And if he did, where was the Cessna? A pilotless plane at low altitude in hilly terrain would surely not have travelled too far.

The puzzle deepened twelve years later with the chance discovery of the downed Cessna. In 1987 George Foster, a scallop diver, came across the wreckage of Gibbs's plane about 300 yards offshore, lying at the entrance to Fishnish Bay in the Sound of Mull. So the aircraft had definitely crashed, but how had Gibbs managed to abandon it before it sank, swim ashore and then climb a hill only to die from exposure? To get there he would have had to cross a main road when the obvious thing to do would be to wait for a passing car. If he had been exhausted and disorientated after reaching land then it would have been understandable if he had been found there. But if he did swim to the shore, then walk a considerable distance, he clearly still had control of his faculties even after battling against the tide. So why not do the obvious thing and flag down help?

But can any theory account for all the known facts? Perhaps Gibbs was not flying the plane when it left the Glenforsa airstrip. This does not explain why he was later found dead on a hillside, but it would solve one riddle: why Gibbs was found in a different location from the Cessna. Felicity Grainger, however, told the Fatal Accident Inquiry, held in Oban in June 1976, that Gibbs unquestionably got into the plane and took off in it. As the only other person known to be present, she would surely have reported if a third party was involved.

So could Gibbs have landed elsewhere and allowed another person to pilot the plane? This is undeniably a possibility, but it doesn't explain the crashed Cessna which had certainly suffered a serious impact. If there was a second pilot, where is the body? And where else could Gibbs have landed his plane without being noticed? And even if these two events occurred why did Gibbs end up dead of exposure on a hillside which had been previously searched and was within sight of the Glenforsa Hotel?

So what are we left with? There certainly are weird aspects to Gibbs's disappearance. In the first place, there is the day that Gibbs took off and vanished, Christmas Eve, a significant date long before the arrival of Christianity. In the pagan calendar it marked the end of the five dark days when the sun stood still in the sky and time came to a stop before the world was born again. It was a time when the veil between this world and the next was raised and those beyond came in close contact. Maybe not significant on its own, but it could be when linked to the day on which Peter Gibbs's body was discovered. Incredibly, 21 April is the holy day of Mull's key saint, Malerubha, after whom Tobermory, the main town on the island, is named. It was Malerubha who, centuries ago, travelled the west coast of Scotland driving pagans out of their old religious sites.

Then there is the area where Peter Gibbs's body was found, on a spot known as Pennygown. Traditionally, this was the haunt of fairies that lived beneath the hill. It is also curious that Gibbs's Cessna was last seen flying over Pennygown before it vanished. Today we link strange lights up above with UFO sightings, but in times past they were known as fairy lights and have been recognised as a strange phenomenon for centuries. Unidentified lights in the sky were noticed at the time Gibbs disappeared. Roger Howitt said, following the discovery of Gibbs's body, 'My wife and I maintained all along that we saw lights dying out in the Sound of Mull which could have been the plane, but at the time we thought he was still in it.' If those lights were not the doomed Cessna then what were they coming from? And why did the plane end up in the water when the last sighting of it was heading away from the sea over Pennygown?

Could it have been a case of alien abduction, with Peter Gibbs removed from his plane by extraterrestrials then, weeks after, returned to a Mull hillside? In the United States, just a few weeks after Gibbs's disappearance, forestry worker Travis Walton was taken aboard a strange craft and days later dumped on the roadside in a state of shock. His account is controversial, but does bear similarities to the Gibbs incident.

Or was Gibbs's body left as a warning to others? It was lying in a spot where it was certain to be found. In an area so very close to the hotel, but distant from his plane, that it was bound to raise awkward questions. But if so who was the warning intended for? There is no evidence that Gibbs was interested in the powers of the occult or obsessed by the existence of other dimensions. But maybe these strange forces found him. Could there be some unknown vortex of power that can swallow people? And did it suck out of this world the Eynhallow tourists and the Flannan lighthouse keepers, but for some reason disgorged Peter Gibbs back onto a lonely hillside? A solution hard to accept, but that at least takes in all the facts and stands closer scrutiny than the verdict of the Fatal Accident Inquiry. That Peter Gibbs had, quite simply, died of 'exposure' and that there was, in fact, really no mystery at all.

SEVEN

The Devil's spawn

ARE VICIOUS ATTACKS on horses proof that witchcraft is alive in Scotland today? From across the country there have been incidents of horses with their genitals mutilated or strange marks cut into their bodies. In 1994 a 2-year-old gelding was hit on the head with a claw hammer as it grazed on an Uddingston farm. A year earlier stables at the same place were broken into and the mystery attacker hacked off the tails of two tethered horses. The incidents were part of a series of strange attacks with no obvious motive. A horse was knifed and left bleeding from an eight-inch wound following an almost identical attack at another farm a few months earlier. Soon after, a horse was shot in the head and a second animal suffered a bullet wound to the flank. In 2002 a fresh wave of attacks swept across north-east Scotland, home in the past to the secretive horse-whispering societies which themselves adopted bizarre occult-style rituals. In the fields where the assaults had taken place, police found freshly built cairns – small mounds of stones with the remains of burnt horse hair and candles. Pentacles and double-headed axes, symbols used by followers of the black arts, were carved into the ground. To practitioners of witchcraft horses are sacred animals and can be used to create powerful magic. But attacks on animals have not been confined to horses. In 1995 a sheep with a wound which suggested that its rectum had been cored out was found in a field close to Edinburgh Airport. Its throat had also been slashed which suggested a ritual aspect to the animal's death. Though it had been mutilated in other ways there was surprisingly little blood on the body. Cats also have a strong link to ritual magic and there have been many incidents of pets disappearing in mysterious circumstances, and of half-dismembered cats discovered with their legs or heads cleanly removed as if by a cleaver. In Aberdeen in 2000 a woman was seen trying to steal pet cats from the gardens of domestic houses, eventually making off with one with a pure white coat, a colour viewed as particularly symbolic in ritual magic. Witchcraft has a long and dark history in Scotland. It stretches back to pre-Christian times and has taken many guises. To some it is mere devil worship, but to others it is a powerful and uplifting spiritual path though no one would deny that in the wrong hands it can become a force for evil.

There's no doubt that even today witchcraft activity has infected many areas of Scotland. Attacks on animals are only the more obvious sign. In 1976 a minister of the United Free church in Bo'ness clamed that the black arts, including Devil worship, were being practised in the town. During the investigation into the brutal killing of a school girl in Dalkeith in 2003, there were suggestions in the press that Satanists were involved. Though this may have been little more than speculation it shows how fear of the black arts has not gone away. But there is little doubt that some strange things are going on in the towns and cities of Scotland. In the 1980s police in Perth discovered a strange collection of ritual objects in a cemetery at Kinnoull Hill which suggested that black magic rituals were being carried out among the gravestones. The articles found included a sheep's head, dead rats and a ritual knife. They were discovered, by a groundsman, hidden in a box concealed beneath a table-shaped tombstone. The cemetery dated from the seventeenth century, but had long gone out of use for burials. The police commented: 'there have been no complaints about any midnight activities and at this stage we are keeping an open mind. It might have been a bit of mystical nonsense.' Those involved, however, were never identified. To some this shows that a conspiracy involving people at the very top of society is taking place. There have been claims that rock music lyrics are filled with 'satanic' messages. And that even major companies use the numbers '666', the 'mark of the beast', in their phone lines, product numbers, barcodes and the like. But the suspicion that powerful groups are involved in black magic is nothing new. Just a few hundred years ago it was claimed that a cousin of the King was heading a black magic cult which planned to take over the kingdom of Scotland.

The Earl of Bothwell was a close associate of King James VI. He was even entrusted with Scotland's security when in 1590 James sailed to Scandinavia to bring home his bride Anne of Denmark. However, he fell out of favour on James's return when James began to suspect Bothwell of plotting against him. At this time Europe was in the grip of a witch craze. It was believed that there were hundreds of thousands of witches all of whom were in direct league with the Devil. James was convinced that there existed an organised conspiracy of witchcraft, but even he must have been surprised to learn of the extent of his cousin's involvement in the occult.

Bothwell's link to witchcraft was exposed through a long twisting trail which started when Agnes Sampson, a 'white witch', confessed to having attempted to kill James by magic. She also implicated Dr John Fian, who acted as Bothwell's secretary, in her murderous plot. Agnes then tied Bothwell into events by admitting that he had consulted her about the future and, in particular, how long the king was likely to live. Fian was arrested and tortured with the Spanish boot, a vicious, yet simple, instrument of terror. Two sets of metal plates were fastened around each leg and pulled tight. The 'boots' were then battered using a metal hammer. The pain was unbearable and Fian was smashed about the limbs till, as one witness reported, the marrow spurted from his wounds. Incredibly, Fian still refused to confess to involvement in witchcraft. But far from convincing his torturers of his innocence, they reasoned that the Devil must be helping him to overcome the pain. They opened his mouth and discovered two pins stuck in the roof, a charm to stop him confessing. When they removed them, Fian broke down and admitted he was a witch. He told the King of gatherings of witches at North Berwick Kirk where Bothwell, disguised as the Devil, stood in the pulpit and told them of his plans to commit regicide, and how they had by magic raised a storm to try to sink the King's ship on its way back from Denmark. Fian was returned to the cell where, he later reported, the Devil came to him dressed in black. He demanded that Fian keep the oath that he had sworn to him. Fian replied, 'I have listened to you too much and by the same you have undone me therefore I utterly forsake you.' In a chilling retort the Devil warned him, 'Once you die you shall be mine.' Was it coincidence that a few hours later, in the early morning, Fian managed not only to get out of his cell but also clean out of Edinburgh Castle? He was later recaptured near his home in Tranent, but he had undergone a remarkable change and withdrew his confession to witchcraft. Even though the Spanish boot was applied with even greater ferocity he refused to admit to anything. He was put on trial, found guilty, strangled and burnt. The finger of suspicion now seemed to be pointing at the Earl himself.

Bothwell already had a reputation as a man interested in the occult. He openly consulted astrologers and fortune tellers and was alleged to practice necromancy, the raising of the spirits of the dead by magical rites. But claims that he took on the guise of the Devil at a coven meeting in North Berwick Kirk and led an organisation of witches rested solely on Fian's confession, which was of course extracted under extreme torture. And while John Fian and Agnes Sampson were executed Bothwell escaped punishment. The suspicion lingered that Fian had been sacrificed to protect a coven of highly placed witches. And that when he fled Edinburgh Castle gaol he had been met by coven members and even the Devil who had promised some amazing rewards if he kept his silence.

Witchcraft has been a constant then in Scottish life. And Scotland featured not only in the earliest cases of witchcraft, but also the last when, in 1944, a Scottish psychic was charged under the Witchcraft Act. Helen Duncan, born in Callander, was a well-known medium who became notorious because of her prosecution during World War Two. Mrs Duncan not only received messages from the spirit world, but also produced through her mouth a material called ectoplasm which allows a spirit to take on a solid form on this earth. One evening in Portsmouth in 1941 Helen Duncan informed one of the audience that she had a message from her son. Through Duncan he told his mother, 'My ship has been sunk'. The woman had no idea that her son's ship had gone down. Nor as it turned out did any other relatives of the crew as the authorities had kept the fact a secret. Helen Duncan's message was accurate. The ship in question – HMS *Barham* – had been torpedoed by a German U-boat. News of Mrs Duncan's clairvoyance reached the ears of officialdom who took the view that the medium posed a threat to the security of the nation. Of course, they did not present it in that way and the charge under the 1735 Witchcraft Act was of 'pretending to raise the spirits of the dead'. But if secrecy was not their concern why go to the lengths of prosecuting one medium and wait three years till 1944 to take action? It seemed to be taking paranoia to an extreme, but some have suggested a more sinister reason.

Spiritualist circles claim that Helen Duncan was a confidante of Winston Churchill and leading military figures. That she was used (as the wartime German government did) to detect the movement of Nazi warships and troops. It is a fact that Churchill was enraged by Duncan's prosecution and wrote to the then Home Secretary asking, 'What was the cost of a trial to the state in which the Recorder was kept busy with all this obsolete tomfoolery?' If Duncan had indeed been consulted by members of the government they could never afford to admit to it at the time nor are we likely even now to know the truth behind the prosecution.

Duncan was found guilty and sentenced to nine months imprisonment in Holloway gaol. A stiff sentence which points to the fact that contacting spirits was not the real motive behind the prosecution. It is also noticeable that Duncan was kept under observation after her release and police officers attended a number of her séances. Spiritualists believe that it was a confrontation with police at a meeting in Nottingham in 1956 which led shortly after to her death. She was cremated at Warriston crematorium in Edinburgh.

Helen Duncan was a well-intentioned medium who was simply attempting to contact the dead rather than using magic to control forces from other worlds – unlike the infamous Aleister Crowley, who claimed Scottish ancestry, married in Dingwall and for several years made Scotland his home. And it was in an eighteenth century Scottish mansion that he made his most dangerous contacts with the 'other side'. Boleskine House lies on a wooded hillside on the eastern, more sheltered, side of Loch Ness. It was the ideal retreat for 25-year-old Aleister Crowley who, though still a young man, had already carved a reputation for himself as a master of the black arts. He was labelled the 'Beast' and 'the wickedest man in the world'. Strangely, Crowley had been brought up in a strict Christian sect, the Plymouth Brethren, but abandoned his early faith to become a member of a key occult society, the Golden Dawn. Crowley was soon in charge of the organisation. He showed a real ability to put into practice strange rituals which convinced many that he truly did have magic powers. But Crowley wanted to go further and put himself into contact with entities which even experienced practitioners shied away from. To carry this out he needed a secluded location, far from prying eyes, where the rituals he wished to carry out could be prepared in secret. So he took out a lease on isolated Boleskine House. If Crowley is to be believed his time on the shores of Loch Ness was a great success. He held black masses and practised weird rituals, engaging in what many would regard as obscene deeds. This was all part of Crowley's belief in 'chaos magic', a device to open the mind to influences from other dimensions, contacting forces and entities from other spheres and allowing them into this world no matter what the consequences for the individual. The true magician, if he wants to control the forces of darkness, must take risks, or so Crowley argued. It seemed to work. He was so successful that events soon got out of hand. The spirits he raised in the darkened rooms of Boleskine House were not willing to be confined to the building but spread to the surrounding countryside. One of the men he hired began to lose his mind and tried to kill him. Another began to shake uncontrollably as if his body was being taken over. His housekeeper fled the place, terrified. More bizarrely, when Crowley wrote down the names of two demons on a butcher's bill, the unfortunate man cut through an artery in his arm and bled to death. True or not, there is no doubt that Boleskine House earned a reputation as a place to avoid. In March 2000 a film producer making a movie about Crowley asked a minister to bless the crew after a series of bizarre incidents. Beetles, sacred insects in black magic mythology, appeared out of nowhere in droves. Glass lights exploded for no apparent reason and there were constant equipment failures. Everyone involved was plagued by recurring dreams of Crowley and his weird rituals. It is claimed that Crowley put a curse on anyone who tried to deal with his private life even though when alive he craved publicity.

But for strange occult practices Crowley has a rival in the equally infamous Thomas Weir. The life and death of Thomas Weir bring together all those elements of the paranormal that still puzzle us today. Was he a Satanist, devil worshipper or black magician? Weir was no figment of the story writer's imagination. He was a man with a footnote in history, who notoriously blew smoke in the face of James Graham, the Marquis of Montrose, as the nobleman, a fanatical royalist, was on his way to his place of execution in 1650. Later Weir became a magistrate and Captain of the Edinburgh City Guard. He had also by the 1670s earned a reputation as a God-fearing citizen. A renowned preacher, Weir was a frequent visitor to the homes of the leading families of the capital to lead them in prayer. It was remarked that husbands had no hesitation in allowing him to visit their wives when they were not at home. He had such a saintly reputation.

So had Weir been living a double life for years? Or at some point did he and the sister with whom he lived simply go mad? Out of the blue he confessed to having been for fifty years a servant of the Devil. But it was the details he gave that shocked Edinburgh society. He confessed to having sex, not only with his sister, admitting that they had lived together as man and wife, but with the wives and daughters of leading members of the city council, many of whom he knew as friends. He claimed he had done this by occult means, using a magic staff the Devil had gifted him, to appear in their bedrooms in the dead of night. Most bizarre of all, he described how he had sex with a horse in a farmer's field.

The first reaction of friends was that Weir had gone mad. But though they hoped that he would eventually shut up, the opposite happened. His protestations of guilt grew more determined. Whenever he had the opportunity he denounced himself to anyone who would listen. Weir had become a scandal and the city authorities were left with no other choice but to arrest him, lock him in the Tolbooth and charge him with witchcraft. Had he begun to contradict himself, claimed that he had been seized by a fit of madness, or simply kept quiet, he would in all likelihood have been set free. But Weir would not play that game. He continued to announce his guilt, give details of the weird practices he had engaged in and describe his meetings with the Devil.

The authorities were being pushed into a corner, one from which there was no escape, especially when Weir's sister Jane began to admit to the same occult crimes. Weir was brought to trial, found guilty and executed, as was his sister. Though, curiously, the witchcraft charge was dropped and Weir met his death on the grounds of 'incest, sodomy and bestiality'. It was Jane alone who was branded as the consulter of 'witches, necromancers and devils'. It was a calculated act. Weir's high-ranking friends had no wish to be linked to a servant of Satan. And rumours of a conspiracy were soon sweeping the capital. It was claimed that a secret group of wealthy men had forced a double to take Weir's place and Weir had been seen, very much alive, staff in hand, walking the streets of surrounding villages. It was suggested that he was the leader of a secret occult group that worshipped the Devil, and that the members of the group were trying to save their leader by any means. Even at the time it was recognised that there was more to the case than met the eye.

So was it all in Weir's twisted thoughts? There are several puzzling features about his account. Sex with a horse seems on the surface the admission of a deranged mind. But on the other hand, this strange act was, in fact, part of ancient pagan rites. The Kings of Ulster in past times ritually copulated with a mare to achieve long life. Weir, in fact, had fought in 1641 with the Puritan army in Ulster against royalist Catholics. By that time he had, according to his own account, already become a follower of Satan, but he may have learnt of this strange practice during this period. Furthermore, as we know from events in the twenty-first century, horses are viewed as sacred animals by various occult groups, which suggests there was a real purpose to Weir's bizarre act. And then there is Weir's description of a strange airborne machine: the 'flying chariot' sparking flames which, in seconds, carried him from Edinburgh to Dalkeith in broad daylight for a meeting with the Devil, his master.

Clearly something had disturbed Weir's mind. But were these real events for all that? Had he become mixed up with strange entities of some twilight world? Although at first Weir talked freely about the Devil in the later part of his time in gaol he became reluctant to describe him though he still chatted unreservedly about his own crimes. Had he been warned to stay off the subject? Or did he realise that if he tried to explain exactly who the 'Devil' was he simply wouldn't be believed?

Maybe in the twenty-first century we would wonder whether Weir was genuinely involved with Satan or had simply gone out of his mind. But can we afford to feel superior on this matter? Accusations of witchcraft still have the power to shock, as the case of Scotswoman Carole Compton in the 1980s and events in Orkney in the 1990s show. Carole Compton hit the headlines in November 1983 when she was suspected of being a witch. Or so it was claimed in the popular press. Compton, a 21-year-old from Aberdeen, had been working as a nanny with the Ricci family at their holiday home near Bolzano in the north of Italy. Events at Bolzano were to contribute to her later arrest and trial. Several fires had mysteriously started at the house during the time she was employed there in July 1982. No one was injured. However, when she took up a new post in August 1982 at Mario Cecchini's home on the island of Elba fires erupted the day after she arrived.

Suspicion fell on her for several reasons. The fires coincided with her arrival, it was claimed. There seemed to be no other likely suspect and it was felt that the fires had been started deliberately. Furthermore, one blaze had occurred beside the cot of 3-year-old Agnese Cecchini, who Carole had been taken on to look after. Carole was accused of the attempted murder of Agnese, a charge she strenuously denied. It was at this point that the paranormal entered the debate. It was claimed other odd incidents had happened when Carole appeared on the scene. As *The Scotsman* newspaper reported it, 'in the Elba home . . . a statue fell to the ground soon after her arrival, then a glass bowl crashed to the floor without anyone being near it and a cake stand fell from a table'. Even the fire that threatened Agnese hadn't behaved as normal. As a fire investigator explained: 'Normally fires start at the bottom and work upwards, but in this case the flames had travelled downwards. It was very strange.' Professor Antonio Vitolo, a chemical expert, added: 'In the forty-five years of my career I have never seen such an atypical fire.'

There were certainly puzzling factors. The two mattresses beside Agnese's cot were burned only on the outside. And each was burned to the same extent although one was made of wool and the other of horsehair, which burns more easily than wool. Even weirder was the fact that the material woven into the horsehair was burned, but not the horsehair itself.

But these strange aspects hardly justified accusations of witchcraft. So what was the connection? It was alleged that her employer suspected her of having started fires by pyrokinesis: that is, psychic means through the power of thought. How much that was a concoction of the media is unclear. Undoubtedly the paranormal acted as an undercurrent to the trial. That was confirmed when Ciara Lobina, a local faith healer, turned up at the court carrying a large wooden crucifix and a small bottle of holy water, stating that Carole and her mother were possessed by an eighteenth-century witch. Ciara claimed, 'I want to touch them and cleanse their spirits'.

However, as it turned out, Carole Compton was not put on trial for witchcraft or for being a psychic arsonist. Nor was the court in Italy sitting in judgement on whether or not she was possessed of supernatural ability. Carole was eventually acquitted of attempted murder but sentenced to two and a half years for fire-raising, then immediately released to return to Aberdeen. The court's written judgement touched on Carole's alleged psychic ability and commented that, if that were true, why had there been no fires before her arrival in Italy or after her departure? Even though the judges rejected the paranormal as a component the fact that they were forced to mention it reveals the extent to which the psychic aspect had grabbed the attention of the world. The fear of witchcraft, of unknown forces controlled by a 'Master of Evil', still haunts us even today.

And though we may like to consider ourselves in the twenty-first century as far removed from some of the more grotesque forms of prejudice, it is instructive to compare Carole Compton's treatment to that given to Isobel Gowdie from the village of Auldearne over three hundred years ago.

Accused of being in league with the Devil, Gowdie gave an amazing amount of detail in her confessions, made during four separate interrogations between 13 April and 27 May 1662. She confessed voluntarily without any application of torture. This fact coupled with the extensive descriptions she gave of her activities convinced later writers that she could not have invented all the incidents. She must have been talking of events that had actually taken place.

Isobel claimed that she first became a witch fifteen years earlier in 1647 when she was re-baptised as Janet by the Devil himself in a macabre ritual after she had renounced her Christian faith. The ceremony, which took place at Auldearne church, was said to involve the Devil sucking Isobel's blood from her body and using it in the place of holy water. Isobel also explained to her interrogators that she would fly like a bird to the Sabbat, the witches' gathering place, after muttering an incantation. She used magic rituals to raise storms or ruin the crops of farmers who had displeased Satan. Isobel also recounted how Satan would punish the witches of her coven with a beating when they failed him. Here she would take part in various sexual acts with the Devil, who appeared in the form of an animal with a horned headdress. There was clearly a sexual aspect to women's involvement with the Devil, and the confessions extracted from females accused of witchcraft contain frequent descriptions of sexual activity. Isobel Gowdie commented that the Devil's member 'was as cold as ice' inside her and 'much bigger than a normal man's'. He was also capable of satisfying a woman far beyond the norm. That wasn't always the case though and other witches confessed that sex with the Devil could be a painful experience. The detailed descriptions of sexual activity have encouraged some to believe that gatherings of witches did take place, that witches were organised into covens and that their faith was all based on the survival of a pagan cult. The 'Devil' was simply the local 'priest', a man dressed up as a goat or other animal; one of the ancient gods of nature.

But the most frightening aspect to Isobel Gowdie's statements was the suggestion that the servants of the Devil were organised into covens of thirteen witches. This backed up claims that witches were a well-organised conspiracy with strong roots in most local communities, almost in fact like a secret sect. It was this aspect of Gowdie's confession that convinced later writers that what was being dealt with was an organised religion rather than a mass hallucination or mania. It provided a historical pedigree for witch-craft, to which present-day adherents of the craft could point as justification for their beliefs. Isobel Gowdie through her confes-sions – which were rediscovered in the twentieth century – sparked the modern revival of the Wiccan religion with its covens of thirteen witches, and she is regarded as the founding mother of modern witchcraft. She has become a key figure in the develop-ment of modern witchcraft or Wiccan belief. She earned notoriety during her lifetime as a central figure in the Auldearne village witch trials. But, at a time when the witchcraft mania that had swept Europe for two centuries was fading away, her confessions did not appear significant to her contemporaries in the 1660s. By contrast, to the twentieth century writers who came to believe in the reality of witchcraft the Gowdie confessions were of major importance in the understanding of an alleged religion centred on the worship of the horned god, known to us as the Devil.

And fear of witchcraft can still arouse passions today. In the 1990s, on the remote islands of Orkney, claims were made that a coven of witches was holding bizarre rituals in an isolated quarry. Police and social workers were called in, several adults arrested and a number of children taken into care. And an even stranger story emerged. It was alleged that the coven meetings were run by someone called the 'Master' who wore a black cloak and mask. As they danced round him in a circle he would use a stick to pull out anyone he wanted to have sex with. Most bizarrely of all, the 'Master' turned out to be a local minister of religion. Events in Orkney followed on similar incidents in Rochdale, England and in the USA where it was claimed Satanic covens were carrying out gruesome rituals, including the killing and eating of babies. Even though investigators dismissed the evidence there are still those who believe in the existence of Satanism and argue that followers of the Devil are simply too clever to be caught.

There is no doubt that there are individuals in Scotland who might claim to be Satanists, but the key question is whether there exists a widespread and organised conspiracy. Is it true, as one Church of England cleric claimed on a television programme, that 'Satanism is growing'? Scottish churches, on the other hand, have been virtually silent on the matter. And there is no publicly organised religion as there is in the United States, with its Church of Satan based in San Francisco and founded by Anton La Vey. In Scotland's occult circles gossip abounds about the dark deeds of Satanists. However, Satanists by nature prefer to avoid the limelight.

Satanists worship a Christian creation – Satan, the anti-Christ. And worship of Satan brings with it the belief that Satan's power can be used for the individual worshipper's own ends. Satan's aim is world domination and, as part of that, the destruction of the Christian way of life. He is not out to wipe mankind from the face of the earth. In fact the control of mankind is a key part of Satan's strategy. So he desperately searches for followers to help him carry out his plans. That is why Satanism is seen as essentially a mass conspiracy rather than a matter of individual conversion.

In some ways Satanism and witchcraft can overlap. While there are 'white witches' there are also 'black witches'. It is a major division within Wicca today, and those who follow the 'dark side' appear hard to separate from Satanists in practice. Both are intent on using the forces of the occult for negative ends, in other words to benefit themselves. There are undoubtedly practitioners of black witchcraft in Scotland though, so far, they have been at pains to distinguish their activities from those of Satanists. But to the public they probably appear as one and the same. Just as in the past our ancestors found it hard to separate the Devil from Satan. It may or may not be true that pagan religion survived into the Middle Ages as a form of worship of the god Pan. But to the Christian churches who wanted to crush the worship of Pan, the Devil and Satan were one and the same. So between 1400 and 1700 they carried out a merciless war on Satan's earthly army and around 1700 the Christian's war against Satanism ground to a halt. So for the last three hundred years Scotland's Satanists have been allowed to go about their business in relative peace. However, they have yet to declare their allegiance to the public and therefore the only conclusion that can be drawn is that they remain very few in number. Is the power of witchcraft simply a figment of the imagination? Or does the Devil really exist? And are the sacred rituals witches practise truly capable of affecting the world around us? It has even been suggested that illnesses like Aids, far from being the product of our own world, have been the result of bizarre occult rituals going completely wrong. That, through opening a portal to another world, black magicians have allowed not only strange entities but malignant diseases to enter our world.

For centuries people have believed in the power of ritual cursing to affect others. The extent to which individuals will go to achieve their ends is shown by a discovery on the hill called Arthur's Seat in Edinburgh in 1836. Three schoolboys found, in a small tunnel, hidden by three upright slates, seventeen miniature coffins arranged in three layers. A single coffin lay on the top suggesting that there were more to be added. When the coffins were opened an even stranger find was made. Inside each one lay a tiny doll, fully dressed, in funeral clothes with its boots painted black. Someone had clearly gone to a lot of trouble to create a realistic funeral scene as the coffins had even been lined with cloth and the lids nailed down with small brass tacks. Furthermore, from the varying state of decay, it seemed that the objects had not been put there at the same time, but separately, perhaps even centuries apart. So what had been their purpose? Ritual magic was one obvious answer. Witches were believed to use realistic clay or wooden images of the victims on whom they wished to inflict harm. Placing a lifelike doll of the person against whom you had a grudge in a coffin in the ground had obvious implications. But cursing is by no means a thing of the past. In the 1990s one Scottish psychic involved in helping those who believed they were under ritual attack commented, 'A spell is really a form of negative energy. You can create it simply by having bad thoughts about someone. However, some people go further and work with occult powers to put a spell on individuals they have a grudge against. Signs that you have been victim of a spell can be falling ill, your business getting into difficulties and constant family arguments.' And even today a doll can exercise a baleful influence. Psychic medium Katrina told of the small wooden figurine, about twelve inches high, which became notorious as the 'voodoo doll'. It seemed to bring bad luck to whoever owned it. Katrina agreed to look after it for a while and put it on a display cabinet by the staircase. Several unfortunate incidents followed. The doll toppled from its shelf and broke several mirrors. Her son tripped and fell down the stairs under the watchful eyes of the mysterious doll. A relationship broke up. All these events seemed to coincide with the arrival of the doll. Eventually the owner buried it and, at least for the moment, the earth has appeared to act as an effective barrier to its influence.

So even today the power of witchcraft can seem very real. There can be no clearer evidence than the accounts given by those who have been involved as practising Wiccans in the current movement. In the 1990s Dougie Bain, a high priest of a 'White Wiccan' coven and opposed to Satanism, found himself on the wrong side of those still following the teachings of the 'Great Beast', notorious black magician Aleister Crowley. To show their displeasure these disciples of the dark side sent a warning in the form of a bizarre entity called a gollum. A gollum is created by black magicians using soil from an ancient graveyard. Using strange rituals the black magicians resurrect the outward form of a dead person and put inside an evil spirit. It is then sent to terrify those who they believe need to be taught a lesson. Dougie Bain spent the whole night crouched in a corner of his Edinburgh flat with the gollum standing over him. It was only when the sun rose that the attack came to an end. Dougie had managed to defeat the power of the gollum by using his athame, a sacred knife consecrated by Wiccan ritual.

But are any of us safe from the servants of the Devil? Those aware of the power of witchcraft ritual, and who believe they may be the target of attack, make a regular habit of creating a psychic ring of defence around their person or home to protect themselves against evil influences. The Devil, it seems, has not given up the struggle and still has an interest in recruiting followers to his earthly army. Is modern disbelief in the power of witchcraft simply allowing him to have it all his own way?

EIGHT

A land of mystery

EVER SINCE COLUMBA encountered a strange beast at Loch Ness in AD 565, Scotland has been seen as a land of mystery. A country where weird things happen. But Scotland's reputation as a mystic centre could have an even longer pedigree. Incredible though it may seem even Jesus, it is claimed, while a young man travelled to Scotland's mysterious Glen Lyon to discuss arcane matters with religious 'wise men', mystics who claimed to be in communication with other worlds. In the 1300s the weird organisation the Knights Templar fled to Scotland, the country they regarded as their mystical homeland, after being accused of witchcraft and Satanism by the King of France. They became a powerful force in the country, even playing a key role in defeating English forces at the Battle of Bannockburn. It is not surprising to learn then that even Scotland's ancient throne, the Stone of Destiny, on which successive Scottish kings were crowned, has an aura of mystery. It was by tradition the rock that the biblical Jacob used as a pillow and then dreamt of a ladder leading from earth to heaven, a magical key that opened closed doors to other dimensions. It may explain why Edward I was so determined to remove it to England. And was it coincidence that within three years of the stone's return to Scotland in 1996, the first Scottish Parliament in three hundred years was set up? In the last century Scotland attracted an assortment of people, like black magician Aleister Crowley, who believed that the land bordering Loch Ness was a prime location for contacting spirits from the beyond. During this period occult circles across Europe were coming to recognise that Scotland was a candidate for the legendary 'Atlantis of the North', an island that had been the centre of an advanced civilisation, similar to the Atlantis described by Plato, and which had been destroyed by an almost identical catastrophe. The mystical link continues into the present. In the 1990s, Bonnybridge, in the heart of Scotland, became a world focus for sightings of unidentified flying craft, mysterious lights and alien-abduction incidents.

Scotland seems awash with mystical sites. Locations where beings from other worlds and dimensions can make contact with us. Places where unexplained power is generated. Take the mystery of standing-stone circles. Many still remain, but there is no doubt that over thousands of years many more have disappeared. At one time in the past there probably existed a network of circles stretching across Scotland. But those that remain are compelling evidence that our ancestors were driven by a determination to build these stone circles at specific locations. Stonehenge is a massive construction, a testimony to the technical skills of ancient man. Callanish, on the island of Lewis has a more complex and intricate layout. However, the purpose of both Stonehenge and Callanish remains a mystery. Archaeologists have suggested that they were put in place to keep a log of the movement of heavenly bodies, particularly the sun and moon.

But that hardly seems the whole story. Why would people with the skills to build Callanish need such a cumbersome structure to chart celestial activity? And the smaller circles, which form the vast majority of those set up, certainly could not have served this purpose. However, other explanations also tackle the imagination.

That standing stones were beacons to ancient astronauts; or even marked the landing sites of these visitors from distant planets. But one fact stands out even though most archaeologists choose to ignore it. Stone circles link with an unknown energy force running below ground, a force that can be detected through dowsing. In fact stone circles seem to channel and focus this energy to a quite extraordinary degree. The greater and more complex the stone layout, the more energy that is present and generated. Intricate layouts, like Callanish, perhaps, should be thought of as temples of energy that impacted not only at ground level, but could also be focused upwards even leading to suggestions that our ancestors were engaged in an attempt to contact other worlds and dimensions. They were, in fact, sending out signals to distant civilisations.

And this underground force has never gone away. Dowsers have identified different types of energy that can be found running through our homes even now. 'White' energy appears to encourage good health. A network of such energy lines spreading across Scotland could have brought much benefit to the land. But there is also 'black' energy, which today can be found at rubbish dumps, disused coal mines, nuclear establishments and cemeteries. It radiates out and runs through our homes to cause illness and depression. The physical effects can be quite dramatic. In 1995 an annex of Craigpark School in Ayr, used for pupils with special needs, had to be closed because of unexplained sickness to both students and staff. Despite extensive investigation by health and building experts the cause could not be detected. Dowsers, however, confirmed that the annex was a crossover point for several lines of intense underground energy. Ley lines which bypassed the main school building, but by chance focused on these smaller classrooms lying in the school grounds. This concentration of energy caused the physical and mental health problems which disrupted the life of the school, and eventually led to its closure. But this phenomenon can lead down even stranger pathways. Black energy, psychics believe, is used by evil beings from other dimensions to enter our world. This could explain why some buildings become the target for poltergeist activity. It can also be harnessed by magicians of the dark side to work evil in the world.

Our ancestors seemed to have a deep understanding of this natural energy force. Many buildings, especially churches and cathedrals, right into medieval times were constructed to link into this mysterious underground power, as ancient stone circles had been thousands of years before. This urge to locate sacred buildings at specific sites could explain the mystery of Rosslyn Chapel.

As buildings go it doesn't look imposing. But for generations it has fascinated those obsessed by the occult, including leading members of the German Nazi party. There is no doubt that Rosslyn Chapel, situated some eight miles south of Edinburgh, contains bizarre secrets. Hidden messages that we are only just beginning to unravel. Its walls are decorated with thousands of mysterious symbols, some in the shape of small statues. Others are occult designs carved into the walls and pillars of the church. But the enigma doesn't end there. The nave of the church is only ninety-five feet long, but beneath the chapel extensive vaults stretch the whole length of the building. Only a part of these vaults has ever been exposed, and it is not possible to enter one large section because it is blocked by tons of rubble. There are no plans as yet to excavate because of the technical problems of removing such a vast quantity of material from a confined area. It is probable that in the distant past the vault was filled in deliberately. There must have been something precious that a group of people were determined to conceal. But what could be so important that it had to be hidden and at the same time preserved for future generations? It is claimed that the unopened crypt holds earth-shattering documents about the life of Christ. And even the Holy Grail, one of the most mystical of all Christian objects – the cup that Jesus is said to have passed round at the last supper. Its mystic power has fascinated occult practitioners through the centuries.

Underground passages, only recently discovered, run from Roslin Castle, situated below the chapel, to the surrounding countryside. There can be little doubt that these may lead to the chapel itself though their actual route has still to be located. It seems that these passageways were not intended for escape but could have been used for religious rites of some kind – practices kept secret and revealed to only a few trusted initiates.

But exactly why in 1446 William St Clair chose this spot to build his mysterious temple is unclear. It may have had a previous history as a sacred site, one stretching back to pre-Christian times. For Rosslyn Chapel is clearly not simply a monument to Christian belief. It is far stranger than that. The building, from the outside, looks half finished, as if the architect was stopped in his tracks. But that would be a mistake. It appears that the chapel was quite deliberately constructed in this manner as part of a mystic plan. It was intended to represent the long-lost temple of Solomon. The Temple, described in great detail in the Bible, was seen as a key source for arcane and hidden knowledge. Its strange secrets influenced the beliefs of the Knights Templar, the early Masons and many occult societies. The St Clair family, and through them, their creation, Rosslyn Chapel, fit closely into this circle. The family had close links with the Templars and later on the Freemasons. This emerged as early as 1736 when a St Clair was made hereditary Grand Master of Scotland's Masonic lodges.

To some mystics Rosslyn Chapel is one of the world's seven omphalos: paranormal locations where this world and other worlds interact. But if Rosslyn is one of the omphalos this is not its only secret. There must be much more if, as suggested, it attracted the interest of leading members of the Nazi Party. For an explanation we have to search centuries back with the origins of the mysterious Knights Templar. The Templars had been founded on 25 December 1119 as an organisation to protect pilgrims who were travelling to Christian sites in the Middle East, especially Jerusalem. The Templars had a close, even mystical, link with the legendary Temple of Solomon. They were known at first as the Poor Fellow Soldiers of Jesus Christ and the Temple of Solomon. Eventually this was shortened to Knights Templar. The link with the Temple was critical to the development and mystique of the organisation because of the secret knowledge, and so power, traditionally connected with the building. At some point, it is alleged, during their occupation of Jerusalem in the twelfth century, members of the Templars excavated beneath the temple and discovered several astonishing documents and artefacts. There were finds that would have rocked the world had they ever been made public. In fact, they never were revealed, leading to speculation that it might have been a false lead, a deliberate smokescreen, intended to hide the fact that the Templars were determined from the very start to follow unorthodox beliefs. Rites and practices that bordered, and maybe even crossed into, the realms of black magic. Outwardly committed to Christianity, it was widely suspected that they were inspired by a mixture of pagan and occult practices. They were said to worship a talking head, engage in obscene sexual rites and hold unorthodox views of the true relationship between Mary Magdalene and Jesus. It was claimed that the Templars possessed documentary proof of Jesus's real role in the world which was so shocking that making it public would have destroyed Christianity. And that they had evidence that he had married and had children. Though the contents of these documents were kept secret, they shaped the organisation, beliefs and secret rites of the Templars.

And these beliefs were brought right to the heart of Scotland's ruling families. A close link was established between Scotland's monarchs, the Knights Templar and the St Clair family who were eventually to build Rosslyn Chapel. There is a strange, almost mythical tale, which involves King Robert the Bruce and William St Clair on a deer hunt. They chased a white deer, but could not catch it. King Robert challenged his nobles to a bet that none of their hounds could kill the deer. Only William St Clair took up the challenge. He set his dogs after the deer, calling on Christ, Mary and St Catherine to assist him. The dogs drove the deer into a burn where the animal was brought down. Even though its meaning may be lost to us, the account, which is certainly fictitious, was clearly intended as a sign of a mystical bond between Bruce and the St Clair family. Bruce had welcomed the Knights Templar to Scotland and the St Clairs had close links with the organisation. One of the Templar founders, Hugh de Payen, had married Katherine St Clair. It gives more credence to the belief that the Knights Templar were a key element in Bruce's success in 1314 at the Battle of Bannockburn, fought by tradition on 23 June, the feast day of St John the Apostle, an inspirational figure for the Templars. That link is surely more than coincidence.

On Bruce's death it was a member of the St Clair family who

was instructed to take Bruce's heart to be buried in the Holy Land. In fact, William St Clair did not complete the journey as he was supposedly attacked as he travelled through Spain by a band of Muslims. However, because he and his fellow knights behaved so bravely, the account goes, he was not killed and was allowed to return to Scotland. Bruce's heart was interred at Melrose Abbey, or so we are led to believe. To some, however, that tradition does not ring true and it has been suggested that, in fact, Rosslyn Chapel is the real burial place of the Bruce's heart given his link with the St Clair family and the Knights Templars. There have been even stranger stories circulating linked to the secret knowledge of the Templars; that Bruce's heart was being taken to the Holy Land in order to carry out a secret rite. The rather easy way in which the enterprise allegedly failed certainly leaves room for doubt over the course of events. Was it possible that the Templars believed that by using the Bruce's heart in a magical ceremony some mysterious force could be contacted? Even Bruce himself. Was that one of the secrets of Rosslyn Chapel?

The sacred rites of the Templars influenced a range of mystic societies including the Freemasons and Rosicruicians, and eventually filtered into the occult societies of the late nineteenth and early twentieth centuries. These societies developed links with right wing political circles across Europe, particularly, but not only, in Germany. This may explain one of the strangest incidents of the Second World War. In May 1941 Rudolf Hess, Adolf Hitler's deputy, made a bizarre solo flight to Scotland. He apparently missed his intended destination, the Duke of Hamilton's family seat at Dungavel House, south of Glasgow, and crash landed in a farmer's field near Eaglesham. He was taken prisoner and his real identity soon unmasked. However, the reason for Hess's flight has never been properly explained though it has been linked with secret peace deals to end Britain's involvement in the war. But could the truth have been even more bizarre? The interest of leading members of the Nazi Party in the occult is well known. Hess was a member of a German organisation known as the Thule Society. The Thule Society not only was interested in pagan myths, but also had contacts with occult societies across Europe, including

Scotland. A member of the Thule Soiety, Hans Fuchs, visited Rosslyn Chapel in the 1930s and afterwards gave a talk to the Edinburgh Theosophical Society, a mystical organisation founded in the late nineteenth century by the Russian psychic Helena Petrevona, also known as Madame Blavatsky. Through his occult contacts Hess, and leading Nazis, would have been well aware of the mystical significance of Rosslyn Chapel, especially the rumour that it was the burial site of the Holy Grail. And had been informed too of the several documents and artefacts supposedly buried beneath the chapel. If they did not understand the significance, they were aware of the hundreds of figures carved into the stonework in the chapel's interior, and of the mystical significance of the magical dimensions on which Rosslyn Chapel had been built.

Granted that Hess could have been aware of the occult importance of the chapel what role could it have played in his mystifying flight to Scotland in May 1941? One argument has it that Hess was attempting to get hold of magic artefacts that could be used to influence the outcome of the war. Leading Nazis had already amassed a collection of mystic objects including the spear said to have pierced Christ's side as he lay dying on the cross. It was not simply the prestige of owning objects with a powerful symbolic meaning. Occultists believed that using these objects in a magic ritual could actually influence events on earth. That is the whole point of magic. Controversially, it has been suggested that Hess planned to go to Rosslyn Chapel to carry out some mystic ritual assisted by sympathetic individuals in Scotland. It might even have been the intention to conduct joint magical ceremonies to establish some occult link between Scotland and Germany and so influence the course of the war. Some leading Nazis may have convinced themselves that it was possible. Such beliefs are not new and continue to this day with all kinds of sects holding vigils to summon up power to save the world. More likely is the suggestion that Hess believed he could get his hands on secret historical documents which would radically change the way the history of Europe was usually taught.

Central to this historical time bomb was proof that Jesus married and had children, and that these children escaped, after his death, to France and the descendants of these children formed the ruling houses of Europe. If this could be confirmed as true, it could have had a dramatic impact on the warring nations' attitude to one another though whether it would have been enough significantly to change Britain's involvement in the war is doubtful. There were other issues at stake. Hess's mission probably would not have been based on Rosslyn Chapel's significance alone, but it could have played a part if he had contacts with similarly minded persons among Britain's ruling elite. Although the real reason for Hess's flight is much disputed, more details are continuing to emerge though it may be some time before we learn what really happened. We may then be in a better position to assess its occult significance. Attempts by the Nazis to destroy secret societies like the Freemasons seem at odds with their supposed interest in the occult. But there is no doubt that leading Nazis did consult astrologers and even employed people who used remote dowsing techniques to locate enemy warships. Members of the SS undoubtedly took part in occult rites and worshipped old Norse gods, particularly Odin, the god of war.

So it would be wrong to dismiss the occult aspect to the Hess affair. Despite the fact that for the last two hundred years we have passed through a period of rapid technological change, the influence of the mystical has also, strangely, been alive and well. The West may pride itself on its rational approach yet all types of occult groups and alternative lifestyles thrive. The idea that our leaders may be influenced by ideas other than practical down-to-earth ones may at first glance appear unlikely. Among US presidents Ronald Reagan consulted an astrologer, Abraham Lincoln a psychic and Jimmy Carter publicly admitted to having seen a UFO. Winston Churchill had several psychic experiences. Lady Dowding, wife of Hugh Dowding, the commander-in-chief of Fighter Command during the Battle of Britain, was a practising medium. Dowding regularly consulted her and shared his wife's enthusiasm for the 'other world'. Queen Victoria actively involved herself in spirit phenomena. Cherie Blair, wife of the British prime minister, Tony Blair, consulted mystics who claimed to be in contact with the 'beyond'. Even present members of the

British royal family have been involved with psychics. And the list could go on. In fact, there is a long tradition of Britain's rulers making use of unorthodox sources. The relationship between Elizabeth I of England and the psychic John Dee, and James VI's fascination with witchcraft, are simply the best known. Later monarchs were more secretive on the matter as public tastes changed and interest in the occult came to be seen as less acceptable and even strange.

So Rosslyn Chapel may be living proof that history is more complex than we believe, especially with regard to the influence of the occult on society. Its significance may explain why, as recently as the 1990s, Prince Charles came to open Rosslyn Chapel's newly established museum. But he was not the first monarch to have shown a keen interest and was following in other royal footsteps. As far back as 1847 Queen Victoria visited Rosslyn. She made a point of warning the St Clair family that the chapel must not be allowed to fall into a state of disrepair. They took the hint and a start was made on restoration work. Queen Victoria was a strange person. To her Victorian subjects she appeared reserved and strait-laced. However, as her personality has gradually been revealed in the century since her death a rather different character has emerged. John Brown, her servant at Balmoral, and also a close confidant, acted as her personal medium. Victoria had an intense interest in consulting the spirit of her dead husband, Prince Albert. Something she did every day, not only on domestic issues, but also on matters of state.

But then, of course, the real interests of public figures often does not emerge till well after their death. And so there may be a long wait till we learn the truth behind the decision to build Scotland's most controversial piece of architecture. But could there really be a link between the ancient mystery of Rosslyn Chapel and Scotland's new parliament building? The 'temple to democracy' designed to see in the new politics of twenty-first century Scotland. To discover the truth we have to go back several hundred years.

There is a mysterious tale connected to the founding of Holyrood Abbey, close to the spot where the new Scottish parliament will stand. In a strange foreshadowing of the later Bruce and St Clair deer chase, King David I in 1128 was hunting in the shadow of Arthur's Seat when he was confronted by a male deer, a white stag with prominent antlers. The stag threw David to the ground, wounded him in the thigh and would have killed him if a crucifix had not suddenly, and miraculously, appeared in his hands. The stag, faced with the cross, turned and ran. That night David had a vision that having been saved by divine intervention he should, in repayment, build an abbey at Holyrood. In this way the Holyrood site was from an early date firmly fixed as a mystic location through a series of events that go beyond this world and have clear pagan, as well as Christian, elements.

Is it simply coincidence that Scotland's new parliament is being built in the same mystical location? The saga so far has caused general puzzlement. Starting at an estimated cost of £40 million the projection of the actual cost had by August 2003 risen tenfold to £400 million. But no one was sure why or appeared able to stop it. People were further perplexed by the parliament's bizarre shape which some compared to an upturned boat although, as was observed, looked on from above it appeared as a pyramid. To others it had the appearance of the 'all seeing eye' of the god Horus, a favoured magic motif of the ancient Egyptians.

Imagination may have been getting out of hand, but there was no doubting that there existed somewhere and with somebody an obsessive determination to build at this location when other sites seemed to offer a better choice. There was already available the former Royal High School building on Calton Hill. It could have been occupied almost immediately, but was dismissed as too small. Sites in Leith and elsewhere would have offered a less awkward construction task, and were easier to access than a city-centre site. They were brushed aside with little discussion that leaves not much doubt there was a fixed view that the new parliament-building must be situated at the foot of the Royal Mile, a site within the shadow of Arthur's Seat and within view of St Anthony's Chapel, reputedly linked to the Knights Templar. Could the location have been selected because of its mystic association? In the area where David I's enigmatic confrontation with a stag took place and Holyrood Abbey was built as a consequence.

It has been argued that the decision to site the new building at Holyrood was not taken by Donald Dewar, not even by Scottish politicians, but by Tony Blair and a few close associates. If this is true it is to be wondered why Donald Dewar stuck so tenaciously to the project as it turned into the most bizarre of living soap operas. As Scottish National Party MP Alex Salmond pointed out in a press release, 'Donald Dewar seemed to have an enormous attachment to personally creating a new piece of architecture for future generations.' Despite a lifetime spent in public affairs, Dewar was surprisingly reclusive. His entries in reference books like *Who's Who?* are short and uninformative. They don't even mention his keen interest in art. He lived a notably, admirably, sparse life. But on his death even those who thought they knew him well were astonished when they learnt that he left an estate worth well over £2 million. He had gathered a collection of Scottish Colourist paintings worth in excess of £400,000. Dewar was no doubt aware that the Colourists were strongly linked to the Celtic revival in the Scottish arts, which took place in the early years of the last century. Artists from the Colourist school were frequent visitors to Iona, an island that had earned a reputation as a mystic centre where entities from other worlds were reportedly seen, encounters claimed by the artists themselves. Iona has continued as a spiritual inspiration up to the present; Labour leader John Smith was buried on Iona after his sudden death in 1994.

Wherever Dewar's interests may have lain, by the time he became first minister of Scotland, Holyrood presented him with a real problem. Way behind schedule – it was supposed to be in use by 2001 – and way over budget, doubts surfaced over whether the winning entry in a competition held to choose a design for the building was in fact the one that was going to be built. It seemed to have been changed out of all recognition and no one seemed sure quite how it had happened. In a new democratic Scotland, there is no doubt that it was strange that neither Scottish politicians nor the Scottish public were given an opportunity to decide where they wanted the new parliament. Or what kind of building should house it.

If Donald Dewar had any doubts about what was being done in Scotland's name, he hid it well. On a visit to the site in April 1998, he enthusiastically extolled the historic significance of the location. He said in a press release:

> The start of the archaeological work is another milestone on the road to establishing Scotland's Parliament. It is Scottish Office policy to conduct appropriate archaeological and historical work in advance of new building and the site, at the heart of so much Scottish history, offers an unrivalled opportunity – before the site is developed – to examine the reality of that history in detail. Historic Scotland has already examined documents and maps to establish as far as possible the history of the site.

A statement which shows that Dewar was not only aware of the historic significance of the location, but was also revelling in it. But while he clearly saw the new parliament as a continuation of that historic link, it leaves a tantalising question. Did that include the mystical backdrop with which the area had been so intimately connected? If that could be answered, the puzzle surrounding the new Parliament's location would be solved.

Sadly, the two people most publicly associated with the Holyrood project, its architect Enrico Miralles and Donald Dewar, died within months of each other. Many awkward and unanswered questions died with them. The heat, though not completely taken off, was certainly turned down. Some Labour supporters were quick to suggest that any criticism of the project was an unwarranted attack on the 'Father of the Nation', Donald Dewar. So now we may never know if the decision to site the new parliament at this spot was a deliberate act taken because of its mystical past. Or the effect of some kind of unconscious force, working on people's minds and drawing them to the area.

Though we may never solve the enigma of Scotland's parliament, it does suggest that our present and future may be shaped by forces we simply fail to recognise. And that our past may be far stranger than we believe. Many involved in the occult argue that we are mistaken about our history. That advanced civilisations existed long before ours, reached our own technological level, then vanished. And, incredibly, there could be the evidence in Scotland to support what seems on the surface a bizarre view of our history. So could the puzzle of Scotland's vitrified forts be proof that a technologically advanced society was destroyed in a nuclear war thousands of years ago? And could the miles of underground tunnels which exist in many areas of Scotland, our 'prehistoric' monuments and even the remains of underground cities lead to the same conclusion? That, following a nuclear holocaust, the survivors sheltered in subterranean accommodation till it was safe to return to the earth's surface. Some argue that the craters visible on the Moon are not the remains of extinct volcanoes, but evidence of a bombardment by weapons of mass destruction. And that Mars, which so clearly was at one time capable of sustaining life, was reduced to its present lifeless state not by natural erosion of its atmosphere, but by a destructive war.

We may think we know our past, but how much can we be sure of? Historians are not even certain of basic facts about important civilisations that allegedly thrived a little more than three thousand years ago. When archaeologists are unable to supply a convincing explanation of how an ancient civilisation, without mechanical transport, succeeded in building a stupendous monument like the Great Pyramid can we be so sure of what really happened in the past? And Scotland is packed full of enigmas that add further twists to the puzzle.

The mysterious vitrified forts of Scotland, which can be found as far apart as Clickhimin in the Shetlands and Moat of Mark in Dumfries, seem to contradict the traditional view of the past as taught by archaeologists. These enigmatic remnants of an unknown race have puzzled scientists ever since they were first brought to public attention. Built thousands of years ago from chunks of neatly carved solid rock, they were at some time in the distant past blasted by a great force of heat. The temperature was high enough to melt the rock structure of the fort, turning it into a glass-like mass. Why, and how it was done, remains an unsolved riddle. But there seems little doubt that it was done deliberately.

Archaeologists, unable to explain it, suggest that it may have been carried out for ceremonial purpose. But why go to the trouble of constructing a solid fort which common sense suggests was intended as some kind of defensive measure and then turn it into a weaker structure? It's a puzzle. Scientists agree that blasting stone blocks with intense heat would have no benefit, simply reducing the internal strength of the rock. But the most mystifying aspect is that incredibly high temperatures would have been required to reduce rock to a fluid – as high as 1,100 degrees centigrade.

On the face of it, it seems hard to understand how a technologically 'primitive' people could have had the knowledge to generate such phenomenal temperatures. But that it did happen is undeniable. The evidence exists to prove it. The forts have been dated to up to 2,500 years old, but that relates to the date of the last inhabitants. Evidence suggests that they could be considerably older. Maybe thousands of years older. The dating of the construction of these forts, as with so many ancient structures, of which there are no written records cannot be certain. The paradox of Scotland's vitrified forts has raised speculation that only the heat generated by a nuclear explosion of some kind could have caused it. The state of the rock has an uncanny resemblance to the effect on buildings seen after the impact of atomic weapons in the Japanese cities of Hiroshima and Nagasaki. Such an interpretation would rewrite the past and force us to take a dramatically different view of how man and our current civilisation came into being. An equally dramatic explanation could lie in the heavens. There are stone carvings made in Scotland, generally dated to the time of the Picts, but which may describe events from an earlier period, which show people running from an object careering across the sky. This could be a comet. It could be something man-made. The Indian Vedas, which are thousands of years old, describe machines that fly, and even how to make one. Even so the thought of stone forts in Scotland being attacked by advanced flying machines may be hard to swallow. Until we consider the history of European colonisation of Africa. Here, technologically advanced nations collided with countries at a less developed state. To end resistance to foreign rule, tribal villages in Africa were attacked by European planes dropping high-explosive bombs on mud and stone built structures to force the inhabitants into submission. In ten thousand years time how comprehensible will that appear to our descendants? But it is a fact that, though we have sent men to the moon, in other parts of the world people live in accommodation made of earth bricks and barely scrape a living.

So have we simply been misinterpreting the past by projecting our own view of the world's development even when it contradicts what we can see with our own eyes? There is evidence from across Scotland of secret underground tunnels, bunker-like constructions dating from unknown centuries past. Maes Howe, a giant conical-shaped mound in the Orkneys was built of massive stone blocks that form a narrow chambered entrance and a protected interior some thirty-five feet in diameter. The labour involved must have been intense, if only simple tools were used, but similar examples can be found in Ireland. Unable to explain why our primitive ancestors would go to such trouble, archaeologists describe it as a burial mound. However, if Maes Howe is linked with the vitrified forts another solution may offer itself. These earth-covered, thickly built structures would have been ideal protection against radiation exposure or almost any level of explosive force. In fact, these buildings are anything but primitive and reflect a very advanced level of society. They also suggest protection rather than another purpose. Furthermore, there can be little doubt that there were at one time many more structures like Maes Howe, but they have either fallen down or been raided for building materials over thousands of years. It is pure chance that Maes Howe survived.

Just a few miles north of Maes Howe, there is further evidence. Skara Brae, dug deep into the ground, and usually designated a Stone Age settlement, could be viewed in a different light. Generally considered to have been buried by accident, the series of ten carefully stone-built huts, with connecting stone passages, makes more sense as homes built to protect against some kind of aerial menace. Even archaeologists accept that Skara Brae was abandoned in a hurry, though they argue it was because of a dust storm or similar incident. Yet the evidence from Maes Howe, the vitrified forts, Skara Brae and elsewhere could also suggest a determination to avoid attack or natural calamity from the sky.

Present-day Scotland is full of protected bunkers, some wholly below ground, others partly above, which will be used in the event of nuclear or other attack. Can we be so sure that our civilisation is the first to seek to protect itself from dangers from the sky? In the case of our ancestors this might have been a succession of debris falling from a disintegrating celestial object, even a planet, as some experts have suggested took place in the recent past. A catastrophe which caused the flood and devastation of humanity recorded in the Bible and in many supposed worldwide 'myths'. One writer, Comyns Beaumont, even argued that a large meteor impacted with the island of Mull and created a massive detonation. Disregarded at the time, investigation by scientists over the last forty years has shown that throughout history the earth has been hit many times by large pieces of space debris. Evidence of fresh impact craters emerge all the time. In 1908 a huge explosion, believe to have been caused by a comet, devastated thousands of miles of Siberia. A series of similar incidents covering a relatively short period could have forced our ancestors to seek protection in bunker-like dwellings.

The truth is, 'How much do we really know about our past?' What we are taught is that we evolved over millions of years from a single-celled organism. Essentially that life on earth has been a generally upward progression from simplicity to complexity and the technologically advanced society we live in today. But there is evidence that challenges that. Objects that appear 'out of time'. Artefacts discovered in our own backyard that throw huge doubt on man's origins, and Scotland's past. As long ago as 1844 a gold thread was found inside a lump of rock millions of years old quarried close to the village of Rutherford on the river Tweed. Some years later a leading scientist of the day, Sir David Brewster, reported to the British Association for the Advancement of Science the discovery of an iron nail in the middle of a block of sandstone chiselled out of a Dundee quarry. This rock was over 350 million years old. These finds were ignored because they went against religious belief, that the world had been formed a few thousand years before, and contradicted the theory of evolution which suggested that Man had been around for a relatively short period. But these finds were not isolated discoveries. And similar 'out of time' objects continue to emerge. In 1968 in Utah a sandal imprint was found on a piece of shale when it was split open. The shale was over 250 million years old. In 1972 a trail of human footprints was discovered that overlap with those of dinosaurs which lived over a hundred million years ago. But, according to scientists, dinosaurs died out millions of years before Man walked the earth. A growing body of evidence suggests that our history is far more complex than we are led to believe. And that an advanced civilisation could have been around a long time ago with Scotland as one of its main bases, then been destroyed by natural disaster or some nuclear war.

One fact is clear. We need to look more closely at our own history and the influences on us today. The enigmatic stone structures of Scotland, and objects found 'out of time', suggest that our past is no open book. And the experience with the Scottish parliament-building at Holyrood suggests that mystic influences, maybe less than wholesome, which shaped man in former eras are still alive and with us today. Scotland remains, as it has always been, a land of mystery and unanswered questions.

NINE

They could have been serial killers!

IN THE EARLY 1980s there were two murder trials that completely transfixed not only their respective communities but also Scotland as a whole. The background made it inevitable that public attention would be intense and media coverage unrelenting. There were three factors in these cases that made them stand out from the run of murder cases: the four women murdered were either completely unknown to the killers, or random acquaintances; there appeared to be no motive for any of the killings; the women were the victims of fate when they strayed into the paths of two of the most evil killers in Scottish criminal history. To these must be added a fourth, even more chilling, factor – police firmly believed that if the men had not been caught after committing two murders apiece they would have become serial killers, perhaps even rivalling the Yorkshire Ripper, Peter Sutcliffe, for the number of women slain.

The other similarities between the two killers are equally striking. They both grew up in affluent, professional, middle class families, a background rare in murder cases. Both were young men who had disappointed their ambitious parents by their lack of educational achievements and their lifestyles. Both had experienced behavioural problems in their adolescent years. Both were – to the casual observer – polite and helpful. Both were good looking and attractive to the opposite sex, with girlfriends who stood by them from the moment of their arrest to the end of their trial. Both – to some extent – were inadvertently 'put in the frame' by their doting and protective mothers. And, of course, both murdered two women.

*

The detectives who found Catherine McChord's body at three o'clock on the morning of 1 October 1982 in Braeside Place, Cambuslang knew they were dealing with a cold, calculating and brutal killer. The body of the 36-year-old taxi driver from Carmyle in Glasgow had been stuffed into the luggage compartment of her cab. She had been stabbed twice in the back of the head and three times in the chest, suffering what one forensic scientist described as 'extreme violence'. In a bizarre twist her ignition key, an inhaler and a cigarette lighter had been arranged in a straight line on the driver's seat. This laying out of the victim's possessions was one of the hallmarks of a ritual murder. And it was not the only bizarre aspect of the crime: it later emerged that the killer had spent an hour alone with the corpse in her taxi.

Almost immediately, police had a significant lead to investigate. They were somewhat surprised to discover that the victim had a conviction for a serious crime. Mrs McChord had been found guilty of a £143,500 fraud involving a Spot the Ball competition in the *Scottish Daily Express* and sentenced to three years in prison. This, detectives reasoned, could mean that she had been the victim of an underworld hit. In Glasgow, with its reputation for blood feuds among the criminal classes, such revenge attacks were relatively common. The police urgently pursued this line of inquiry, but it turned out to be a red herring. It appeared that the McChord murder was completely motiveless, a fact that chilled the blood of the senior officers in charge. They knew this was a man who was likely to kill again.

At the same time that the underworld connection was being pursued, a massive murder hunt was under way in the local area. Rutherglen CID office was quickly transformed into an incident room and a police caravan was sited in Braeside Place. Detectives from other areas were drafted in to help, and this allowed more than sixty officers to get involved in the laborious, but necessary, tasks of knocking on doors, checking alibis and collating evidence. Appeals were published in local newspapers asking witnesses to come forward. A taxi like the one driven by Mrs McChord was parked in areas she had worked in to jog memories. In fact a number of people did remember seeing her that night, helped by her conspicuous appearance – she was always immaculately dressed, wore lots of jewellery and, invariably, a wig. Yet police were nevertheless disappointed by the response from the local community, and some officers attributed this to the victim's conviction for fraud.

Another problem was that the night of the murder was very wet and, as is the norm when it is raining heavily, cabbies have a large number of hires covering short distances. It proved difficult to locate everyone that she had picked up. Other promising lines of inquiry proved fruitless, such as the questioning of Glasgow's 130 or so female cabbies to determine if they had picked up anyone suspicious. As time went on the number of officers involved dropped to twelve as leads were exhausted and the stream of new information dried up. But the men in charge of the investigation were deeply concerned. They felt it was only a matter of time before the killer struck again.

Their fears were justified a matter of weeks later when Cambuslang, a quiet suburb to the south of Glasgow, experienced one of the most shocking murders in Scottish criminal history. Elizabeth Walton was a nursing sister who lived in the area with her husband and children. She was a hard working, highly respected member of the local community; a model citizen without a stain on her character. After a much deserved night out on 2 December 1982 in Glasgow city centre with a female friend to celebrate her recovery from illness, Mrs Walton made her way home by train. Her train got into Cambuslang station just after eleven. Her normal practice was to phone home for a lift but this time she decided to walk to her house, which was less than half a mile from the station. She never reached her destination. An assailant, hidden by shrubbery, pounced and knocked her unconscious. He then dragged Mrs Walton into thick undergrowth next to West Coats primary school – the school attended by her 9-year-old daughter – where he strangled and savagely beat her. When she was dead the killer stripped off her clothes and mutilated the body with a knife. Still not content with his handiwork he then 'decorated' the body with the knife by slashing her wrists and cutting her thighs. The killer also tied her clothes in knots. These were the tell-tale signs of a ritual killing. It is little wonder that hard-bitten detectives later described the murder of Elizabeth Walton as one of the most sadistic they had ever encountered.

This breed of murderer is often referred to today as a 'signature killer'. Criminologists such as Robert Keppel argue that the signature killers are not satisfied with simply killing a victim and departing the scene. Often driven by violent sexual fantasies, they have a compulsion to leave their personal stamp on the victim. As Ted Bundy, the notorious American serial killer, pointed out it could be whatever the killer 'gets his rocks off on'. It is clear that the Cambuslang double murderer fits neatly into Keppel's classification of the signature killer. In his classic book, *Signature Killers*, he points out: 'I've seen lust killers who have a need to bludgeon to the point of overkill, others who carve on the body, or signature killers who leave messages written in blood. Some rearrange the position of the victim, performing post-mortem activities which suit their own personal desires.' Given this profile the need to catch the perpetrator was greater than ever.

With the tight-knit community of Cambuslang now in a state of shock, police efforts to find the killer intensified. In addition to the control room in Rutherglen police station the incident caravan was reinstated to assist in the investigation and to reassure the public. The caravan was a hive of activity with witnesses, police and forensic specialists coming and going throughout the day and into the night. Door-to-door enquiries resumed with forty detectives and many uniformed officers working flat out. Strathclyde Police even took the decision to draft in a team of detectives from the elite Serious Crime Squad.

But as so often happens in murder cases the police got a break. A very lucky break. Only seventy-two hours after Mrs Walton was killed a local man, one of many who had called to assist, walked into the caravan with a piece of information. Information that might crack the case. Was this the breakthrough the police had been praying for? The witness, Iain Scoular, aged 24, was personable, good looking and well dressed; and he came from a highly respected family. This was not the profile of the crank who pesters the police with dubious information and spurious confessions during high-profile murder cases. He told detectives that, at about 11 p.m. on the night of 2 December, he had been walking home from the pub when he saw a strange man acting suspiciously near the spot where Elizabeth Walton had been murdered. At the time, he said, he thought little of it and went straight home. The officer in charge of the investigation, veteran detective Chief Inspector George Dunwoodie, instructed his officers to follow this up in the usual way by checking out the lead and, given that Scoular had been in the vicinity of the crime scene around the time of the murder, his detectives spoke to those closest to him to verify his story. It was at this stage that police discovered there was more to Iain Scoular than met the eye.

*

Iain Scoular was a disappointment to his parents, despite their obvious devotion to him. His father, John, was a chartered accountant who had been the financial director of a big company in the motor trade and his success in business had enabled him to provide well for his wife, Jean, son Iain and his daughter. The family lived in a new house on a small private development in

Cambuslang, and were liked and respected by all those who knew them. But despite his comfortable, middle-class background Iain was a boy with problems. At school he was described as immature, and tended to hang around with children younger than himself. He also told lies constantly and was referred to a psychiatrist as a result. Although his parents had high hopes for him he left Cathkin High School with a single O level, in woodwork, with only the prospect of unskilled work. Following a number of nondescript jobs he ended up as a fork-lift-truck driver with a local company.

Much of his social life centred around visiting neighbourhood pubs, such as the Kirkhill Arms and Finlay's Bar, where he frittered away large sums of money on fruit machines. Indeed the problem became so bad that he decided to hand over his pay packet to his father on a Friday night to curtail his spending. Despite his apparent lack of interest in girls during his teenage years he met a young woman at a country-and-western night in a local club in July 1980, when he was 22, and they fell deeply in love. The object of his affection, Irene Anderson who was also from Cambuslang, described Scoular as 'the perfect gentleman . . . he was never pushy or fresh and did not try to have sex with me.' Ignoring the disapproval of Scoular's parents about Irene's background – she was brought up in a council house and worked in a factory – the couple got engaged after a ceremonial exchange of rings in Anderston bus station in Glasgow.

Although he was an adult and engaged to be married Iain Scoular's mother still kept a protective eye on him. She admitted to 'old-fashioned views' on the family and would wait up for her adult son and daughter if they were out for the evening. In fact, she would go out in her car to look for them if they were late home. Iain Scoular even felt it necessary to hide his collection of pornographic magazines from his over-protective mother. It is therefore ironic that an ever-vigilant and caring mother would play such a large part in convincing the police that her son was a double murderer.

*

Following Iain Scoular's dramatic appearance in the incident cara-van, detectives began to notice cracks in his story. They questioned him no less than ten times in eight weeks, which provoked his father into instructing the family solicitor to write to the Chief Constable to complain that his son was being harassed. But it did no good. Chief Inspector Dunwoodies's team was like a dog with a bone and had no intention of letting go.

It was information provided by Jean Scoular that sealed her son's fate. She told detectives that he had not returned home until one o'clock on the night of Elizabeth Walton's murder. Indeed she remembered the time clearly because she had been out in the car looking for him and they subsequently had a heated argument about him being out so late. Scoular, of course, told police that he got back home shortly after eleven. This piece of evidence was crucial and changed the course of the entire case.

Now exposed as a liar Scoular desperately changed his story. He claimed that he had not gone home at eleven but had visited a friend's house to watch a video; police discovered this was also a lie. His next claim was that he had crossed the road to avoid the 'suspicious stranger' who, he said, scared him and had then gone to a local park to sober up. This seemed unlikely because, if he was afraid, why go to a park late at night where he could have been mugged?

With a definite suspect police could now explore other avenues. There was scientific evidence: hairs from Mrs Walton's musquash jacket were found on a pair of Scoular's trousers – along with bloodstains, grass and mud. The blood was from the victim's group and the grass was identical to that at the scene of the murder. And the draw-cord from his anorak was missing – it may well have been the ligature used to strangle Mrs Walton – and police noted that he was unable to account for its disappearance. The police also found witnesses who identified Scoular as the man seen running at full pelt through Cambuslang shopping centre not long after the murder had taken place.

Although detectives were not convinced there was any conn-ection between the McChord and Walton murders another dra-matic interview with Scoular's mother helped to change their mind. In an emotionally charged atmosphere at Rutherglen police station Jean Scoular threatened to walk out after being grilled by detectives. She accused police of lying and, clearly at the end of her tether, made a statement that would put her son in the frame for the McChord slaying: 'It's a wonder you are not blaming him for the taxi murder. It's as well he was at home with his father and I that night.' This was completely at odds with Scoular's version of events and was compounded by evidence from two witnesses who identified him at an identity parade as the man they had seen running away from her taxi on the night of the murder. It was also established that Mrs McChord had been stabbed by a left hander and Scoular was left handed. And it was surely no coincidence that Scoular lived only a few hundred yards from the scene of both murders.

After a preliminary hearing in Glasgow Sheriff Court in February 1983, the trial of Iain Scoular for the murders of Catherine McChord and Elizabeth Walton began at the High Court in Glasgow at the end of May. He pleaded not guilty and lodged a special defence of alibi in both cases. During the fourteen-day trial the jury of nine men and six women heard a mass of evidence from the prosecution and were shown horrific photographs of Mrs Walton's naked body as she lay dead on the embankment. The proceedings had no visible effect on Scoular who exhibited a complete lack of emotion throughout the whole process. This mirrored his behaviour when being interrogated by police who reported he was always polite, helpful and calm. In fact, on one occasion he even halved his sandwich and offered it to the startled officer sitting across the desk. The only time he lost his cool was during questioning by the prosecution about his sexual inadequacies. Psychiatrists who had examined him came to the conclusion that, as well as being a psychopath, he was completely impotent.

While the jury members were considering their verdict, Scoular sat alone in his cell reading a novel, apparently without a care in the world. When he returned to the dock he again showed no emotion as the jury brought in a guilty verdict on both charges. He even nonchalantly popped a sweet into his mouth as the verdicts were being read out. The judge, Lord Allanbridge, handed down life sentences for both murders, with a recommendation that Scoular should serve at least twenty years. He said: 'Both attacks were of a brutal nature in cold blood and the second killing was particularly horrifying. I consider you an extremely dangerous young man.' The officers who had worked on the investigations agreed with these sentiments. Indeed one said of Scoular that, 'He was the nearest thing we have seen to an evil, emotionless murder machine. God knows what might have happened if he had not walked into the murder caravan to tease us and arouse our suspicions. He could have been another Yorkshire Ripper.'

But there was at least one person who still cared for him at the end of the trial: fiancée Irene Anderson, who had grown close to the Scoular family in the face of adversity. She told one newspaper, 'I can't stop loving him. I wish I'd married him sooner.' The reality is that signature killers like Scoular develop a growing taste for murder and rarely stop until they are caught. Miss Anderson could well have been a victim of the man she loved.

***

It is every parent's worst nightmare. An argument with a temperamental teenager results in the young person storming out of the house and they are never on good terms again. Not because their relationship has broken down irretrievably, but because the youngster has come to harm. The anguish must be unbearable and, thankfully, such cases are extremely rare. Yet it happened in Ayrshire and the result was the most sensational murder case in the county's long history.

The story begins one hot afternoon in July 1984. The scene is the Rise Hotel in Ayr's Eglinton Terrace, a street close to the seafront and at the centre of the town's thriving bed-and-breakfast trade. A middle-aged man is unpacking, but he is not a resident. He is the owner of the hotel, which he had bought only seventy-seven days before when he moved back to Scotland after a career spent farming in Africa. The man comes across his teenage daughter's records and puts them to one side. At that moment his daughter comes in and starts to browse through her precious collection. Her father takes the view that she should be helping with the unpacking and tells her so; after all they are her possessions and the work he is doing is for her benefit. Clearly homesick for her former life in South Africa, she is more highly-strung than usual. An argument ensues and the girl storms out. It was to be the last time they ever spoke.

The young woman was Kay Wyllie, an attractive 19-year-old who had returned, perhaps unwillingly, to the town where, at the age of 10, she had spent two terms as a boarder at the exclusive Wellington School. Her father was Douglas Wyllie, who was born in Ayr and had decided to come home to the old country after a lifetime spent in farming in Southern Rhodesia, Zambia and South Africa. Apart from family connections, one of the main reasons for moving back was the assurances friends had given them about the lack of crime in Scotland; a complete contrast with South Africa, where it was often dangerous to venture out, especially after dark.

Kay did come back home that day, but only to get ready to go out again. At around six o'clock her father saw her ironing a pair of jeans but, stung by their earlier row, she deliberately ignored him. She left the hotel saying that she was going for a swim at the Marine Court Hotel leisure complex in Fairfield Road where she was a regular customer. In fact Kay did not go to the hotel but went instead to see her boyfriend, Russell Anderson, at his parents' pub – the Cochrane Inn at Gatehead near Kilmarnock. This was entirely predictable: Kay Wyllie spent a lot of time with Anderson. Despite a part-time job in the Domino Kitchen Centre in Ayr's Sandgate she knew very few people in the town, apart from those she met while out with her boyfriend. The couple stayed in the pub until closing time and then drove to the luxury bungalow owned by his parents near Dundonald. But Anderson's grandmother was concerned that Kay's parents would be worried that she was out so late and suggested that she should return to Ayr immediately. Therefore, a few minutes later, at 12-45 in the morning, she was driving – on her own – along the Kilmarnock to Barassie road. Although he thought little of it at the time, Russell Anderson was sure she was going straight home.

Douglas Wyllie was also sure that she would be returning home that night. Despite their tiff, Kay's welfare was still his top priority and he left a light on in the front hall for her. But when he woke at half-past-six the next morning he saw that the light was still on and, instinctively, knew that something was wrong. Overcome by worry he phoned not only friends, but also the police and local hospitals. He spent the rest of the day searching the car parks of pubs and nightclubs for her car and went to the Anderson's hostelry in Gatehead looking for clues. It was becoming clear that something was seriously amiss, and it was time for the police to take a hand. Within forty-eight hours they found an abandoned car in Ayr's Wellington Lane, a back street less than a quarter of a mile from her home. It was Kay Wyllie's white Mini City.

This was the signal for the start of a major police operation and dozens of officers were assigned to the case. But it was a member of the public who made the discovery Kay's parents had been dreading. Two days after the car was found Stuart Miller, a farm labourer, found her half-naked body in a ditch next to a lovers' lane in Dunure, an isolated fishing village seven miles south of Ayr. A forensic examination would later reveal that she had been strangled by her white bra while being pinned down on rough gravel. The killer had then dumped her in the ditch and the corpse with her jacket and sweatshirt. There were no indications from under her nails that she had scratched her killer, nor were there any signs of sexual contact between them. To this day police have no idea how she met her killer. However, Kay's mother, Isabella Wyllie, later said that she would never have stopped for a stranger in the middle of the night, much less have gone to Dunure with him.

At first Russell Anderson was the prime suspect, and he was interrogated by police for several hours before being eliminated from their enquiries. This was par for the course: the spouse, partner or lover invariably comes under the official spotlight when someone is murdered. The police now widened the net and compiled a list of twenty suspects. Reflecting the apparently motiveless nature of the crime, a huge team of forty detectives and a similar number of uniformed officers were assigned to the case. The police worked round the clock following up leads, interviewing witnesses and questioning suspects. After eleven days of intensive investigations they got the break that all detectives need. From this point on their focus would be on an 18-year-old who, although he had racked up a considerable number of petty offences, did not have a reputation for violence. His name was Andrew Cameron.

It is highly unusual for people from Cameron's background to be involved in crime. Born in Hartlepool in the north-east of England he was the second of four children. His father was an engineer and, reflecting the peripatetic nature of his work, the family moved several times during his son's formative years, firstly to Mossblown then back to Hartlepool and then to Clydebank. Finally, in 1983, the Camerons settled in Troon where they bought a large detached house at 6 Sarazen Drive. In a prestigious estate with fine views over Royal Troon Golf Course the property, by the standards of 2003, would cost in the region of £400,000. To the outsider it must have seemed like the Camerons were living the middle class dream.

Yet Andrew Cameron was a troubled young man. Indeed he was a one-man crime-wave. By 1984 he had a lengthy record for breaking into and stealing from vehicles. In addition, his behaviour was often highly erratic. On trial at Ayr Sheriff Court on fifteen separate counts of breaking into cars he suddenly leapt from the dock, jumped over the railings outside the courtroom and landed on the floor of the building twelve feet below. If it was an attempt to escape it failed miserably; he ran straight into the clutches of a plain-clothes policeman. His criminal tendencies must have been a source of constant anxiety for his parents, particularly his mother who often had to look after the family on her own as her husband frequently worked abroad. It may have been the stress caused by Andrew's constant lawbreaking that drove her to report her son to the police for taking her car without permission. Little did she know this would implicate him in the murder of Kay Wyllie.

The police picked up Cameron on 17 July in his favourite watering-hole; the Anchorage Hotel in Troon which, with its lively bar and night club, was a popular haunt of young, single people looking to meet members of the opposite sex. They cautioned him for taking away his mother's car and, with nothing to lose, asked him about his whereabouts on the night Kay Wyllie was killed. His answers surprised them. He told them that he had been driving around breaking into cars in Tarbolton, Mossblown and then Ayr. While driving past Wellington Lane he said that he saw Kay's white Mini and a man walking away from it towards the beach. When the man disappeared from sight, he siphoned petrol from the car and stole other items, including a digital clock. Although he denied ever having met Kay, detectives were suspicious and carried out a range of forensic tests. To their delight the tests proved positive. Cameron's fingerprints were found on the inside of the driver's window. Police found the petrol cap from Kay's car in the front garden of Cameron's house. A fibre of clothing was discovered in the back seat of the car which, according to forensic scientists, matched the fibres on an anorak owned by Cameron. It was later established that the anorak was of Japanese make and that only eighteen of them had ended up in Scotland. Of these only three came to Ayr – and were sold at the What Every Woman Wants shop in the High Street.

This evidence pointed clearly to Andrew Cameron. But, on its own, it was not nearly enough for a successful prosecution. Detectives racked their brains for new leads until, in September 1984, they decided to publish a photograph of a digital clock taken from Kay's car on the night she died. The reasoning was that the murderer might either be using the clock or had tried to sell it. The picture of the clock was published in national and local newspapers, and it elicited an amazing response. The police received a letter that completely contradicted Cameron's story and convinced them that he had killed Kay Wyllie. It read:

To whom it may concern,
Last week as I read the article about the murder of Kay Wyllie in the *Ayrshire Post* I suddenly realised that you have got it all wrong. The murderer didn't take the clock. I did. I thought I had better put you in the picture. I hope you catch the bastard.

To prove it was not a sick hoax, the author of the letter also enclosed the keys to Kay's car. The police were jubilant; the letter had breathed new life into an investigation that had started to falter. But they needed to speak to the thief and, to encourage further contact, a further article appeared in the *Ayrshire Post* offering immunity from prosecution if the anonymous correspondent came forward. The offer did the trick. About a month after the letter was received two boys – one from Dalmilling in Ayr, and the other from Waterside, near Patna – contacted the police and confessed that they had broken into the car on 4 July 1984 and stolen a number of items including the clock. More significantly the boys told police that they broke into the car a full sixteen hours before Andrew Cameron claimed he had stolen the clock and the other items. He was now revealed as a liar; a liar who wanted police to believe his fingerprints were found in the Mini because he was a thief, and not because he had killed Kay Wyllie.

By now there was no doubt in the minds of the detectives working on the case: Cameron was their man, and they duly reported their findings to the Procurator Fiscal. The only problem was the evidence, or lack of it. The Crown Office in Edinburgh has responsibility for prosecuting murders in Scotland and was not convinced that the case against Cameron was strong enough. It spent months weighing and testing the evidence, but did not give the green light for a prosecution. During this period a senior detective went to the Fiscal's office in Ayr every week to see if the Crown Office had made a decision. But it was all to no avail; the powers that be would not be moved. It is easy to criticise the Crown Office for its perceived inaction but it was acutely aware of the dangers inherent in a shaky prosecution; if he got off, he could not be retried for the same offence under the double-jeopardy rule. Meanwhile, police in Ayr had their own nightmare scenario to contend with. Cameron was free to kill again.

*

Nancy Nicol was a happy-go-lucky 19-year-old from Kilmarnock who, like many girls of her age, enjoyed dancing, a drink with her friends and the company of young men. She worked in a clothing factory in Troon, a routine job that she and many of her colleagues found more than a little boring. For someone with her sense of fun there must have been, from time to time, a temptation to give work a miss and to spend the time enjoying herself. This is exactly what happened on Friday 2 May 1985 when she and a workmate, Lorna Connelly, decided on the bus to work that they would spend the day touring Troon's pubs, clubs and amusement arcades. They met other girlfriends in a pub around three o' clock in the afternoon, and it was clear to the newcomers that Nancy was already drunk. The girls played pool and continued to drink before moving on to other pubs in the area. Eventually the group ended up in Pebbles Hotel, which Nancy left at around 10-50 p.m. An hour later a taxi driver saw her chatting to a young man outside Greggs the Bakers, a man she had first met five days before on another night out. It was Andrew Cameron.

Nancy was not the only woman Cameron had shown an interest in that day. Allison Bainbridge of Alexandria near Glasgow was staying with her sister in Troon and had been out for a meal with her husband. He was staying in a different house and walked back with his wife in the direction of her sister's house. In normal circumstances he would have taken her all the way home but on this occasion he left her to walk the last stage on her own. She was walking along Harbour Road when a man holding a can of beer came out of a bus shelter and started to follow her. Mrs Bainbridge, who was on her own, was understandably alarmed and hurried as quickly as she could to the safety of her sister's house. At an identity parade she picked out Andrew Cameron as the man who had followed her.

Nancy Nicol, an attractive blonde, did not return home that night. Nor did she turn up the next day. Her parents, William and Agnes Nicol, who had already suffered the tragedy of losing two baby daughters prematurely, reported her missing. An intensive police investigation ensued and, when police realised that Cameron was the last person seen with Nancy, there was fresh pressure for him to be arrested for the murder of Kay Wyllie. But, once again, the Crown Office decided there was insufficient evidence. It would now be up to the police to come up with the evidence needed for a successful prosecution.

Six days after Nancy Nicol disappeared Andrew Cameron was picked up by Detective Chief Inspector Robert Redmond and Detective Sergeant James Brown. He refused to go to the police station and so the two officers questioned him in an unmarked car parked in a Troon street. But his story contained a number of inconsistencies. In one version he claimed he necked with Nancy in a phone box and then had intercourse with her in an alleyway. While in another he said that he took Nancy home and they had sex on a couch after eating supper and watching a video. He also claimed that he walked Nancy back into the centre of Troon where she got into a car with a man he did not recognise. Because of these inconsistencies the two detectives took him for questioning at Troon police station. At the station the interrogation was taken over by the top detective in the area: Chief Superintendent John Fleming. Although Cameron was well used to police procedures, and was not easily intimidated, this was of a different order: the police were under pressure to solve both cases and were prepared to use all the resources at their disposal to get a result.

Fleming and his colleagues knew from the interviews carried out with Cameron months before in relation to the Kay Wyllie case how difficult he found it to get his story straight. In one statement he claimed that he saw Kay's empty Mini, immediately drove up to it, siphoned petrol and stole a number of other items. However, in a subsequent statement he said that when he first saw the car there was a man with 'curly hair and long sideburns' inside and that he had to wait until the man got out and left the scene before carrying out the break-in. He also gave a detailed description of the man despite the fact that it was dark and he was more than seventy-five yards away.

After a day of detailed and painstaking questioning there was a dramatic breakthrough. According to police, Cameron confessed. In response to questions from Chief Superintendent Fleming about Kay Wyllie's murder he is alleged to have said: 'I remember arguing with her. I think I punched her and then I choked her.' When Fleming asked why he had done this Cameron replied 'Because she argued. I can't remember about what. It was ten months ago.' Later the same day Cameron confessed to killing Nancy Nicol and dumping her body in the sea near Royal Troon's clubhouse. According to police he said:

> She's in the water. I remember waking up in the morning. My shoes were covered in sand my trousers were wet up to the knees I think. I think I can remember where I put her. I think I can show you where it happened. It was like the girl last year as well. It just happened. I don't know why it happens. I don't mean it. I just lose the head then I blank it out of my mind. I forget all about it.

Shortly thereafter, at around half-past-eleven that night, Cameron went with police to South Beach in Troon. According to the officers who accompanied him he was shaking with fear – one detective noted that he had never seen anyone so frightened. Cameron asked for, and was given, a torch. After looking around to get his bearings he pointed out to the Firth of Clyde and said, 'There – she's in there.' The police could see little in the dark, but marked the spot that Cameron had indicated. He was taken back to Troon police station and the next morning, with his solicitor present, charged with the murder of Kay Wyllie.

In the days after Cameron's confession the search for Nancy intensified. Police put all the resources they could spare into looking for what they now realised was a corpse. They even called in the Royal Navy: a helicopter using highly sophisticated equipment joined the search, but found nothing. A team of six police divers, tied together by a seventy-foot line, scoured the sea up to sixty yards from the shoreline. Again their search drew a blank. As with Kay Wyllie's body it was a member of the public who would make the ghastly discovery. Some weeks later, a man and his son were out whelking on the rocks at Little Craigs near Troon when they saw something in the water. It was Nancy Nicol's body which, after a month in the sea, was now in an advanced state of decomposition. Andrew Cameron could now be charged with a second count of murder.

Andrew Cameron spent five months on remand at

Longriggend Young Offenders' Institution. He spent some of his time writing tender love letters to Kathleen Chisholm, his 18-year-old girlfriend. According to the young woman this was typical of him: 'Andrew was a very special boyfriend', she later said, 'I could never have believed he was capable of murder. He was gentle and kind. He never treated me badly in any way.' This view of Cameron must have been considered naive by the police who dealt with him. In fact they firmly believed that Kathleen Chisholm would have been his next victim.

Despite attempts by the defence team to get the trial moved to Glasgow proceedings began at Ayr's High Court on 2 September 1985. Media interest in the case was unprecedented and, understandably, it also caught the imagination of the public with people queuing from seven o' clock in the morning to get a seat in the courtroom. Reflecting the importance of the case to the authorities the prosecution was headed by the highest law officer in the land, Peter Fraser QC, the Solicitor General. The defence team was no less formidable and was led by Nicholas Fairbairn QC, the colourful and often controversial veteran of many high-profile murder trials, who would also become a government minister in the late 1980s. Fairbairn was assisted by Joe Beltrami, the legendary defence solicitor from Glasgow and a man with unparalleled knowledge of the criminal justice system. With more than one hundred witnesses cited to give evidence the proceedings were likely to be long and complex. It is little wonder that the *Ayr Advertiser* described it, with some justification, as 'Ayr's most dramatic trial this century.'

With the benefit of advice from his legal team Cameron pleaded not guilty to both murder charges and to the breach of the peace charge relating to Allison Bainbridge. He lodged a special defence of alibi. During the thirteen days of the trial much of the prosecution's case rested on the confessions Cameron allegedly gave to the police. This was a time before the landmark Police and Criminal Evidence Act, which stipulated that interviews with suspects had to be taped, and that accused persons are entitled to have their solicitor present while they are being questioned. This did not apply in the case of Andrew Cameron, and it was strongly argued by defence lawyer Nicholas Fairbairn that the police simply wore the accused down to such an extent that he would admit to anything, even murder. When he was in the witness box, Cameron testified that police had bullied him into making statements; in fact he even went on to say that they had punched and slapped him to extract a confession. He said, 'I have done nothing. I am innocent. The police just picked on the easiest person, it's not fair.' While he admitted having sex with Nancy, he stated that he walked her back into the centre of Troon and saw her get into a Ford Escort with a man he did not recognise.

At the end of the trial on 18 September 1985 the jury of eleven men and four women filed into the room set aside for their deliberations. Many of its members must have been in two minds about Cameron's guilt, as it was by no means an open-and-shut case. There were no witnesses to either murder. There was limited forensic evidence in the case of Kay Wyllie, and none at all in respect of Nancy Nicol. There was no apparent motive for either murder. While Cameron had clear criminal tendencies, he had never been violent before. The prosecution case hinged largely on Cameron's confession, which came after a lengthy period of interrogation by senior detectives and was recorded in police notebooks without Cameron's solicitor present. Understandably the jury took time to reach a conclusion, emerging after four and a quarter hours to deliver its verdict: guilty, on both counts of murder. But the members were far from unanimous; in fact Nicholas Fairbairn believed that the split may have been only eight to seven in favour of the guilty verdict.

The trial judge, Lord Ross, imposed a life sentence on Cameron with a recommendation that he should spend at least twenty years behind bars. While he pointed out that Cameron was a dangerous young man from whom the public had to be protected the judge added that the murders were senseless and committed for no apparent reason, a view shared by many observers. As he was led away Cameron sobbed loudly and shouted that the CID 'are all liars'. But there was to be one more dramatic twist. The defence team produced a witness who had not been heard at the trial – a witness whose evidence may have swayed some members of the jury. Mrs Ruby Steed of Prestwick claimed that she had seen Kay Wyllie in a car with a man only a short time before the teenager was murdered. And it was not Andrew Cameron. Mrs Steed said she had been going to her home in Prestwick with her husband after a night out when she saw the couple in a white Mini around one o' clock in the morning. The car had stopped at a pedestrian crossing and as she crossed the road she looked into the car and saw Kay and a young man. She was absolutely certain it was not Cameron. The official reason for her not being called was that she had come forward too late and could not be cited three days before the trial started as the law required. Fairbairn believed the real reason was that she would have contradicted the other witnesses. He argued that if the jury had been able to hear Mrs Steed's evidence his client would not have been convicted, and he gave notice of Cameron's intention to appeal.

The dramatic news of the conviction was immediately relayed to the outside world. The main local paper, the *Ayrshire Post*, had already gone to print and 1,500 copies had been run off. But when the verdict came through it scrapped them and ran the paper with the Cameron verdict on the front page. The *Daily Record* carried the story on its front page as did the *Glasgow Herald* and *Scotsman*. The aftermath brought a great deal of resentment to the surface. Nancy Nicol's parents took the view that their daughter would not have died if Cameron had been charged with the murder of Kay Wyllie at an earlier stage. Nancy's mother Agnes said: 'My lassie died because they dragged their heels. He should have been arrested or even watched twenty-four hours a day so he couldn't kill someone else.' The Nicol family was backed up by Kilmarnock MP William McKelvey who strongly criticised the authorities for their perceived inaction after Kay's death. The Wyllie family had also been traumatised. After the trial Douglas and Isabella Wyllie found they could no longer face living in Scotland and moved to Zambia. There Douglas found his own, very touching, way of keeping Kay's memory alive: 'In Africa' he said ' I drive out into the plains and call out Kay's name. It makes me feel better. It's some form of consolation.'

On the other side of the fence Cameron's mother, Marion,

believed there had been a miscarriage of justice and said she would do everything in her power to prove his innocence. Her son, she stressed, 'was no murderer'; he was, she believed, the victim of a conspiracy. But her efforts were to no avail. An appeal against his convictions was considered by the Court of Criminal Appeal in 1987 but was rejected. Cameron suffered another hammer blow in June 2002 when his sentence was increased to a minimum term of thirty years by the High Court in Glasgow. The reason for this was that courts were obliged to review the punishment element of sentences under European human rights legislation and the judge concerned, Lord McEwan, took the view that his sentence should be set at the higher end of the tariff. Andrew Cameron will be in prison until 2015 at the earliest.

TEN

Deadlier than the male: four murders that shocked Scotland

MOST MURDERS ARE committed by men, the more aggressive and combative of the two sexes. So when a woman kills, or is somehow caught up in a murder, the resultant publicity is far more extensive than would be the case for a similar case involving a man. There have been four cases in recent years, all very high profile and all equally shocking. Three involved women being convicted of murder while the other saw a woman accused of murder and conspiracy to murder cleared after her lover was convicted of killing her husband.

There are of course much older examples of Scottish women being convicted of murder; cases that in their day alarmed and horrified the public. In June 1923 a 13-year-old paperboy from Coatbridge, John Johnston, was first strangled and then bludgeoned by Susan Newall in an apparently motiveless attack. It is not clear if he was killed by these assaults and there is some evidence that Newall set his body alight while he was still alive. After the boy's corpse was seen in the family's living room by her daughter, Newall wrapped it in a blanket and took it to Glasgow in a cart. She was caught thanks to the observational skills of a Glasgow schoolgirl, Helen Elliott, who noticed a foot sticking out of the cart. At her trial Susan Newall tried to blame the murder on her husband but the jury spent just over half an hour deliberating on the evidence before bringing in a verdict of guilty. Sentenced to death, 30-year-old Newall was hanged in Glasgow's Duke Street prison on 10 October 1923, the only female to suffer this fate in Scotland in the twentieth century.

Another gruesome case occurred in April 1934 when 8-year-old Helen Priestley from Aberdeen was strangled, tied up in a sack and dumped in the close of her own tenement building. Even more disturbingly, it also appeared the child had been raped. After a huge police investigation Helen's upstairs' neighbours, Alexander and Jeannie Donald, were arrested. After detectives had questioned Alexander Donald he was released and his 38-year-old wife – herself a mother – was charged with murder. Police found strands of Helen's hair in the Donalds' flat and other vital forensic clues that pointed to Jeannie Donald's guilt. But how could a woman have raped a girl? Scientists took the view that she had been defiled by a poker or similar instrument. The motive? To make police think the perpetrator was male. At her trial at the High Court in Edinburgh she was convicted of murder and sentenced to hang. However, after an appeal, the sentence was commuted to life imprisonment. In fact she served only ten years in prison and to her dying day Jeannie Donald never disclosed why she had so callously killed an innocent child.

*

Perhaps the best known modern murder involving a woman is that of Sheila Garvie who was convicted, along with lover Brian Tevendale, of killing her husband Max Garvie in May 1968. This case had it all: sexual deviance, infidelity, jealousy, money and people drawn from a wealthy background. Understandably, it was a murder that electrified 1960s Scotland, and some commentators even described it as the crime of the century.

Max Garvie was a wealthy young man. He owned a farm, West Cairnbeg, in Fordoun, Kincardineshire, traditional farming country in an area known as Howe of the Mearns and immortalised in Lewis Grassic Gibbon's novel *Sunset Song*. In 1954, aged 20, he met Sheila Watson, a vivacious and outgoing 17-year-old at a summer dance in Stonehaven town hall. She came from the other end of the social spectrum and had once lived on the Balmoral estate where her father was a stonemason in the service of the Queen. Max fell deeply in love with the slim, attractive blonde and a year later they married. They were blessed with three healthy children and to the casual observer seemed to have it all: a young family, a luxury home, three cars (including a Jaguar), servants and even a private plane. Sheila, in particular, loved life at West Cairnbeg and quickly grew accustomed to the luxuries her husband could provide.

But there was a dark side to Max Garvie. A very dark side. He became obsessed with nudism, and by the 1960s was travelling to camps in Britain and abroad to indulge his new passion. He forced his wife and children to go with him and to take part in naturism, often against their will. Garvie also bought land in Alford, Aberdeenshire, planted trees on it and set up his own nudist colony. His exotic tastes in the bedroom soon became evident. There were orgies with his naturist friends in a house on the colony that became known as 'Kinky Cottage' and Sheila, reluctant at first, soon became an enthusiastic participant. Max Garvie also developed a taste for deviant sex: he regularly sodomised his wife and took photographs of her in the nude, which he would proudly show to his cronies. After a time Sheila became depressed by his behaviour and started to take tranquillisers in disturbingly large quantities.

But Max Garvie had no intention of curbing his appetites. If anything they became even more depraved. He met a young barman, Brian Tevendale, through their membership of the Scottish National Party and they quickly became close friends. Tevendale often stayed at Garvie's home and it became apparent that his genial host wanted Tevendale to have sex with his wife. Although there was certainly an attraction between Tevendale and Sheila Garvie, nothing happened for some time and Max Garvie eventually dragged her naked into Tevendale's bedroom one night in September 1967 when she had consumed a lot of alcohol. They had intercourse, an outcome that gave Max Garvie a considerable vicarious thrill. But Garvie, who had strong homosexual tendencies, also wanted to have sex with the handsome Tevendale, who was then aged 21. He made several passes at him, including on one occasion walking into his bedroom wearing only a nightgown, which was open at the front.

Around this time Tevendale introduced Max Garvie to his sister, Trudi Birse, who was married to a policeman. Birse was instantly attracted to the handsome farmer and later said, 'You could feel the electricity in the air.' She and Garvie began a torrid affair and this eventually led to four-in-a-bed romps, with Sheila Garvie and Brian Tevendale – Birse's own brother – making up the foursome. To ensure that the harmony of these arrangements was maintained, Garvie even procured a girl for Trudi's husband, Alfred Birse. There was no doubting the strength of his attachment to his mistress: Garvie later cruelly told his wife that he got more pleasure from Trudi 'in a fortnight' than he had had from Sheila in all their years of marriage. If Birse was unavailable, Max Garvie and Brian Tevendale would often toss a coin to determine who would sleep with Sheila that night.

But despite Max Garvie's liberated approach to life and love he was simply not prepared for what happened next; Sheila and Brian Tevendale had fallen for each other. When Garvie realised the strength of their attachment he immediately terminated his relationship with Trudi Birse and demanded that Sheila do the same with Tevendale. She refused and was subjected to violence and intimidation from her husband. At around the same time, and in a clear attempt to warn him off, Tevendale was slashed on the face by a man thought to be working for Max Garvie. Although Sheila left the marital home on a couple of occasions to live with her lover she returned, apparently taking seriously her husband's threats that he would shoot Tevendale and her children.

Then, suddenly, on 15 May 1968 Max Garvie went missing. In the absence of evidence to the contrary, the police treated his disappearance as a missing-person enquiry and even published details of his disappearance in the *Police Gazette*: the notice read: 'Spends freely, is a heavy drinker and often consumes tranquillisers when drinking. Is fond of female company . . . deals in pornographic material and is an active member of nudist camps . . . may have gone abroad.' But the truth was that Max Garvie was dead, a fact that Sheila Garvie acknowledged to her mother, Mrs Edith Watson, immediately after his disappearance. Sheila Garvie also told her mother that she had 'a strong man at her back', a clear reference to Tevendale. But it took Edith Watson three months to contact the police and it seems she only did so when her daughter said she was going to live with Tevendale and would be taking the three children with her. Mrs Watson disliked Tevendale intensely and she had also made a promise to Max Garvie, her son-in-law, to keep the children away from him.

Armed with Mrs Watson's information the police promptly arrested Sheila Garvie, Brian Tevendale and an alleged accomplice, Alan Peters, and charged them with murder. Tevendale was able to lead police to the body, although he claimed that he had only helped to hide it and that Garvie had been killed by a rifle shot after a struggle with Sheila. And so the scene was set for one of the most high-profile trials of the twentieth century.

Even though this was the end of the so-called 'swinging six-ties', the whole affair had stunned – and titillated – this rather tra-ditional area in north-east Scotland. When the trial started at the High Court in Aberdeen on 19 November 1968 there was great interest from local people and newspapers paid large sums for photographs of the Garvies and Tevendale. Such was the attention focused on the case that the Solicitor General for Scotland, Ewan Stewart QC, took charge of the prosecution. In court the three accused all entered pleas of not guilty, blaming their co-accused for the murder. It was a dramatic trial with huge queues snaking outside the courtroom hoping for a space on the public benches. Indeed the whole country would be agog at the details of the couple's life together, especially their sexual activities.

In court Sheila Garvie maintained she knew nothing about the murder of her husband. She testified that on the night of his death they had made love and fallen asleep together. She was then wak-ened by a tug on her arm and saw Brian Tevendale – who was car-rying a rifle – and a fair-haired young man in her bedroom. She claimed that she was bewildered by their presence in her bedroom and had no idea what the gun was for; it 'never entered her head' that he might shoot Max. Tevendale then took her into the bathroom and told her to stay there. She heard thumping noises but did not think they were gunshots and only discovered the awful truth later. She had not gone to the police to report the murder because she felt morally responsible for Tevendale – who had fallen deeply in love with her – and wanted to protect him.

But her account of events, delivered in nine gruelling hours in the witness box, lacked credibility. There was a mass of evidence to the contrary. Sheila Garvie stood to gain financially from her husband's death. There were two life insurance policies worth £55,000 (a very substantial sum in 1968), the house at West Cairnbeg, the three cars, personal possessions and income from the farm. She would be a wealthy woman in her own right as well as being free of an unfeeling and often brutal husband. There was also the fact that she continued to have sex with Tevendale in the three months between Max Garvie's death and her arrest. Why would a wife keep up a relationship with a man who had so brutally slain her husband? It was also noted that Brian Tevendale had been best man at the wedding of Alan Peters soon after Max Garvie was murdered and that Sheila Garvie was matron of honour . . . a further sign of the bond between the two.

But the evidence that did more than anything to undermine Sheila Garvie's story was provided by the other man in the house that night: Alan Peters. A rather timid 20-year-old, Peters was a close friend of Brian Tevendale and appears to have been both mesmerised and intimidated by him. In his evidence he told how he and Tevendale went to the farmhouse, which they entered through a side door and were met by Sheila Garvie. They had a drink together and Sheila Garvie then said, 'I'll show you where to go.' The two men went upstairs and waited in a room. Forty-five minutes later Mrs Garvie returned and told them, 'He's asleep now.' Peters said that he and Tevendale (who was carrying a rifle) then went to a bedroom where a man was lying face down, asleep. Tevendale then smashed the man's head twice with the butt of the rifle, put a pillow over his face and shot him through the pillow. They put the body in the boot of Peters's car and went back into the house, where Sheila Garvie made them coffee. Peters said he saw Tevendale and Garvie kiss passionately on the lips. He and Tevendale then took the body to Lauriston Castle, St Cyrus, Kincardineshire where they buried it in a culvert and covered it with a pile of stones.

It was this version of events that the jury believed. Sheila Garvie and Brian Tevendale were found guilty of murder on 2 December 1968, while the charges against Alan Peters were found to be not proven. Interestingly the jury brought in a unanimous verdict for Tevendale but only found Garvie guilty by a majority. In any event, they were both given life sentences. Before being taken to prison they were allowed a few minutes together and no one who saw them could doubt their love for each other; they kissed passionately, vowed to marry and, in tears, were parted. And so ended one of the most sensational murder cases in Scottish legal history.

Both Sheila Garvie and Brian Tevendale were released from prison in the late 1970s. By that time she had made clear that she did not wish to see Tevendale again. Tevendale subsequently married and, in 2002, was reported to be running a pub in Perthshire. Garvie, who wrote a book about her experiences in 1980, married on two more occasions but both marriages ended in divorce. She is said to be living alone with her dog in a quiet cul-de-sac in Stonehaven, ten miles from Kinky Cottage.

*

Despite her subsequent notoriety, Nawal Nicol was never found guilty of murder, nor of any other crime. But she became a source of endless fascination for the media when her husband, 29-year-old Stuart Nicol, was murdered by Jason Simpson and Muir Middler in Ellon, Aberdeenshire. The case had much to commend it to the tabloids: a brutal killing, infidelity, greed, jealousy and a dark-skinned woman motivated by a seemingly insatiable sexual lust. It was little wonder that the press nicknamed her the 'Black Widow'.

The basic facts of the murder are not in dispute. One night, in early June 1994, Stuart and Nawal Nicol had gone to a nightclub in Ellon with their friends, Simpson and Middler. On the surface nothing seemed amiss and the Nicols even had the last dance together. All four of them went back to the couple's home and Simpson and Middler – who had been drinking all day – stayed until Nawal Nicol went to bed. They returned half an hour later and, when Stuart Nicol answered the door, Simpson held him and Middler stabbed him four times in the chest with a survival knife. One blow pierced his heart, killing him within seconds. The killers dumped the knife and their blood-soaked clothes in a wood, where they were later found by police.

At their trial in September 1994 both men were found guilty of murder and given life sentences. There was a further bizarre twist when Frank Nicol, father of the murdered man, got a phone call offering to have Simpson and Middler murdered in Perth Jail. The caller said that two cons were willing to murder both men for a fee of only £400 each – quite clearly the value of human life is not highly rated in the criminal underworld! Mr Nicol turned down the offer flat. As he explained, 'I want them to rot in jail. I want them to serve every minute of their life sentences.'

Despite the guilty verdicts against Simpson and Middler, the Crown took the view that the case was far from over. In fact prosecutors were in the process of preparing a case against Nawal Nicol for murder and incitement to murder. It was only when her trial on these charges started in the High Court in Forfar in June 1995 that the astonishing allegations against her were revealed in full. It was suggested by the prosecution that 21-year-old Simpson had been having a torrid affair with Qatar-born Nicol, a woman eight years his senior, and had been driven to kill because of his lust for her. Indeed it was claimed that Nicol had made love to Simpson only four days before the murder. It was also alleged that Nicol had offered Simpson and Middler – who was also said to be her lover – £25,000 each to murder her husband.

In the witness box Jason Simpson testified that Nawal Nicol had been plotting for some time to kill her husband. At first, he said, she had dropped hints about 'getting rid of her husband'. Initially he presumed this meant getting a divorce, but he claimed she actually meant something quite different and more chilling: 'It eventually began to dawn on us that she wanted to kill him and was asking us to help.' Simpson alleged Nawal Nicol had even devised a number of different strategies for the foul deed. One plan involved pushing him over cliffs at Slains Castle in Aberdeenshire, the setting for the Dracula story – it was alleged that Nicol had dreamt up this plan after she had seen a television documentary about vampires. Another of Simpson's allegations was that she planned a mock burglary with her husband being murdered when he disturbed the intruders. A third scheme involved tampering with the brakes on his car.

Simpson denied that Nawal Nicol had offered him money to kill her husband and he also claimed that he had only gone to the house on the night of the murder to warn Mr Nicol of his wife's intentions. He went on to say that when they were in the house he turned round to see Middler stabbing Stuart Nicol with a knife. Nawal Nicol's lawyer, Donald Findlay QC, accused Simpson and Middler of being 'out-and-out liars'.

The Crown may have been persuaded by Findlay's arguments, or perhaps realised that the chances of a guilty verdict were slim. In any event, on the second day of the trial there was a dramatic, and wholly unexpected, twist. To gasps from the crowded public gallery, the prosecution dropped all charges against Nawal Nicol. She was, Lord Johnston said, free to go. At first Nicol looked bewildered but, after regaining her composure, she smiled and whispered 'thank you'.

Although the legal proceedings had reached a conclusion it was far from the end of public interest in Nawal Nicol, the so-called Black Widow. In fact there was what can only be described as a tabloid feeding-frenzy – a frenzy caused in part by her shameless behaviour. Her husband's death left her, at the age of 30, a wealthy woman. She got more than £100,000 from the sale of the marital home in Ellon, and received tens of thousands from insurance policies. She was also paid £10,000 by the Criminal Injuries Compensation Board for the loss of her husband. She wasted no time in spending her windfall. After buying a luxury flat in Ayr and filling it with fine furniture, Nicol took expensive holidays and partied hard, telling one newspaper she had more than fifty lovers in a year.

But it was her cosmetic surgery that attracted most attention. She paid £6,000 for an operation to have her breasts enlarged from a 34A cup to a 34D cup, and had liposuction on her thighs. The results delighted her and, wearing a micro-mini skirt and a skimpy top with a plunging neckline, she told the *Daily Record*: 'I have nothing to be ashamed of. I had the operation in a Glasgow clinic. It was money well spent. I did it for me, no one else, but the guys certainly seem to approve. Yes it was money I got after Stuart died but I was entitled to it. Remember, I had nothing to do with his killing. Any other grieving widow would receive a cash payment, so why shouldn't I?'

The family of her late husband most certainly did not approve. His mother, who had been granted custody of Stuart and Nawal Nicol's son, was livid and said of her daughter-in-law, 'She's a waster. It is blood money. She's parading around having a life of luxury paid for by my son's death. I just cannot believe her and what she will do next.'

Yet by 1997, three years after the murder, Nicol's cash reserves were draining away. So, no doubt helped by her breast enhancements, she moved to Spain to begin a new career as a stripper. According to one of her close friends this new occupation suited her down to the ground, 'She's going to be a stripper and she'll be a sensation – she loves showing off her breasts.' But her new career in the Spanish sunshine proved a disappointment. After working in go-go bars she graduated to a seedy brothel in San Antonio, Ibiza where she stripped for the male clientele. This work was clearly uncongenial and in October 1997 she was back in Ayr and living in a downmarket rented flat with second-hand furniture – a far cry from her former life of luxury.

Her downward spiral continued and by 1998 she was performing in a lap-dancing pub, called the Fantasy Bar, in Edinburgh. But few customers even noticed her, and even fewer were prepared to pay the £10 charge for a lap-dance. Her best days had gone for good. As one member of staff said: 'Nawal isn't the youngest or prettiest girl we have here and she finds work hard to come by on midweek nights when the place isn't so busy. Guys tend to ignore her if there are younger girls about.' The

Black Widow's fifteen minutes of fame – some would say infamy – had come and gone.

*

The trial judge said it all in his summing-up: 'To don rubber gloves, arm yourself with a knife and then burst in on a neighbour and slit her throat in the course of a sustained attack, as it turned out all for the sake of some £20 or £30, a miscellany of personal items and some gift vouchers is a crime of almost unimaginable depravity.' It is perhaps even more shocking that the murderer was a girl aged only 20 and that the victim, a neighbour, was herself aged only 22. This tragic crime took place in Aberdeen in October 1999 and stunned the good citizens of that city with its senselessness and cruelty.

The victim, Melanie Sturton, lived in a bedsit in Great Western Road. She hailed from Ballater on Deeside and was a student at Aberdeen College. She also worked part time as a care assistant at Nazareth House, an old people's home in the city run by nuns. Melanie came from a loving, close-knit family and was clearly devoted to the elderly people she helped to look after. She was small and had a gentle disposition and was gradually overcoming the shyness and lack of confidence that a slight facial-paralysis had brought in its wake. All in all Melanie Sturton was a daughter any parent could be proud of.

The contrast with her killer could not be more marked. Originally from Inverbervie, a small town close to Aberdeen, Pamela Gourlay was a cold, selfish young woman with a drug habit that had left her deeply in debt. This was despite a job as a chef in an Aberdeen restaurant, an income from dealing cannabis that netted her more than £300 a week and occasional stints as a beggar. Gourlay lived in a bedsit in Aberdeen's Great Western Road to which her boyfriend Kris Taylor (24), a regular heroin user, was a frequent visitor. The bedsit was on the floor above a similar room occupied by Melanie Sturton.

Like most of her other problems Gourlay's involvement in murder started with drug taking. On the evening of 8 October she and Taylor had been at a friend's house where they had both smoked cannabis and taken Temazepam. They left in the early hours of the morning and on the way home made unsuccessful attempts to get money from two cash machines. Taylor later said that he watched videos until five o'clock in the morning before falling asleep. But Gourlay, anxious to get her hands on ready cash and probably still high from the drugs she had taken, was wide-awake. Donning two pairs of plastic gloves and a sun hat she sneaked downstairs and knocked on Melanie Sturton's door. Although still in her night-clothes, Melanie was awake as she was getting ready for work. But, when she answered the door, she knew immediately that something was wrong and tried to keep Gourlay out. But her efforts were to no avail. Gourlay forced her way in and, in the course of a desperate struggle, slashed Melanie's throat four times with a razor-sharp kitchen knife. Melanie's screams were so loud that a neighbour on the floor below clearly heard them.

The fact that she had just murdered an entirely innocent human being in such a callous fashion did not faze Pamela Gourlay. Without bothering to check if Melanie was dead or alive she covered her heavily bloodstained body with a duvet and a rug and then, coolly and methodically, gathered up everything in the flat that she thought might be of value. A compact-disc player, two bank cards, some gift vouchers, a purse and items of jewellery. Gourlay calmly returned to her bedsit with these ill-gotten gains where she took off her blood-covered clothes. The next morning she and Kris Taylor headed for Aberdeen's main shopping area in Union Street as if nothing had happened. She even tried to beg money from passers-by for the bus fare. According to Taylor, Gourlay was her 'usual cheery self'. Gourlay used Melanie's bank card and PIN number to steal £10 from a cash machine and she spent the Marks and Spencer gift vouchers stolen from the flat to buy her aunt a vase. Her demeanour remained calm for the rest of the day. She met her parents for lunch – which she paid for with the money stolen from Melanie Sturton – and, according to her mother, was 'fine and cheery'.

But all that was soon to change. Melanie's body was discovered on 11 October and a murder hunt was launched by Grampian Police. As part of their routine enquiries Detective Constable Janice Falconer interviewed Gourlay as a potential witness on 12 October and, two days later in an attempt to eliminate her from enquiries, interviewed her again and took a routine DNA sample. According to police, she was happy to co-operate up to that point and to go voluntarily to police headquarters; one officer described her as 'pleasant, plausible and controlled'. But there was a dramatic change in her mood when police obtained warrants to search her bedsit and the homes of her mother and sister. According to detectives, she became quieter and more withdrawn and said that she wanted to go home. Her sense of foreboding was fully justified as police found much to incriminate her in the bedsit – in particular a Sabatier boning knife with Melanie Sturton's bloodstains on the blade and handle. The police also found a blood-stained jacket and latex gloves as well as a number of Melanie's possessions.

Pamela Gourlay was now on a murder charge. She was strip-searched by two female officers and, through a vale of tears, asked them 'What if you have done the worst thing in the world?' She was then taken for a formal interview, which was video-recorded by police. Gourlay wept throughout the interview process and made a dramatic admission to the detectives who questioned her, 'I murdered Melanie. I slit her throat.' She said that her unfortunate victim had begged her to stop. She was unable to offer any explanation for her actions, 'I don't know what was going through my head' she told police.

But by the time of the trial at the High Court in Aberdeen in March 2000 she had changed her mind about her guilt. In the dock, charged with murder and facing a life sentence, she tried to put the blame on her erstwhile boyfriend, Kris Taylor. This of course completely contradicted the confession in the video-taped interview with Grampian Police, which was shown to the jury of ten women and five men. It also contradicted evidence from her mother who testified that her daughter told her during a telephone conversation from prison that she was the sole killer. Mrs Eileen Gourlay recounted how Pamela Gourlay told her: 'It was me. I am sorry mum . . . They'll give me fifteen years mum. I am so scared.' Mrs Gourlay put it to her that someone else must have been involved, but she was insistent: 'I am telling the truth' was the tearful reply.

Mrs Gourlay then told the court how, only a few weeks later, her daughter had a completely new version of events: 'She told me it was Kris that done the murder and she took the stuff out of the girl's flat.' The justification for this *volte-face* was quite simple – she claimed that she was frightened of Taylor and did not want to 'grass' on him. She was also worried about what might happen to her family if she told the truth. Therefore in the initial phase of the investigation all her instincts told her that she should shoulder the blame but as time went on and the trial drew nearer she decided to tell the truth as 'everything seemed to be getting more real'.

For his part Taylor vehemently denied any involvement in either robbery or murder. There was one piece of evidence linking him to the crime but it was rather tenuous – a DNA test of a blood-stain on Melanie Sturton's front door revealed that it almost certainly belonged to him. But Taylor insisted that he had never been in the bedsit and could offer no explanation as to how it had got there. It would now be up to the jury to decide if Gourlay's version of events was credible. After two-and-a-half hours the members of the jury returned to the courtroom where the foreman announced they had found her guilty by virtue of a majority verdict. Gourlay showed no emotion but Melanie Sturton's relatives uttered a single word, a word that spoke volumes for their state of mind: that word was 'yes'.

In passing sentence the judge, Lord Marnoch, noted that detention for life was mandatory for a murder conviction. But given the nature and circumstances of the crime he went on to say, 'I have decided to mark the gravity of your offence and the degree of depravity, and also the genuine lack of remorse and the sense of outrage which your crime engendered in any right-thinking person. It is appropriate, despite your youth, that I recommend to Scottish ministers that you serve a minimum period of fourteen years detention before being even considered for release into the community on licence.' To loud applause from the public gallery, and shouts of 'bitch', Gourlay was led away to start her new life behind bars.

There is a postcript to the story. Gourlay made an attempt to get a new trial on the grounds that she had suffered a miscarriage of justice because the trial judge, Lord Marnoch, had interrupted her evidence 186 times. Although this plea was rejected by the Court of Criminal Appeal in Edinburgh she later persuaded it to quash the recommendation that she should serve a minimum of fourteen years behind bars. The effect of this was that she would only have to serve a 'normal' life sentence, which would have meant an earlier release date. This decision horrified Melanie Sturton's mother who described it as a 'kick in the stomach' and complained bitterly that no one was able to speak up for her daughter in court.

But there was a final twist. Under European human rights legislation, judges in Scotland must now specify the length of time murderers should spend in jail as a punishment for their misdeeds. In October 2002, Gourlay found herself back in the High Court where Lord Marnoch confirmed his original minimum sentence of fourteen years. He said 'It seems to me that this murder was severely aggravated by the element of premeditation involved, by having financial gain involved and by the ruthlessness of its execution.' He went on to say that he also took into account the 'total lack of remorse' shown by Gourlay. This decision, understandably, was welcomed by her victim's family.

*

If murders by women are rare the chances of a mother and daughter committing the crime together seem almost outwith the bounds of possibility. But, in June 2003, Isabell Carvill, aged 37, of Rutherglen, and her 17-year-old daughter, Gemma Valenti from Hamilton, made legal history by becoming the first mother and daughter to be convicted on the same murder charge in Scotland. Even more astonishingly they were not the first murderers in the family. In 1993, Frances Carvill, Isabell's sister and Gemma's aunt, stabbed Daniel Currie to death in Glasgow, was convicted of his murder and given a life sentence.

The story of the mother-and-daughter murder began in a house in Blantyre, Lanarkshire in July 2002. Three women, Carvill, Valenti (then aged 16) and their close friend Isobel Black arrived at a party to celebrate a friend's win on the horses. But the mood quickly turned sour when another guest, 32-year-old Kenneth Finnie, made indecent remarks to the three women. He followed two of them to the toilet, at which point one of the women thrust a glass into his chin breaking his jaw in three places. With Finnie helpless, Gemma Valenti then grabbed a knife and plunged it deep into his heart. As he lay dying from the stab wound, he was subjected to a prolonged and frenzied attack as his assailants kicked and punched him, stamped on his head and hit him on the head with a bottle. Shortly after the attack they were seen wiping his blood off their faces.

Despite the enormity of what she had done Valenti was almost flippant when she was the subject of a medical examination to gather forensic evidence. She said to officers, 'I'm daein' nae mair murders if you've got tae go through this. I should have learned frae my Auntie Frances. She did eight years for murder.' Indeed the trial judge, Lord Bracadale, took the view that the teenager was the most vicious of the three assailants and sentenced her to life imprisonment with a recommendation that she should serve at least twelve years before being eligible for parole. For her mother, Isabell Carvill, he may have taken account of the fact that she had attempted to resuscitate her victim and handed down a life sentence with a minimum term of ten years. Isobel Black was convicted of attempted murder and given seven years. The next day one tabloid newspaper spoke for many when it described Carvill and Valenti as the 'she-devil and her spawn'.

Kenneth Finnie's family was outraged at the sentences. His mother, Margaret Finnie, said, 'I am not happy. They should never get out at all. We have still not got over Kenneth's death and probably never will.' His father, Alex, agreed, 'The sentence was pure rubbish. It doesn't matter if they are all women. Life should mean life.'

The Carvills might well be categorised as Scotland's most dysfunctional family. Three female members of the clan have been convicted of murder. And Gemma Valenti's father – a man she is said to idolise – has served an astonishing total of thirty-seven years in prison for a variety of offences. Indeed did the background of these women lead inexorably to a life of crime? Is there something in the genes that predisposes them to carry out despicable acts, or can we attribute their behaviour to the way they were brought up? It is the old nature versus nurture debate in another form. Neil Murray QC, Isabell Carvill's advocate, pointed out in court that she had a background and upbringing that people would not wish on their worst enemy. Gemma Valenti had a 'hellish' family background, according to her lawyer, Jock Thomson QC, and up to three weeks before the murder had been staying in a children's home, describing her time in care as the happiest period of her life. Isobel Black's lawyer noted that his client had suffered abuse and chronic depression, and also had a drug problem. Their chaotic lifestyles were even reflected during the four-week trial. Carvill turned up drunk one day and Black twice slept in.

We may never find the answer to the nature-nurture question. It may or may not be in the minds of Isabell Carvill and Gemma Valenti as they serve their sentences in Cornton Vale prison near Stirling (in the short term at least they are more likely to be focusing on the appeal against their convictions, announced in August 2003). But there is sure to be one thought uppermost in their minds: their relative Frances Carvill hung herself in Cornton Vale after serving eight years of her sentence for murder.

ELEVEN

The gay slasher

HE WAS CHUBBY, squat with his hair an unkempt mess. The sort of person who would look away rather than meet you eye to eye. But he could dress smartly, possessed a certain glibness and a good deal of cunning. By the time he was living in the Ayrshire town of Kilmarnock in August 1991 he had already walked free from a murder charge. But, as often happens, his narrow escape from a lengthy gaol sentence had not led him to rein in his activities. Rather it accelerated them, as it suggested to him that he could get away with anything. Including murder.

Kilmarnock is not the most picturesque town even on the sunniest day. But it does have a certain warmth about it, a lived-in feel. People know how to enjoy themselves, which is what 18-year-old Barry Wallace set out to do on the evening of 4 December 1999. At the time Barry was working as a shelf stacker in Tesco, having left school, Grange Academy, in May of that year. With Christmas approaching a night out with workmates had been arranged at the Foxbar Hotel in the town's London Road. As he set out for the party he told his parents not to expect him back that night as he might stay with a friend. Barry then met up with his pal Lewis Caddis for a few 'warm up' drinks. So, by the time he'd passed the later part of the evening with his Tesco mates at the Foxbar, he was in a pretty merry state. In fact, as far as Barry was concerned, the night was not yet over so he turned down the offer of a lift home. Instead, he waved goodbye to his fellow workers with the news that he was heading up to the Expo nightclub in West George Street to catch any friends still about. It was a walk of only a few hundred yards. That appears to have come to nothing, or maybe Barry changed his mind because he was next seen in a queue for a taxi in the centre of town. For some reason he got into an argument with a man there and left. Fate had intervened. At 1.45 a.m. a CCTV camera near the Foregate, also in the town centre, caught Barry heading in the direction of Green Street. He was very drunk at the time. It was later discovered that Barry was four times over the legal limit for driving and was most likely in a very confused state. He could have been heading for his parent's house at Cumbrae Drive, in the affluent suburbs of the town. But it was a distance of over two miles, so on that wintry night it was unlikely that Barry would have welcomed the walk home.

Barry did not return home on Sunday. Nor had he appeared by Monday. No one seemed to have any clue as to where he might have got to. His parents, understandably concerned, reported six feet two inches Barry as a 'missing person' to the police. It was 6 December.

A 'missing person' could be many things. Someone taken ill and rushed to hospital. An injured person lying in an out-of-the-way spot, unable to move. A runaway. Someone who has lost their memory. The Scottish police forces have thousands of such cases on their books any and every day of the week. But they don't make grim discoveries every day.

Monday 6 December. It was no more than a routine training session in the waters of Loch Lomond. Central Scotland's underwater police unit was carrying out one of a regular series of practice dives at Rowardennan when they made the unexpected find. A left arm, clearly human, was discovered in about fifteen feet of water close to the pier. Further search brought to the surface a severed leg. Detective Superintendent Douglas Neilson announced that, 'It certainly looks as if somebody has been killed and dismembered. We have not yet established the identity of the man. The arms and leg do not appear to have been in the water for very long'. The murderer had certainly failed to put real distance between himself and the crime, but that was down to simple bad luck. Who could have expected the police to be there so soon after the evidence had been dumped? Someone not familiar with the area, it seemed. One local resident, John Bannerman, claimed, 'It's a stupid place to dump a body. It's a regular haunt for police divers and is a very popular tourist area.' The police were less sure and Neilson gave his view that, 'Had our underwater diving unit not happened across those limbs during a training dive they may never have been found and that is possibly what the person, or persons, who disposed of these may have been counting on. If this is the case he or they will probably be very nervous at this time knowing that the parts have been discovered.' The killer, however, was far from feeling nervous. He was too busy, as it turned out, trying to cover his tracks.

But where was the rest of the body? And did the parts found so far belong to one person or two? The police set up base on the loch side and began a fingertip search along the bank. Divers continued to look in the area close to the pier, once a docking place for ferry steamers, then fallen into disuse and only recently renovated. More finds were soon made. On Tuesday 7 December a right arm was located and, on Thursday 9 December, a right leg. All the limbs had now been found. A preliminary examination suggested that they belonged to the same person, but scientific tests would be carried out to confirm it. Key parts of the corpse, the head and torso, had still to be located, but while the investigation continued the police trawled through the missing persons' files for any description that matched the victim. They had by now a general idea of the dismembered person, pieced together by judging the age and height from the body parts found. They believed that the limbs belonged to a white adult male, aged between 18 and 50, height between six feet two and six feet four.

At this stage in the investigation the police had made no clear link with Barry Wallace's disappearance. In fact, Barry's parents, Ian and Christine Wallace, were telling reporters that the police were fairly sure that the remains in the loch were not those of their missing son.

But the next discovery suggested that the killer was either careless or so arrogant that he believed that nothing would link him to his victim. At around 8.30 a.m. on 16 December Margaret Burley, walking her white West Highland terrier along Barassie beach, near Troon, made a horrific discovery. It was her dog that first drew her attention to it by sniffing at the object. As Margaret later explained it 'was a face inside a cream-coloured polythene bag. The bag had split.' Margaret could not believe that what she had found was real. On the way home – she lived near the shore – she met a neighbour, William Auld, who she told of the strange find. They returned to the beach together and found the 'face' still in the bag. Unsure that what had been discovered was real, Mr Auld flicked the bag with a stick. It opened a bit more, enough to give them a better view. They could now have no doubt that what they were seeing was a severed human head. They covered it with a bread basket lying close by and reported the grisly discovery to the police. Dr James Mann, called in to examine the find, reported that he did not believe that the victim had been dead for long. The police noted that the object had been placed inside a Scandinavian Seaways carrier bag and that there were no other body parts in the vicinity. These were to prove significant clues.

The police quickly linked the find in Barassie with the horrific discoveries at Loch Lomond. In fact, it changed the whole direction of the inquiry. Although clearly suspicious, the limbs in the water could have been the result of an accident. Swimmers have been cut up accidentally in the past by a propeller. It didn't seem a likely explanation, but the police are always cautious and reluctant to release information. In fact, they had guessed from the start that it was no accident. Limbs cut off by a passing boat don't normally find themselves inside a plastic bag. But stranger things have undoubtedly happened. With the finding of a head, it was a completely different matter. Only a third party could have put parts of the same body in separate areas of the country. If, of course, the head and body matched. The police now set out to discover if they did. Central Scotland police were quoted as saying 'Either the head and limbs belong to the same person, or we've got two dismembered corpses lying around Scotland in pieces at the moment, and that really is stretching credibility. What's not known is whether there is a link to Barry Wallace, but we will know that soon.' DNA technology was going to be used to scientifically prove it one way or another.

In Kilmarnock the parents of Barry Wallace had no immediate reason to connect the events in Loch Lomond with the disappearance of their son. It was miles away for a start and so soon after he had inexplicably vanished. How could a young man who was widely liked be connected to such a gruesome discovery? The incident at Barassie changed all that, and delivered a cruel blow to such devoted parents. Bizarre and harsh as it must have seemed, Barry Wallace, with his life ahead of him, had been cruelly murdered and even more brutally dealt with after death. It was only the start of a terrible journey for Barry's family.

The police are very familiar with local criminals. Who they are. Where they stay. Their friends and habits. Most crimes are carried out by people who belong to the area. So when the murder of a young man in Kilmarnock took place, detectives immediately turned out the files on local suspects. One name stood out like a sore thumb: William Beggs, who lived where he had been since he moved into Kilmarnock, at Doon Place. The first-floor flat was immediately put under police surveillance.

Thirty-six-year-old Beggs was something of an enigma. He came originally from County Down in Northern Ireland and had grown up and gone to school there. One of his teachers described him as 'A good pupil, well mannered, above average intelligence. A quiet lad. Don't recollect any behavioural problems.' So where did it all start to go wrong? Beggs came from a respectable middle class home: 'Fine Christians', their Baptist minister called them. His father, also called William, lectured at a local college. Winifred, his mother, taught at a primary school. Nor was William an only child. He had the emotional support of two younger brothers and two sisters. But there may have been a less than tolerant attitude towards drink and sex. Most likely Beggs developed doubts about his sexuality at an early age, but could not admit to himself that it wasn't young women who aroused his interest. His was not the sort of home where those interested in their own sex would be welcomed. Maybe it was genuine revulsion against his own feelings that led Beggs to campaign against the extension of homosexual rights to Northern Ireland. Or maybe a cynical ploy. He certainly had political ambitions.

But he could not hide his true nature from friends and acquaintances. They were becoming increasingly aware that some odd thoughts were running through Beggs's tortured mind. One former pupil from the Quaker school Beggs attended in Lisburn claimed, 'Beggs was treated with almost blanket hostility. Ostracised by almost everyone in the form. Nobody would sit near him, particularly women, because he made people very uneasy. He really was a creep.' Although the girls avoided him, it was not women that Beggs was turning his unhealthy attention to.

Even murderers have to start somewhere. And it usually isn't by killing. The serial killer often begins with crimes wholly unconnected to his later activities. Beggs came somewhere in between. He didn't assault his first victim, but clues to his later behaviour were plainly there. On a Duke of Edinburgh camping expedition, a young man sharing a tent with Beggs woke during the night to find razor blades in his sleeping bag. Beggs was left to sleep on his own, thereafter. His unsavoury reputation intensified when he was seen hanging around secondary schools in Portadown, trying to strike up conversations with young male students. Around the same time he was attacked after exposing himself to young boys. The emerging pattern of weird behaviour could no longer be kept a secret. Even those who had given Beggs the benefit of the doubt dropped him.

But, of course, to the twisted mind, other people's disapproval, even disgust, at their nature does not stop them attempting to act out their fantasy. They just try harder to hide it. And that's how it was with William Beggs. In 1982, aged 19, having gained nine O levels and two A levels he left Ireland to start a course in public administration at Teesside Polytechnic in Middlesbrough. He wasn't exactly a dedicated student. Beggs failed his second year exams, got through on resits, and eventually in 1987 graduated with a third class degree. His fellow students found him quiet, 'a bit of a closed book' one called him. But in other ways Beggs was active. He was elected to the Student Executive Committee and even became northern chairman of the Federation of Conservative Students. His behaviour is strangely reminiscent of Dennis Nilsen, the gory killer who was, at the same time, active in his trade union. Beggs was, like Nilsen, leading a double life. The public face of a right wing, authoritarian, anti-homosexual masked a secret, hidden agenda of frequenting gay meeting places. The strain of balancing both lives must have been enormous. Something had to give. The first to go was Beggs's political ambitions. He left both the Student Executive and the Federation of Conservative Students over the issue of Ireland. The Teesside students, he claimed, were anti-British and he abandoned the young Tories after the Anglo-Irish agreement.

He was now free to focus on his sexual activities and these burst into life in various bizarre manifestations. Reports of cutting young men with a razor led to a police inquiry, but no charges. His victims were too anxious to avoid publicity. But these incidents only whetted Beggs's appetite for more. In May 1987 the body of 28-year-old Barry Oldham was found in a secluded country lane in North Yorkshire. His throat had been savagely cut with a sharp implement and there had been an obvious attempt to dismember the body. The killer had either been disturbed in his work or had not been adequately prepared for the task. His bungled efforts could most clearly be seen around Barry's head where his murderer had tried to separate it from the torso. Barry Oldham was a homosexual and had clearly gone willingly with his killer to the spot where he was attacked. Enquiries by the police revealed that Barry had met a man at a gay disco and returned with him to his flat. His partner was identified as William Beggs. Police digging brought out the earlier incidents in which homosexual lovers of Beggs had been slashed with a razor. In June 1987 he was charged with the murder of Barry Oldham. In addition, he faced five separate counts of wounding. Beggs, true to his self obsession, denied the charges and, in Oldham's case, claimed that he had acted in self defence. Beggs may have convinced himself that it wasn't really his fault, but the jury were not willing to believe him. He was found guilty of murder and on two counts of wounding.

But a fatal mistake had been made. Fatal for Barry Wallace growing up in Kilmarnock, and for the future peace of mind of Ian and Christine Wallace, blissfully unaware of events taking place in a faraway courtroom. The prosecution had linked the wounding charges with the murder of Barry Oldham to build up a pattern of behaviour. It was not a course of action the judges who heard Beggs's appeal approved of. They took the view that to join the incidents in this way and present them to the jury was prejudicial, not allowing Beggs a fair trial. After only eighteen months in gaol, Beggs's conviction was quashed and he was set free. Others were nearly to die, and Barry Wallace to lose his life, because three appeal judges in London inhabit a world where using common sense is frowned upon. As Superintendent Tony Fitzgerald, the head of North Yorkshire CID, remarked: 'When we caught Beggs we seriously thought we had caught a serial killer in the making. We thought we were lucky because we had managed to catch him after his first killing.' It seems strange, given police concerns, that there was, at least, no retrial.

No doubt glorying in having escaped justice, Beggs returned to Ireland, but did not stay there for long. It has been suggested that he was chased out by extremist loyalists who resented his claimed association with the defence of Ulster. But it is more likely that he was simply too well known to be able to carry on his clandestine activities. He needed a new hunting ground. Incredibly, he managed to obtain a post as an Estate Management Officer with Kilmarnock and Loudon District Council. Applicants, presumably, were thin on the ground though it shows what a glib, persuasive, presentable individual Beggs could be when the occasion required. One wonders what the members of the interviewing panel think of their choice now.

Beggs may have avoided a gaol sentence for his murderous activities, but he could not escape the impulses surging through his mind. In August 1991, back to his habit of cruising gay clubs,

Beggs picked up Brian McQuillan at the Lorno Disco in Glasgow. Beggs must have been at his usual persuasive best because McQuillan willingly accompanied him back to his Kilmarnock flat. Once he had McQuillan safely in his private lair, Beggs's true nature, aroused by his sexual passion, burst into the open. McQuillan woke to find Beggs standing over him, slashing at his legs with a razor, shouting in a rage 'things will be over soon. You have made me do this.' Blood was pouring from several wounds on McQuillan's body and had splattered on the bedroom wall. He grasped that if he didn't get away immediately he would be killed and, though naked, dived through the window of the flat to escape.

The incident had been too public to escape notice and Brian McQuillan was willing to testify. Beggs was arrested and examined by a psychiatrist from Carstairs State Hospital. Found guilty at his trial, he was pronounced a 'danger to the public' because of his 'abnormal personality'. His gaol sentence, however, was still a comparatively light one of six years, and, in spite of being 'a danger to the public' he was released after three. Beggs's parents seemed blind to their son's vicious nature, mounting a campaign against the Scottish prison authorities over alleged mistreatment of their son.

After his release in 1994, an unabashed Beggs returned to Kilmarnock, even choosing to live at the Doon Place address in the Bellfield housing scheme where he had assaulted Brian McQuillan. Situated in a cul-de-sac on the outskirts of Kilmarnock it provided quick and easy access to the main roads out of the town. Paisley University took on the ex-con who gained a place on a computing course and eventually graduated with a Master's degree in information technology, a qualification that helped him get a job at a Sykes call centre in Edinburgh. His fellow students at Paisley were less easily taken in by Beggs than the various authorities and employers who dealt with him. They nicknamed him 'Fred West', after the notorious Gloucester killer, and bet each other that they would hear of him in the papers one day. His neighbours too had had enough of Beggs and his sordid activities. They were attracting too much outside attention. Local gangs targeted his car because of his openly homosexual inclinations and unsavoury behaviour. It was widely known that he was regularly bringing young men back to his flat. Wild rumours circulated about what was going on inside.

But, like many sadistic killers, Beggs appeared quite unaffected by the anxious ripples his presence was causing. When neighbours tried to have him removed from the area, he responded by buying his flat. In spite of the unwanted attention his car was receiving, he made no attempt to remove it, but installed a video camera to monitor it. He continued to attend his local church and, ever the keen camper, led camping trips into the countryside.

By December 1999, however, perhaps even William Beggs was starting to wonder how long this carefree life could continue. Maybe only a corner of his warped mind maintained some hold on reality, but he could no longer avoid the fact that he was coming to the end of the road. There had been clear hints in the media that he was involved in some way in the murder of Barry Wallace. It wasn't too hard to guess that he might top the police's list of suspects. He was not aware, however, that the police had obtained a warrant to search his flat and, on the surface, appeared calm, even attending an office party on the evening of 16 December. The police broke into his house the following day, 17 December, while Beggs was on his way to work, at his call centre job in Edinburgh. The block where he lived was sealed off and his apartment thoroughly searched. Eventually over five thousand items were taken away for further examination. Interviewed by detectives, neighbours reported that they had heard the sound of sawing on the night that Barry Wallace disappeared.

As Beggs drove to work that morning he could not have realised that it was going to be his last day of freedom for some time. At some point during the afternoon Beggs became aware of a BBC broadcast that his flat had been raided. He must have believed that, once again, Lady Luck was on his side, that he had been given the chance to evade justice. Having slipped the police net Beggs drove through the night to Luton Airport. In the car park he abandoned his vehicle then travelled to Heathrow Airport. Under the assumed name of W. Frederick, he took a flight out to Jersey and from there to Dinard near St Malo in France. By 27 December he had moved to Amsterdam where, having engaged a lawyer, he surrendered to the Dutch police. At the same time, he announced his intention of fighting extradition to Scotland, claiming that he would not receive a fair trial.

There were some back in Scotland who agreed with him. Beggs had been publicly branded in the media as the chief suspect. According to the press, there was little doubt as to his guilt. His picture was everywhere. Typical of the strange stories that circulated were claims that Beggs had covered himself in liquid chocolate as a protest against extradition, then tried to commit suicide by choking on a chocolate bar. Joseph Beltrami, who relishes taking on high-profile cases, claimed that the media frenzy would make it impossible 'for rational jurors to expunge all this information and prejudice from their minds'. There were others, however, who believed that Beggs had brought the situation on himself because of his sordid activities over many years. And Beggs had shown that he was more interested in trying to escape justice than in proving his innocence.

Meanwhile back in the real world, the misery left in his wake was flowing strongly. The search was continuing for Barry Wallace's torso. Having discovered Barry's head miles from Loch Lomond, the police were faced with the possibility that the torso had also been disposed of in the Kilmarnock area. Police searched local rubbish dumps, but it was a chance find that brought the hunt to an end. There had been a number of reports of suspicious objects, all of which had to be followed up. A stretch of the river Doon, which runs through the area, was searched when on Thursday 6 January 2000 two women reported seeing a body in the river. If it was a body, it was never found, though whatever it was it could not have been that of Barry Wallace. It was from Loch Lomond that the mystery of the puzzle was solved. On Saturday 8 January a passer-by reported seeing a suspicious object floating in the water at Manse Bay near Balmaha. When investigated it turned out to be the missing remains of Barry Wallace. Detectives now believed that they were in a better position to discover how Barry had met his death.

Piecing together the evidence from Barry's remains and Beggs's known behaviour, detectives believed that they had a clear idea of how Barry died. But it was not till the trial in October 2001 that the public heard for the first time the full extent of Beggs's shocking behaviour and his deliberate attempt to cover his tracks. Encouraged, in a drunken state, to come back to Beggs's flat by the suggestion either of a party or of more drink, Barry was at some point, early in the morning of 5 December, handcuffed. Probably when he had fallen asleep or was too drowsy to grasp what was happening. Or maybe Beggs tricked him into putting on the cuffs, as the serial killer John Wayne Gacy did with his victims in Chicago. Beggs may even have been familiar with Gacy's case. The prosecution led by Alan Turnbull, attempted to present a particular scenario. Turnbull suggested to the jury that Wallace's hands had been handcuffed behind his back, that his ankles had also been bound and that he had been kept in this position face down on the bed. It was claimed that the marks on Barry's limbs suggested that this was the position in which he had been held before death. It is possible that Beggs spiced a drink with drugs, as Brian McQuillan believed had happened to him before he was assaulted. In any event, Beggs succeeded in getting Barry where he wanted. In a situation where he could not fight back. He was then repeatedly slashed with a razor and may have been choked to death. Or even have died of a heart attack overcome with fright. Dr Jeanette McFarlane, a forensic pathologist, said that Barry's injuries were of a type that 'would be associated with a sexual assault of some sort'. She also told the court that Barry had suffered injuries to his face before death, bruises which could have followed a punch or fall. The evidence, however, as to exactly how Beggs murdered Barry Wallace was open to various interpretations. Only Beggs himself could provide the full answer and he was denying it all. Some facts are clear though. Barry's arms had been punctured by a hypodermic needle. He had been brutally sodomised causing severe internal injury. After Barry was dead, Beggs used a saw to dismember the body, finishing the job with a kitchen knife and snapping some bones with his bare hands. There must have been a lot of blood at Doon Place. Immediately after, Beggs wrapped the severed limbs in plastic bags, packed the body parts into the boot of his car then drove the fifty miles to the pier at Loch Lomond to dispose of them.

The police had gathered substantial evidence from Doon Place to link Beggs to the disappearance of Barry Wallace. It formed a key part of the prosecution case. On the bedside table in Beggs's flat lay a key to a set of handcuffs. In a cupboard outside Beggs's house, plastic bags had been stored. Some of the bags had the same logo, Scandinavian Seaways, as the one containing Barry's head when it was found on Barassie beach. Dried blood had been discovered near the kitchen door-handle, around the washing machine, and on the bedroom mattress and carpet. DNA obtained from these stains matched the gene profile of Barry Wallace. There was only a one in a billion chance of it not belonging to the murdered teenager. Just as significant was the revelation that DNA from two separate individuals had been found mixed together on the mattress. It came from Barry Wallace and William Beggs. A clinching factor was the confirmation that blood on a kitchen knife also belonged to Barry. DNA from Barry was identified under the handbrake of Beggs's car and also on the back of the passenger seat. It also turned out that Beggs was familiar with the area where the body had been dumped. A friend of Beggs, Richard Balfe, a lecturer at Paisley University, who had known the accused for ten years told the court that Beggs knew the Loch Lomond area well and was very fond of it. He remembered that Beggs had drawn his attention to the road to Balmaha, saying 'That road goes nowhere. It's a dead end.' Prophetic words. He also recalled a phone conversation he had had with Beggs at 5.40 p.m. on 5 December, the day after Barry's disappearance. According to Balfe, Beggs said he was driving to Edinburgh and told him that he 'got off with a young guy . . . "a real sweetie". He seemed quite pleased with himself and smug. He was boasting about his sexual conquest.' Balfe was no hostile witness and admitted that he regarded Beggs as 'a mate and good friend'.

The police could also point to a recent effort to redecorate Beggs's flat. And Beggs's actions were significant here. On 7 December, the day following the first reports of the discovery of severed limbs in Loch Lomond, Beggs left work early, claiming illness. That evening, he travelled to Belfast via the 9.30 p.m. Troon ferry. The following day, he called his manager stating that he would be unable to work for the rest of the week. On 10 December, however, he returned to Kilmarnock and was observed buying paint brushes, floor dye and sandpaper at a DIY store. The following day, he bought wallpaper at another store, then returned to Belfast on the Stranraer ferry.

One unresolved question was the fate of Barry Wallace's head. Did he dispose of it at the same time as the rest of the body? Or keep it in the fridge, as serial killer Jeffrey Dahmer did, as some kind of sick trophy? The head wasn't found till 16 December, several days after the limbs were first discovered on 6 December. People living close to the beach at Troon were of the opinion that the head had been placed on the beach as late as the night before it had been found. One woman said, 'I think the head must have been placed there overnight because people walk their dogs there all the time. It surely would have been found earlier.'

Others suggested that Beggs could have thrown Barry's head from a ferry during a crossing from Troon to Northern Ireland. Sean Ward, a Seacat ferry captain, told the court that an object thrown overboard from a ship once it had left Troon could be washed up on the beach at Barassie. It is true that Beggs had travelled to Ireland just after Barry Wallace disappeared using the Troon ferry. Beggs might have used this trip to drop Barry's head into the sea or dump it on Barassie beach. But that would have left a clear week before the bag was found. It seems unlikely that it could have lain there for such a long time without being discovered. Only William Beggs, however, could provide an answer to the gruesome mystery.

Although extradited from Holland, Beggs continued to plead his innocence. At a seventeen-day trial, however, no defence witnesses were called. A different tactic was adopted. In a desperate attempt to defend his client, Beggs's advocate Donald Findlay presented Barry Wallace as a willing partner in a sexual adventure which had gone badly wrong. As he reminded the jury, it is no crime in Scotland to dismember a dead body. Findlay also criticised what he considered a campaign to 'demonise' William Beggs. The jury did not agree with Findlay's explanation of the events of 5 December, preferring to believe a more straightforward version. That Beggs, having somehow enticed Barry to Doon Place, had murdered him. And, afterwards, attempted to conceal the death by dismembering the body and disposing of the various parts. True, the jury's guilty verdict was only by a majority. But the only doubt could have been over Beggs's mental state. Would a normal person have carried out such a vicious crime? The answer must be no, but who would risk the chance of such an unbalanced individual ever being allowed to prowl the streets of Scotland again?

So where had it all gone wrong for William Beggs, in a life that had started out with so much promise? A friend of his parents, James McCormick, a former mayor of Craigavon, claimed: 'He was well brought up and somewhere along the line, when he left home he obviously got in to the wrong company.' The truth is, however, that Beggs was a loner who hid his twisted passions from those closest to him. We may never know why or how his perverted nature developed as it did. But there's no doubt that long before he left his hunting ground of Northern Ireland, he was known as a sick individual. A person who was to be avoided rather than befriended. Once free of the constraints of his family, Beggs was in a position to let his grisly passions rip. What had been unsavoury behaviour developed into something far more sinister. Murderous intent which left two men dead and many more injured. In his flat the blood of fifteen more people were found. They were all identified, but avoided publicity. How many more were attacked by Beggs, but left no clue? And could there yet be other dead bodies, victims of this brazen killer, awaiting discovery in some faraway loch? Time will tell.

TWELVE

The Fiery Cross: Scots and the Ku Klux Klan

HOW WAS IT that a band of friends, holding midnight meetings in a graveyard, were transformed within months into a notorious terror organisation, its name becoming a byword for evil? It is a tantalising mystery, and one that has bizarre links to Scotland. We like to think of Scotland as a tolerant country and the Scots individually as a friendly people. But did our ancient nation inspire the creation of the most sinister organisation of modern times? One which has become notorious across the world. The feared and violent Ku Klux Klan.

On the surface the forces that brought the Klan into existence seem straightforward. The American Civil War fought between 1861 and 1865 came about over the right of the Southern states to quit the United States, set up a separate country and continue with their slave-owning practices. But in the North, the wealthiest area of the country, it was believed that the South had no right to leave. Only war could settle the issue. A violent conflict followed in which hundreds of thousands of soldiers and civilians died. The struggle created a legacy of bitterness on both sides of the divide. But the defeat of the Southern, slave-plantation states of the Confederacy by the armies of the North meant that the black residents of the South were now free men. The North set out to force the South to change its ways. Slavery was abolished. Officials loyal to the North were appointed to positions of power. Blacks were granted the vote and other legal rights so that, on the face of it, the former slaves were now the equal of their erstwhile masters. In practice, the whites bitterly resented not only the control of their homeland by the Northern 'carpetbaggers', but also the very thought of their one-time slaves holding positions of influence. By various means, including threats and violence, sections of the white population set out to show the blacks who was in control.

The Ku Klux Klan became a key part of this white backlash. Klan members fought to undermine the influence of any politician or official forced on the South by the North. And to stop blacks going out to vote. Beaten in war they might have been but the South was not easily going to lose the peace. Even if this meant pandering to those who were prepared to use terrorist tactics to achieve their aims.

The level of violence resorted to by the Klan shocked people even at the time. In one incident in North Carolina, Klansmen shot a mother and four of her five children, murdering the fifth child by jumping on its head. In many other cases, blacks were beaten, hung or thrashed. Eighteen-year-old Maria from Georgia was whipped across her back and arms so brutally that the skin refused to heal. The pregnant teenager was unable to wear proper clothes because she found the friction against her body too painful to stand. Her 'crime' had been to bear a child without her employer's consent, an act of defiance the Klan was called in to punish. But at least Maria survived. In Pulaski, Tennessee a hundred Klansmen rode into town and dragged a black man arrested for alleged rape out of his cell. His body was riddled with bullets and left lying on the town's main street as a warning to other blacks. Lynching, however, was the usual penalty. And the former slave did not have to be guilty of any crime. Simply to have a black skin was adequate provocation. In North Carolina, one black man was dragged from his house, taken to the courthouse in the town of Graham and hung from a tree. A sign warning 'beware you guilty, both black and white' was nailed to his chest.

It is a sad reflection on the times that in most cases even the names of the victims went unrecorded. As in the son and mother who were Klan targets in the same state. The son was taken from the house and shot. The mother was hung by a bed cord from the nearest tree. The young man's body was covered in furniture looted from the home and the whole lot set alight in an apparent attempt to hide the evidence. Incredibly, the youth survived to describe his ordeal. As so often, however, the Klan escaped justice. Even in the most bizarre cases, of which the removal of the flesh of a murdered black man and the hanging of his articulated skeleton from a large oak tree was only the most infamous. Whites who tried to stand up to the Klan were themselves threatened and hundreds were murdered. The brutal killings sent out a message to the former slaves and their supporters not to threaten white control of the Southern states. As a terror tactic, it was highly successful. So successful that the conservative gentry who ran the Southern states began to feel that they might be next on the list and gradually turned against the activities of the Klan.

To outsiders at the time, and looking back from the present, the Klan with its terrifying reputation seems little more than an organisation of redneck thugs. But if we look inside the Klan a stranger story emerges. Although the KKK became the symbolic organisation of violent Southern resistance to black equality it was by no means the only one of its type. Other organisations that sprang up at the same time included the Sons of Midnight, the Pale Faces, the White Brotherhood, and the Order of the White Rose. The Knights of the White Camellia may even have had a larger membership than the Klan. Some have suggested that the Klan's spectacular growth can be attributed to the use of the black arts. Fanciful, maybe, but the Klan spread so rapidly, and was so successful, that it might well be asked whether occult forces were at work. It is clear that the Klan was not simply a terror organisation.

According to the traditional account the Ku Klux Klan began in 1865 as an obscure organisation of unemployed Confederate veterans who lived in the town of Pulaski, in the state of Tennessee. Their aim in creating the Klan was, it is claimed, purely social, but from the very first they engaged in strange nocturnal adventures. They first attracted public attention through their habit of dressing in pure white robes and holding their meetings in isolated graveyards. Klan members adopted the strange practice of hiding beside pathways, stepping out to frighten passers-by with their ghostly appearance. Though they appear at the level of childhood pranks, in fact these apparently inexplicable acts reflected a more sinister intent.

The original 'Pulaski six' were Captain John Lester, Major James Crowe, John Kennedy, Calvin Jones, Richard Reed and Frank McCord. Appearances can be deceptive. There must have been something odd in their backgrounds because the Klan was no run-of-the-mill organisation. They appear to have come from families who were respected locally. They were also better educated than most and had good contacts among local elites. They even held their formal committee meetings in the chambers of a judge, Thomas Jones, father of Calvin Jones. The surnames of some of the original six members of the Klan might not sound obviously Scottish, but according to John Lester they were all of Scottish descent and immensely proud of their Caledonian blood. It was he who suggested that they add the word clan to the title, but spelling it with a 'K' so that it fitted with Ku Klux. However, the reputed Scottish descent might have been a smokescreen to hide rather more bizarre connections with Scotland.

In fact, it is unlikely that Lester alone inspired the use of the term 'Klan'. The Southern states of the US were heavily influenced by a romantic idea of the Scottish clan system which, they believed, stood for brotherhood and supporting one another through difficult times. Even some of the symbols of the clans were adopted by the KKK. For centuries the fiery cross had been used by members of Scottish clans to contact each other in times of emergency. Passed from village to village, it served to warn all clan members of the need to get together. The *crois taraigh*, or Fiery

Cross, had developed from the Old Norse 'fire arrow'. Two pieces of wood, charred at the upper end, were fastened together to form a cross, to which was attached a rag dipped in the blood of a freshly killed goat. The burning of the sap of the wood, mixed with the red animal blood, represented to the warrior mind the deadly force of 'Fire and Sword'. Neither home nor body would be spared when the soldiers of the cross adopted 'Fire and Sword' as their motto. The Fiery Cross was used all over Scotland as late as the sixteenth century and surviving documentation shows that it was sent around the country before the Battle of Pinkie in 1547. Transported to the USA the fiery cross has become the most potent symbol of the Ku Klux Klan: a burning altar 'sanctifying' whichever place the Klan chose to meet. It was the focus of the gathering and served as a warning to its enemies that the Ku Klux Klan was on the march. There has been disagreement over the extent to which the fiery cross was used by the Klan during its early years. Some say that it only became popular fifty years after its formation. However, eye-witness testimony suggests that Klan horsemen rode with flaming torches from the very start. Some in the shape of the cross, though it may not have become a universal symbol until the Klan's later phase.

The name the Klan adopted was certainly strange. Its origin and the meaning are a mystery. Traditionally it was an adaptation of the Greek word *kyklos* meaning band or circle. This was converted to Ku Klux and so the Ku Klux Klan. John Kennedy was alleged to have been the member who suggested *kyklos*. He had apparently studied ancient Greek for a while. Even so that still doesn't explain why 'circle clan' or 'circle band' was chosen as a title. In fact, it only makes sense in a mystical connotation. The circle is a powerful magical symbol and a protective device against evil. It is also significant that the name Ku Klux Klan contains three capital 'Ks' in the title. This is unlikely to have been an accident. Three is a powerful number in occult magic and the letter 'K' is full of magical significance. There is also a curious link between the figure of a circle and three 'ks'. Cut a circle with three intersecting lines and three 'ks' will appear. In spite of what was later claimed, a considerable amount of thought had clearly gone into identifying an appropriate name for the group.

Unaware of its significance, opponents have been quick to brand it as meaningless jargon. However, to the uninitiated all language linked to secret or clandestine groups can be seen as mumbo-jumbo. That is the whole point of using a secret language only fully understood by the initiates. There is no doubt that what this group called itself had a key significance. It resonates with too many occult and mystic links to have been other than deliberate, although even some of its founders may have been unaware of the fact. In any organisation there are always some more in the know than others.

Take the letter 'K' of which there are three in the title. The letter 'K' is associated with so many strange aspects of the paranormal that it is difficult to decide just what area of the supernatural was being embodied in the title. The use of the letter 'K' may have been related to Ka. In Ancient Egyptian religion, Ka was an entity associated with the physical body, protecting and motivating the individual. The Ka lived inside the body. When its 'host' died the Ka survived by inhabiting the tombs of the dead. Does this explain the Klan's early graveyard meetings? The word 'Klu' could have been taken from Kalau, evil Siberian fairies that bring sickness and death to humans, either as a punishment or just for the enjoyment of doing evil. Then there's *Kuth*, in ancient Egyptian mythology, the Darkness, said to have existed as part of Chaos before the beginning. There's also another Greek word *Kobaloi*, from which Klu could have been taken, meaning evil spirits. Ku Klux Klan also has echoes of Klu-Dban one of the five great Buddhist kings. And if a direct American link existed it might have been with the Ku, the mystical 'stone' clan of the ancient Tewa people, living in the area that became part of the state of New Mexico.

The point is not that any one in particular of these directly inspired the choice of Ku Klux Klan, but that in a sense they all did. The title 'Ku Klux Klan' far from being a spur-of-the-moment invention was in fact a highly complex name. It served as a link with all the mystical concepts which attaches the world that humanity operates in to the other world, the 'invisible empire'. It is surely no coincidence that Klan members used the term invisible empire to refer to the Klan and its activities. Rank-and-file members may not have been aware of its occult significance; that this was, in fact, a term used to describe the 'other world' of unseen entities. But the leadership of the organisation must have been.

A mystical name, as Ku Klux Klan surely is, appears at odds with the brutal activities we associate with the Klan. But it finds an echo in the original aims laid down by the first Klan members. It claimed to be an institution of 'Chivalry, Humanity, Mercy and Patriotism' with the aim of protecting 'the weak, the innocent, and the defenceless, from the indignities, wrongs and outrages of the lawless.' Here can be seen a kind of medieval, chivalric code of work, reminiscent of the Knights Templar and, further back in time, the mystical legends of King Arthur and the Knights of the Round Table. However, in the titles of the officers of the order it is clear that even stranger influences are at work. At the head of the organisation there would be a Grand Wizard with his ten genii. A Grand Dragon of the Realm and his eight hydras. A Grand Titan of the Dominion with six furies. A Grand Giant of the Province and his four goblins. A Grand Cyclops of the Den and his two Night Hawks. A Grand Magi. A Grand Monk. A Grand Scribe. A Grand Exchequer. A Grand Turk. A Grand Sentinel.

On the face of it, it sounds almost childish. But there is a clear mystical language being used here as each of the main officers has a magical association. A link which the Klan founders must have been perfectly well-aware of. The Magi were priests of Ancient Persia, leaders of a Zoroaster religion that did, and still does, worship fire. This explains the significance of the fiery cross in Klan activities. Blazing through the darkness of the night, it had a powerful mystic significance. The dragon too was a fire-breathing creature portrayed in many legends. But it was also a highly symbolic animal. In the world of the occult, it is the physical manifestation of hell and a sign of evil. To early Christians, the dragon stood for pagan religions. So was born the legend of Christian St George defeating the pagan dragon. To adopt the dragon as a title of one of their leading positions is a further indication that influences of a mystical nature were incorporated into the Klan at its very birth.

But to use the furies as a title reveals an almost twisted sense of the implications of ancient myth. The furies were conceived from the blood that fell from the castrated genital of Uranus, the Greek sky god, when it fell upon his wife Gaia on the earth. They had a terrifying appearance with notoriously ugly faces and snakes in place of hair. They never smiled and always carried whips and burning torches. They barked liked dogs and delighted to scent human blood and suck it from wrongdoers. Their task was to avenge the murder of family members, an act that fitted in well with the Klan's view of the North as having destroyed the Southern 'family' and deserving of revenge. Goblins are probably better known 'invisible entities' than the furies, but have their own dark side. They form a sub-group of Ireland's 'little people' and are likely to use their magical powers to wreak revenge on anyone who they believe has slighted them. The Cyclops, on the other hand, was an enormous human-like creature, but with only one eye, which was situated in the middle of the forehead. They possessed the knowledge to create thunderbolts used in the war between the gods. As with the Klan, they forged their unique weapon to bring terror to their enemies.

And even the use of the title 'Night Hawk' has a specific intention. In the world of the occult it has a fearsome reputation. It is viewed as a bird of evil omen because of its night-time activity and strange-sounding cry. It is unlucky to hear its call once the sun goes down and if it lands on a house it is considered a sign of misfortune or death for those within. At the top of the Klan sat the Wizard. The wizard is a well known term for a man with magical powers and its use in connection with the Klan, on its own, shows that the organisation began its life with an agenda different from the one that it rapidly adopted.

Rank-and-file members had the most bizarre title of all. They were to be known as ghouls. Ghouls were originally the offspring of Ibis, the Arabic Satan. They live in the desert and attack travellers. And it may be remembered that the original Klansmen would jump out at passers-by travelling on local paths though there is no known evidence of an attack on anyone. Even more curious is that, in European folklore, the ghoul was a creature that lived in churchyards and fed on the flesh of the dead.

Strange though it may seem, the legends associated with these mystic titles were put into practice by the Klan. The fire-worshipping magi were represented by the Klan's fascination with the fiery cross which became almost a religious symbol. The night hawk with its sinister night-time activity and deadly calling card was played out in the Klan's notorious 'after dark' visits. Most sinister of all, castration, represented by the Furies, was a notorious practice frequently carried out by the Klan. It is sometimes seen as a purely sexual crime, carried out against black men accused of the rape of white women, but that it had a deeper significance is shown by the Klan inflicting it on white men who had not been accused of any sexual misbehaviour. This brutal revenge was used by the Klan throughout its history. As late as 1935 members of the Florida branch of the Klan turned their fire on union leader Joseph Shoemaker, who was head of the Workers Alliance. Shoemaker's 'crime' was to start a new political party that seemed to threaten the power of the bosses over their employees. The involvement of the Klan fuelled the conspiracy theorists who believed that the organisation had contacts high up in the government of many Southern states. Shoemaker was arrested on a trumped-up charge and interrogated by the police. As he left the police station masked members of the Klan grabbed him, rode him out of town, stripped and beat him. He was then castrated and died in agony several days later. But Shoemaker's treatment was unusual. The typical victims of the Ku Klux Klan were the many nameless blacks who were suspended from the most convenient tree, castrated while they hung and left to die with their genitals in their hands. On a number of occasions black women also became targets: those who had the temerity to associate with white men had their breasts and faces slashed in a deliberate attempt to disfigure them.

Several of the mythic beings used by the Klan in the titles of their office holders represent entities who, in legend, emerged out of a chaotic present to forge a new future. Just as the Klan saw itself as a new body brought into being to bring order to the South after the 'darkness' of defeat. Even the alleged date of its foundation, 24 December, fits with this picture: Christmas Eve and the birth of the new Christ. But also in pagan times the last of the great 'Dark Days' when the sun stood still in the heavens before it began its rebirth and moved towards spring.

The adoption of these magical and mystical terms was no accident and was heavily influenced by the writings of Sir Walter Scott. During most of the nineteenth century Scott was a favourite author in the South. He inspired in Southern society a belief in the virtues of chivalry, honour and pride. According to the American writer Mark Twain, 'Sir Walter had so large a hand in making Southern character, as it existed before the war, that he is in great measure responsible for the war.' What Twain meant was that, through his novels and essays, widely read in the South, Scott put over a view of society that the educated Southern elite of landowners adopted and lived out. This emphasised the importance of chivalry, good manners and hierarchy. After the Civil War, the South saw a similarity between the destruction of the Scottish clans by English power, as described by Scott, and their own defeat by the wealthier Northern states. His work was especially popular in the Southern states because so many Scottish and Irish immigrants had settled there.

It was the educated and wealthy slave owners who were most powerfully influenced by Scott, but because they set the trend his influence spread right through society. The 'Southern gentleman' with his perfect manners and courteous behaviour towards women was a creation of Scott's. But belief in chivalry and brotherhood could be turned in another direction. If the 'code of the South' was under attack from outsiders then it could become the duty of the 'Southern gentleman' to defend his honour. To gather with his friends and comrades to repel the threat. And so was born the Ku Klux Klan which was surely never intended to be the monster it so quickly became.

But Scott also influenced the South's view of the occult. Scott filled his books with accounts of supernatural incidents. The interplay of the 'other world' with our own often formed a key part of his novels. Scott was fascinated by true accounts of the paranormal and Scottish folklore. He wrote the classic 'Letters on Demonology and Witchcraft' and collected many ancient legends. It was Scott who revived the symbol of the 'fiery cross', popularising it through his widely read poem *The Lady of the Lake*. It's not clear to what extent Scott believed in the reality of the supernatural, but he was certainly convinced that paranormal incidents had an impact on people's daily lives. And through his writings he put across the idea that we should accept the supernatural as part of our real world: that we can interact with the paranormal almost as naturally as we can with another human being. This view of the 'otherworld' and our own world as overlapping comes through in the activities and structure of the Klan. It explains why it could adopt what seem at first glance almost childish tactics yet, at the same time, show another face as a cold and brutal organisation.

But did Scotland influence the formation of the evil Ku Klux Klan in other ways? Was it through the Scottish genius for forming secret societies which acted as a channel for esoteric and hidden knowledge? The link between the Klan and the Masons, especially Scottish Masonry, because of family ties, has been a constant theme; and a controversial one with frequent denials that the two organisations overlapped. As late as 1921 Richard Hanna, deputy to the supreme council of Ancient and Accepted Scottish Rite Freemasonry, said: 'True Masonry insists on just laws rigorously enforced and is ready at all times to assist the constituted authorities in that enforcement, but never to violate the laws in the enforcement process. This Ku Klux Klan is to be avoided as one would a pestilence.' It was an admission that membership of the two organisations did overlap, even if it was only at an informal level. Many suspected that it ran much deeper.

Other influences on the Klan seem equally bizarre. One of the most recognisable characteristics of the Klan is its distinctive costume. The white, flowing robe reaching to the ground, and the tall pointed-white-mask, concealing the face, with two narrow eye-slits. Though it can at times look comical, to others it is a symbol of terror. But this weird apparel was not invented by the Klan. In fact it has an ancient origin. Identical costumes have been worn for centuries in a country far removed from the United States.

In the south of Spain around the city of Seville exists the ancient tradition of the Nazarenes, also known as the Brothers. These religious societies are hundreds of years old and stretch back into medieval times. Every year the 'brotherhoods' parade through the city centre during what is known locally as Holy Week. They dress in flowing robes, with long, pointed masks which cover their faces. Their uniform is identical to that adopted by the Ku Klux Klan. The casual observer might easily mistake them for Klansmen transported to the Old World. Curiously, some of the float bearers wear tartan-style kilts. But can these similarities be anything other than coincidence? It is possible that somehow knowledge of the Seville brotherhoods filtered through to the Klan. Could it have been through the influence of the Knights Templar who were strong in both Spain and Scotland? But what could have been the significance of adopting the style of robe worn by the Nazarenes? There is no obvious answer. It is one more mystery in the strange story of the Ku Klux Klan.

Although the founders of the Klan were heavily influenced by the Scottish magical tradition, publicised by Sir Walter Scott, there is another strand to the story. It is clear that Scottish influence interacted with purely American factors to create a brew of deadly evil. Time and again incidents point to the conclusion that the Klan took for granted the superstitious nature of the former slaves. There could have been a good reason for this. Klan members often had direct knowledge of the religious beliefs and practices of the blacks. So did the Klan, far from viewing the occult beliefs of the ex-slaves as simple superstition, in fact believe in the power of black voodoo and set out to use its own magic to counteract it? Had they summoned help from the Dark regions against Negro magic? Did they themselves believe that the power of magic had been used by slaves to help the North defeat the South and set out to counteract it with their own magic? This would explain why the original founders became desperate to end the Klan when the whole thing got out of hand and turned into an exercise in violent thuggery rather than occult magic. Were there Klan members at the core of the organisation who were literally the servants of the Devil, obeying a master not of this earth?

There is no doubt that strange claims were being made by members of the Klan. According to some freed slaves they were told by Klansmen that Ku Klux included among its members those who had risen from their graves. Could there be any truth in this? It is clear that the Klan was very much made up of representatives of the living. The violence carried out against black, and white, by the organisation testifies to that. But there were also some bizarre stories associated with the Klan's activities. Incidents that make very little sense if it was all down to human actions. In Arkansas mysterious skeletal apparitions appeared ranging from three to twelve feet high, dressed in black or white. One appeared to be using a human backbone as a walking stick. Others were seen carrying their heads in their hands. Some appeared astonishingly thirsty, drinking a barrel of rain water and five buckets of water from a well. In one incident a group of Klansmen forced several black women to strip naked and lie on the road at night. Klan members then danced around the group, uttering strange animal-like shouts and prodding the blacks with canes. It is suggestive of a ritual being performed. This would fit with the activities of the original Klan with its secret graveyard gatherings; occult ritual could have been used, quite literally, to raise the dead from their graves. Equally strange is that in some areas blacks joined the Klan and took part in its activities. Was this a case of the Klan making use of the magical knowledge of their supposed enemies? It certainly suggests that there was more to the activities of the Klan than is usually supposed.

Quite often written threats issued by the Klan to its enemies contained clear 'magical' overtones. One teacher at a school for blacks was warned:

Ist Quarter, 8th Bloody Moon – ere the next quarter be gone! Unholy teacher of the blacks. . . . Punishment awaits you, and such horrors as no man ever underwent and lived. The cusped moon is full of wrath and as its horns fill the deadly mixture will fall on your unhallowed head. . . . When the black cat sleeps we that are dead and yet live are watching you. The far piercing eye of the Grand Cyclops is upon you!

The use of the phrase 'we that are dead' makes it clear that the Klan was threatening to make use of the power of the 'other world'. The question is to what extent, if any, they were able to tap into the power of the occult.

Another letter sent to a Klan enemy in Alabama threatened revenge from 'The mighty hobgoblins of the Confederate dead in Hell', and recited the witches chant from Shakespeare's Scottish play *Macbeth*:

Double, double, toil and trouble,
Fire burn and cauldron bubble.

Then it quoted the last letters of the Roman and Greek alphabet backwards 'Z. Y. X. W. V. U and so from Omega to Alpha', ending with 'Cool it with baboon's blood then the charm is firm and good.' It may appear on the surface as nonsense, but then all magical charms can be perceived as nonsense unless it is realised that it is the combination of words and their links to the otherworld which create the magic. This curse would have been recited several times in a ritualistic chanting manner before being delivered to its intended victim.

Whether or not involved with the occult, the Klan caused havoc in those areas where it gained strong local support. But was it involved in a bigger game? Klan links with key political players was as much discussed in the years after its formation as they are today. Exactly who was running the Klan? Was it really the alleged founders, the 'Pulaski six'? Or was it a conspiracy involving those right at the top of society? It has been suggested that the Klan had contacts with Ulysses S. Grant, the former Civil War general elected to the presidency of the United States (and also from a Scottish background, as his name implies). In January 1869 General Forrest, the Klan's Imperial Wizard, declared that the Klan had been taken over by people who had turned the organisation from its original task. He ordered masks and disguises to be destroyed and the destruction witnessed by the Grand Cyclops for the area. Anybody who went out in disguise after that could not be a member of the Klan. This was, in reality, a first move in attempting to disband the Ku Klux Klan, whose activities across a wide area were getting out of hand and posing a threat to the stability of the Southern states. And, it is said, that this road to disbandment was set on after consultation with Grant, who took office on 4 March 1869 though the presidential election had taken place the previous November.

But why would Northern leaders be involved with the Klan? In fact, there had been slaves in the Northern states as well as in the South and the white leaders of the North were no more willing to see the former slaves in control of the old Confederacy than the Southerners themselves. On top of that many of the leaders on both sides were related and mixed socially. They were part of the same leadership group and, it is suggested, all members of the same secret societies, like the Masons, which certainly had informal links with the Klan in its early years. Were there two Klans or, more likely, a Klan within a Klan? Secret societies are no strangers to the United States. We know that Freemasons played a significant role in the founding of the country, as Masonic signs on the early dollar banknotes show. And as has been recently shown the mysterious horse-whispering societies of north-east Scotland, which practised rituals with pagan overtones, spread to the United States and may also have had a direct influence on the formation of the Klan. Secret societies have been as important in the States as they have been in Europe.

On the face of it the Klan had largely collapsed by 1871 though it had certainly played a part in depriving the former slaves of the fruits of the North's victory over the Confederacy. It was to be nearly a hundred years before another serious attempt was made to give the black population in the South the legal and political rights that the white population took for granted.

For years the Klan seemed almost not to have existed, or, perhaps, it simply avoided publicity. But that changed dramatically in the 1920s following the impact made by the epic film *Birth of a Nation* which romanticised the activities of the Ku Klux Klan. But it was a different type of organisation from that of the original Klan. It had widened its targets to include a whole range of groups and organisations that it considered un-American. It became more commercially aware, making large sums from selling goods to its members. It now saw itself as enforcing a moral code, attacking adulterers and 'loose women'. Violent activity was renewed and anyone believed to be against the Klan or un-American became its target. By 1925 it was claiming a membership of four million. But bad publicity resulting from murder trials and the economic depression of the 1930s almost killed the Klan and, in 1944, it apparently disbanded. Or had it simply gone underground? The rise of the Civil Rights movement in the 1960s led to a revival. Atrocious outrages followed. Four black teenage girls were killed when a member of the Klan bombed an Alabama church where a Sunday school class was being held. Although those involved escaped justice for over twenty years, these criminal acts did much to discredit the Klan. However, the extent of Klan involvement in politics during the period from the 1920s to 1970s and beyond remains controversial. Some have claimed that it delivered votes on a big scale in those states where it had strength and links to local politicians. And that while publicly condemning the Klan even national politicians were willing to use its contacts to win over voters. It was certainly seen as a threat in some areas, which led to a determined attempt to disarm it, either directly by banning its activities or, more subtly, by banning the use of masks. Klan members were often reluctant to be publicly identified. Others, however, gloried in the notoriety. Although its influence may be discounted because its public face seemed so extreme, there is no doubt that it provided an underground link between individuals, some in positions of influence, who were opposed to granting full civil rights to the black population. In the 1980s the Klan was, on the face of it, dealt a severe blow when it was ordered to pay $7 million in compensation. Its headquarters and other assets had to be sold to cover the debt. However, in terms of the money floating in the US political system that was a drop in the bucket. There can be few who would doubt that, should the Klan be required, a river of money would be available to fund a revival. Its memory is still very much alive today as the symbol of white terror. It is one Scottish legacy to America that this ancient land of ours might wish to forget.

THIRTEEN

Murder or accident? The strange death of the Duke of Kent

WAS A REMOTE Scottish hillside the scene of the most infamous crime of the twentieth century? The last sixty years have witnessed various plane 'accidents' which have resulted in the death of a key figure whose activities have become an embarrassment. Among them are Polish prime minister Wladyslaw Sikorski in 1943, United Nations general secretary Dag Hammarskold in 1961 and Sanjay Ghandi, widely expected to become the next prime minister of India, in 1980. And then, of course, there are other 'mishaps' including the death in mysterious circumstances of Princess Diana in a Paris car crash and, closer to home, in the 1980s, the supposed suicide near a lay-by of leading Scottish nationalist William McCrae. So when, in 1942, a Sunderland flying boat exploded on a Scottish mountain and extinguished the life of George, Duke of Kent, the King's brother, had the 'perfect' crime been committed? So expertly planned that till now it has been accepted as a freak accident that, by pure chance, happened to end the life of one of the best known, but strangest, royals of the time.

A plane crash is a very convenient way of disposing of an awkward customer. There are so many moving parts on a plane that it is the ideal sabotage target. There is no room for error, so a few instruments interfered with, or a small explosion, can have devastating consequences. The destruction following the crash of a relatively flimsy machine at high speed, especially before the days of flight recorders, makes it highly unlikely that the would-be murderers, if they plan carefully, are going to be caught. The conspirators can always point the finger of blame at the pilot. 'Pilot error' is a convenient catch-all when the truth may be too unpleasant for the public to hear. Then there is the credulity factor. Who would believe in a conspiracy to murder the King's brother? And even if there were suspicions how could it be proved, especially in the situation of wartime Britain when government control of information had been tightened?

But what reason would there be to have the Duke of Kent killed? And who would dare authorise it? Such a conspiracy would have to involve individuals within the government and security services. Or at least have their tacit approval even if they took no direct part. If there was such a plan then the stakes would have to be very high indeed. The person targeted would have to be a key player in the international politics of the Second World War, as General Sikorski was. But does George, Duke of Kent fit this bill?

Kent enjoyed life in a way those born to a position of privilege take for granted. But it had also led him down some wayward paths. He became a drug addict, womaniser and entered into homosexual relationships. All in all, the brother of King George VI was a bit of a security risk and had already been rescued from potential blackmail and a host of embarrassing incidents. Money had to be paid to a young man to retrieve compromising letters written to him by Kent. At a time when homosexual relationships were illegal, he ran severe risks by visiting same-sex nightclubs.

Had the newspapers of the day been less restrained in their coverage of the royal family, his freewheeling lifestyle would have grabbed a lot of unsavoury headlines. But though he revelled in the high life, partying with star names of the day like Fred Astaire and Noel Coward, there were other facets to Kent's character. Perhaps to compensate for his life of self indulgence, he developed a social conscience. He wanted to learn more about the lives of working class people and, bizarrely, trained as a factory inspector. But he also craved excitement and, after gaining a pilot's licence, took part in various flying feats, earning quite a reputation as an adventurer. When the Second World War came along Kent was anxious to play a full part. Coming from the highest level of society, drug and alcohol addictions were no bar to joining the RAF. He was even awarded the top rank of Air Vice-Marshal.

During the war Kent was given the task of visiting RAF bases, interviewing the flight crews and listening to their complaints. No doubt the top brass believed that having a royal touring the ranks would boost morale while keeping the Duke occupied. Whether anything came of his visits is not clear, but there is no doubt that Kent himself would have liked a more influential role. He could probably see through the part he had been asked to play. He was certainly intelligent, reputedly the brightest of the royals by far. But he could have had no inkling of the disaster that lay ahead when he took an overnight sleeper from London Euston to Inverness on 24 August 1942. His intended destination was the military base at Invergordon on the Cromarty Firth. Officially, his presence at Invergordon was a continuation of his 'visitor's' role. He was supposedly heading for Reykjavik to carry out more grievance investigating. This poses a query because the trip was later described on the crash-site monument as a 'special mission' and, if he was simply continuing his usual duties, this Icelandic visit would not qualify as anything out of the ordinary. So what could this special mission have involved?

According to one source, during a conversation with his close friend – the film star Douglas Fairbanks junior who was serving in the US Navy – Kent asked if there was any way that he could be used as a liaison officer between the US Air Force and the RAF?

Exactly why Kent would have wanted such a position is not clear nor what he intended to do with it. Fairbanks had many contacts and arranged a meeting between Kent and the well known US Air Force general, 'Tooley' Spaatz. The American proposed that Kent fly to the RAF station in Iceland. He would then invite him to the nearby US base and ask him officially for his services as liaison between the two bases. Kent, apparently, agreed to the arrangement. If this is accurate then it must have been cleared at a high level. It seems unlikely that it would have been put together without consultation. Nor does such a role seem to fit in to Kent's more grandiose expectations. These reports may be a garbled version of what was actually going on. It may have even been put about as a cover story. It does suggest that there was more to Kent's Icelandic trip that August than a plan to log yet more complaints.

At Coastal Command preparations for the journey had begun the week before when the crew of a Mark III Sunderland W4026, based at Oban on the west coast of Scotland, received secret orders. According to the plane's rear gunner, Andrew Jack, 'we were a top crew the boys of M for Mike. In those few weeks before that last trip we bagged a U-boat in the Atlantic.' Jack reported that they were told, 'You are being chosen for a special mission. The Sunderland will have to be spick and span.' Coastal Command meant what they said. The Sunderland was 'beached by Gonovan Sands' and her outside was 'cleaned and tidied'. Riggers worked on her night and day. Afterwards the crew 'took her into the air. She was perfect.' The pilot was Australian Frank Goyen who, although only 25 years old, had thousands of flying hours under his belt and was an experienced airman. Since March, Goyen and his crew had been based at Oban as part of 228 Squadron. On Sunday 23 August, Goyen was instructed to take the Sunderland to the RAF base at Invergordon. The plane was flown by a direct route along the path of the Caledonian Canal through the Great Glen to its destination on the east coast of Scotland.

When Goyen landed, he was told that he was to have a famous passenger aboard his next flight. The King's brother, George, Duke of Kent. Goyen also learned his secret destination: Reykjavik. On Tuesday 25 August, just before 1 p.m., the flight got underway. It took a three-mile run along the flat of an unusually calm sea before the Sunderland gained enough lift to creep skywards, carrying with it a payload of fifteen men, over 2,000 gallons of fuel and starting a mystery that has puzzled commentators ever since.

The expected flight path should have allowed the Sunderland to stick to the coast, following the land till the Pentland Firth, at the far tip of Scotland, was reached, then turning west towards the Faroe Islands. But, for some reason which has never been satisfactorily explained, around twenty minutes into the flight the Sunderland abruptly headed inland. It was heard by people as it flew over a river glen known as Berriedale Water, though because of low cloud no one actually saw it. The Sunderland, a lumbering beast of a plane, was attempting to fly in misty conditions in an area peppered with considerable peaks, some above 2,000 feet. The plane, however, seemed to be losing height rather than seeking to leave a good margin between it and the ground and, whether due to poor visibility or not, suddenly found itself faced by a prominence known as Eagle's Rock, a hill about 800 feet above sea level. Frank Goyen no doubt attempted to avoid a collision, but it was too late for emergency action and the Sunderland thudded into the side of the ridge, cartwheeling and disintegrating as the massive wings sheared off, fuel tanks and thousands of rounds of ammunition exploding in a fireball. Incredibly, at least one man survived the impact. Rear gunner Andrew Jack, a 24-year-old Scot from Grangemouth, was thrown free as the rear turret of the plane broke off and took him clear of the explosion.

People arrived on the scene remarkably quickly, given the isolated location, but by then everyone who could be found was dead. Andrew Jack, meanwhile, dazed and disorientated had apparently wandered away from the crash site so the rescuers were unaware that there had been a survivor. His movements, which many years later he recounted in great detail, form a key puzzle in this mystery. Meanwhile at the crash site the scene presented no obvious mystery – just an all-too-clear disaster. Many of the bodies appeared burned beyond quick identification. All except one.

At this juncture the incident had appeared simply as a tragic accident. Many brave and experienced aircrews had been killed in similar non-combat situations. However, the significance of the event was about to be transformed. A local doctor, John Kennedy, arrived. He examined the bodies, all of which had been covered out of respect, checking for signs of life and recognised the face of a well-known figure. For, 'apart from a huge gash on his forehead' the head of the Duke of Kent was unmarked. Kennedy was able to confirm the identification because, rather helpfully, Kent had around his wrist a bracelet with an inscription which read, 'His Royal Highness, the Duke of Kent' followed by his address. In fact, it remains unclear as to who first identified Kent and exactly how he was recognised. Will Bethune, a special constable, claimed that it was he who found the Duke's identity bracelet. In later years Dr Kennedy stated that he had identified the Duke's body from a monogrammed cigarette case and an inscription on his wristwatch rather than from his famous looks. At any event, news of the crash soon spread and within days was reported worldwide. Tributes to the Duke poured in from across the globe.

Such a disastrous incident had to have a cause and something, or someone, would have to take the blame. The official verdict was pilot error. In a statement to the House of Commons on 7 October 1942, Sir Archibald Sinclair claimed that the accident happened because 'the aircraft was flown on a track other than indicated on the flight plan given to the pilot', adding that the plane was 'at too low an altitude to clear the rising ground'. This 'serious mistake in airmanship' was the responsibility of 'the captain of the aircraft'. Sinclair added that 'the weather encountered should have presented no difficulty to an experienced pilot'. Leaving open the possibility that it might have confused a less experienced one.

Pilot error as the explanation fitted well with a statement attributed to the survivor, Andrew Jack. He reportedly claimed that about ten minutes after take-off he heard a voice over the intercom saying, 'Let's go down and have a look.' If this is accurate, it amounts to a serious error of judgement. Why descend through mist and clouds when the standard procedure would have been to climb above it? The crew would have been aware of the pre-flight weather forecast, which indicated that the poor weather was localised. Goyen would have known that all he had to do was to continue on his planned route to reach clearer skies.

But had there ever been an instruction to 'go down and have a look'? Interviewed in 1961, Jack's version was that during the flight he made a routine test of the intercom link to the cockpit, but that afterwards he 'had no conversation with any other member of the crew or captain again'. He certainly did not admit to hearing the comment he allegedly heard. In fact, Jack's account of 1961 gives a clearer, if more sinister, hint of what really happened, and it had nothing to do with Frank Goyen's flying skills.

Kent's death in isolation may have been a simple accident. But if it wasn't isolated? If it was part of a chain then it opens up the possibility that something more sinister was at work. A link in the chain could be the mysterious death in July 1943 of General Wladyslawl Sikorski, prime minister of the Polish government-in-exile in London and commander-in-chief of the Polish forces. Sikorski, despite the contribution made by his countrymen in the fight against Hitler, had become a thorn in the flesh of the Allied governments. Both British Prime Minister Winston Churchill and US President Franklin Roosevelt were desperate to keep the Soviet Union in the war with Germany and part of the Russian 'price' was territorial demands on Poland once the war had been won. Sikorski was bitterly opposed to any concessions to the Soviet Union and had been using the notorious Katyn massacre as a stick with which to beat the Russians. In 1942 occupying German forces discovered a mass grave in the forests around Katyn. Several thousand Polish army officers had been shot in the head and their bodies dumped in pits. There was no doubt, even at the time, that the dead men were prisoners of war held by the Russians, and then executed by them. However, the Russians blamed the Germans for the atrocity and branded Sikorski pro-German. The situation was one of acute concern to Britain and America.

The problem was solved with the death in a plane crash of Sikorski. He was a passenger in a four-engine Liberator transport which went down minutes after taking off from the British airbase at Gibraltar, landing in the Mediterranean almost within sight of the shore. Across European political circles the firm belief was that Sikorski had been assassinated and the plane sabotaged. His death appeared much too convenient for the Allies. And Sikorski had enjoyed close links with the Duke of Kent. Right up to the time of his death Kent had been pro-Polish and was regarded as an ally of an independent Poland. It has even been claimed that Sikorski had offered Kent the Polish throne once the war was over. A symbolic gesture, if it was made. However, had Kent hinted that he was seriously considering it, and the Russians been aware of it, it would have been severely damaging to Anglo-Soviet relations. At the time of Kent's accident the war had been going badly for the Allies. The Germans were still advancing in Russia. The Battle of El Alamein, the turning point in the war, was still two months away. Poland was not an issue that Britain and the US intended to fall out over with their Russian allies.

But months before Sikorski died, and very soon after Kent's death, another mysterious crash occurred also involving a Sunderland. On 4 September 1942, two weeks after the Eagle's Rock incident, a young Scottish journalist, Fred Nancarrow, died in a plane crash when the Sunderland he was a passenger in reportedly ran out of fuel and came down near the island of Tiree off the west coast of Scotland. The plane, like the one in which Kent was a passenger, was from 228 Squadron. Nancarrow specialised in covering aviation and on the day of his death was 'representing his newspaper' on an 'operational flight in a coastal command aircraft'. The engagement had clearly been pre-arranged and Nancarrow 'left on the flight with great enthusiasm, accepting the hazards of the men whose courage and devotion to duty he had so often described in vivid and intimate articles', according to his obituary. Nancarrow had written a history of Glasgow's 602 fighter squadron and was working on another book at the time of his death, but that hardly seems an enterprise that, on the face of it, would put his life in danger. Unless there was some spectacular information that he intended to include in his planned publication.

The sympathies of leading members of the royal family towards Hitler's Germany have been the subject of speculation. In

September 1938, on the return of Chamberlain from Munich with an agreement with Hitler that seemed to provide for future peace, George VI and Queen Elizabeth appeared with him on the balcony at Buckingham Palace to celebrate the event. A clear political statement that they did not want to see war with Germany. But had it gone further? After the downfall of Germany, all those who had attempted to build good relations with the Nazis made strenuous efforts to conceal the fact. However, there is little doubt that, in the first few years of the war, before the defeat of Germany seemed inevitable and for ideological reasons, there were people with influence who wanted to negotiate a peace with Germany. They saw Hitler as a bulwark against both the Soviet Union and a potential international-communist-revolution. It has been suggested that Kent was involved in these peace overtures. He was a close confidante of his brother, David, Edward VIII – who abdicated in 1936 after a very short reign – and who certainly gave the impression at the time that he admired Hitler's Germany.

So had Nancarrow at the time of his death been researching the involvement of the Duke of Kent in the alleged 'Peace Party' plot? It was this shadowy group of top people, including leading politicians and members of the aristocracy such as the Duke of Hamilton, who were suspected of encouraging Rudolf Hess to fly to Scotland in May 1941 to negotiate peace with Britain. Nancarrow's first book, published in 1942, had simply dealt with the exploits of the Glasgow-based 602 fighter squadron, especially its role in the Battle of Britain. He had not touched on either the Hess landing or the death of the Duke of Kent. However, the foreword to the book was written by Sir Patrick Dollan, Glasgow's lord provost. In it Dollan wrote of his 'pleasure of being 'attached' to 602 Squadron since the beginning of the war' and that he had 'met most of the pilots and ground crews on and off duty'. Dollan added: 'I shall always treasure the recollection of hours spent with 602 at the stations and in recreation rooms'. It is clear that Dollan enjoyed a close relationship with the squadron and was in a position to pick up speculation about incidents involving aircraft. He no doubt took a close interest in the mysterious arrival of Rudolf Hess and the death of the Duke of Kent. This interest in aviation explains his link with Fred Nancarrow. And in Nancarrow's book there is evidence that Dollan may have been in a position to learn a lot more about the activities connected with the alleged Peace Party. Opposite page eleven there is a photo captioned, 'Three Leaders of 602 pose with Sir Patrick Dollan at Glasgow City Chamber. Left to right they are Wing Commander Farquhar, Group Captain the Duke of Hamilton and Squadron Leader Johnstone.' The presence of the Duke of Hamilton alongside Dollan points to a potential link between Nancarrow, the Hess landing and Kent's death. Hess had intended landing at Dungavel House, Hamilton's residence lying to the south of Glasgow. The Duke of Hamilton was the man Hess insisted that he wanted to speak to after he parachuted from his Messerschmitt and was captured. Hamilton may or may not have been involved in a peace party, but if he was in touch with Dollan it opens up the possibility that Dollan was in a position to gather information that he could pass to the man with a passion for aviation-related stories, Fred Nancarrow.

Nancarrow's first book effectively ended with the RAF's victory over the Luftwaffe in the Battle of Britain in the autumn of 1941. Patrick Dollan was suspicious of a pro-German peace party amongst the British upper classes. It is not known whether Nancarrow shared these views. However, with his contacts it is possible to see how an air crash in mysterious circumstances, killing a well known royal, could have intrigued an up-and-coming journalist like Nancarrow whose early death at 29 was even noted in the London *Times*. Nancarrow's contacts with aviation and politics could have allowed him to act as a channel for explosive information even in the regime of heavy censorship experienced in wartime Britain.

But in the murky world of high-level politics could Kent's strange death centre not on Hitler's Germany, but the Soviet Union? It was only after the war that the extent to which our security services had been penetrated by Soviet agents became clear, or was at least made public. Whether it was known about beforehand and ignored because of the importance of keeping the Soviet Union in the war against Germany remains unclear. Several of those involved in the spy rings were homosexual, including Anthony Blunt whose activities as a Soviet agent were not publicly unmasked until 1979, and then only with reluctance by the Thatcher government. This could be understandable as Blunt had for many years been in charge of the Queen's vast private-art-collection and even before the war had moved in royal circles. It has also been publicly claimed that back in the 1930s and 1940s Blunt and Kent were lovers. Kent's many indiscretions were well known to the authorities. He was both a blatant liability and a loose cannon. If the government was aware that information was dripping through to the Russians, Kent's involvement with any peace-inclined group, his association with the troublesome anti-Soviet hawk, Sikorski, could have been extremely awkward. In 1942 and 1943 the intentions of Stalin could not be definitely known. Any actions that would weaken Soviet resolve or provide an excuse for a separate peace with Germany would have been stamped on.

So could the rarefied atmosphere of high politics explain another enduring mystery of the crash, the behaviour of Andrew Jack? Jack was the sole survivor of the disaster, owing his life to the fact that the tail section of the Sunderland broke off and threw his rear turret clear of the ensuing fireball. The plane had taken off at 1.10 p.m. from Invergordon and crashed at about 1.30 p.m., twenty minutes later. It had travelled around sixty miles and came down about three and a half miles inland from the coastal village of Dunbeath. There were no witnesses to the impact but several people heard the crash. There is a dispute, however, as to who did what in the immediate aftermath. According to Norman Glass, a local historian, 'an angler . . . three quarters of a mile away' was the first to act. He might have been fishing in the only stretch of enclosed water in the area, Borgue Loch. The fisherman went to the house of a local gamekeeper, James MacEwan who in turn contacted the police. However, those generally credited with raising the alarm are shepherds David and Hugh Morrison, father and son. Hugh Morrison rode on his motorbike to the village of Dunbeath, where the police and Dr John Kennedy were informed of the incident. A number of search parties were apparently then organised. One was made up of local people and representatives of the local military. This was probably the group that met up with David Morrison. According to Morrison's account, 'I myself went towards the spot where I thought the plane had crashed. Within a short time I was joined by a party of village folk'. This group reached the site no later than one and a half hours after the crash. Soon after two special constables, Will Bethune and James Sunderland, appeared. They were followed by a third party that included Dr Kennedy.

As far as the search parties were aware there had been no survivors. But twenty-three hours later, rear gunner Andrew Jack turned up at Ramcraigs, a hamlet beside the A9 main road, a little more than two miles from the crash site. He had, apparently, spent almost a day wandering through the hills. He was missing a jacket, shoes and trousers, all of which he had himself discarded, and was badly burned about the head and body.

On the face of it, to take a day to find your way to safety after a crash on a remote hillside might not seem unlikely. However, when the account of Jack's movements, as he himself gave them, is examined a mystery does clearly emerge. One odd aspect is Jack's reticence about events. He gave only one lengthy interview and that was as late as 1961, nineteen years after the crash, and at which time he was working as an air traffic controller at Prestwick Airport. This may have been natural reserve, but the suspicion has lingered that he was holding back for reasons of his own, especially as he was not called to give evidence at the official inquiry into the disaster. This is an 'oversight' which can only suggest that the information he would have given would have contradicted the verdict of 'pilot error'. Andrew Jack comes across as an honourable man who would not have acted on such a matter off his own bat.

So what were Andrew Jack's movements after the Sunderland collided with Eagle's Rock? In addition to Jack's own version, there is an account given by his sister Nancy in the 1980s. According to Nancy, Jack had told her that 'his turret broke away from the body of the aircraft and was thrown clear'. At this time the plane had not yet burst into flames and he found that he was able to walk, having been fortunate to escape serious injury. Then, however, he saw the Sunderland on fire. Nancy claimed that

Andrew was badly burned attempting to pull seven bodies, including that of the Duke of Kent, from the wreckage. Only one of the seven men was alive, the flight engineer, who was bleeding badly. Andrew had explained to Nancy that he was unable to assist the flight engineer and his only thought was to go for help though he first covered the bodies with tarpaulin. He described to Nancy the desolation of the scene. He was surrounded by mountains and had no idea where he was. Before Andrew left the wreckage to seek help, he lay down and rested. He couldn't remember for how long. Having wandered off and got nowhere he spent the night sleeping in the bracken. The next day as he stumbled along he saw a white crofter's cottage ahead of him and managed to pull himself under a wire fence into the garden. Eighty-three-year-old Mrs Elsie Sutherland found Andrew lying beside her cottage in a state of collapse.

The account given by Nancy adds to details given by Andrew, but also injects some confusion. The main source of information about Andrew's actions in the aftermath of the disaster is an interview he gave in 1961. He never claimed publicly that he had pulled bodies from the wreckage of the Sunderland. And he could not poss-ibly have covered them with tarpaulin even had it been available because when the first rescue group arrived the bodies were uncovered. They did not give any indication either that the bodies had been pulled from, rather than thrown free, from the wreckage. So was his sister's recollection faulty? It might seem so as this was an account given in the 1980s, forty years after the event and by then Andrew Jack had been dead for several years so it would not have been possible to put these matters to him. On the other hand, Nancy stated that she was at home in Grangemouth when the parents of Frank Goyen, the Sunderland's pilot, paid a visit just after the end of the war. She clearly had the opportunity to discuss the crash with her brother. Nancy also drew attention to the fact that Andrew Jack had suffered extensive burns including facial damage. These injuries required skin-graft operations, which were carried out at Bangour Hospital near Edinburgh. There must have been significant burning because, according to Nancy, when she asked Andrew to be the best man at her wedding on 31 December 1942 he was reluctant to do it because of the appearance of his face.

So when could Andrew have received these burn injuries? According to his account, and the description of the site after the crash, his turret was thrown free from the body of the plane. This must have been the reason for his survival. But it also meant that he escaped the explosion which set the plane alight. So his serious burns may not have been received at the point of impact. They could have been received when Andrew, as he told Nancy, scoured the wreckage for survivors. This suggests that Jack, though undoubtedly shocked and injured, was in charge of his senses to the extent that he could attempt a rescue. And, furthermore, that he spent some time after the crash at the site, both of which are significant facts in the context of the following twenty-three hours.

Much has been made of the crash site's remoteness. But within ninety minutes of the incident, not only had witnesses, of whom there were several, gone for help, but also a search party had arrived on the spot. This may have been a site which was not accessible by road and only by rough tracks and on foot, but the definition as a remote site has to be qualified. On the hillside standing, as I have done, at the site of the crash there is a sense of isolation with considerable heights to the south and west. Moorland stretches north-east before running into another hill beyond which are the hamlets of Borgue and Ramscraigs. The only sign of habitation is a crumbling broch at the foot of the hill. But it is by no stretch of the imagination the isolation of a crash site in the Rockies. In fact the plane had come down only two miles from the main road between Inverness and Wick. With my wife I walked the two miles from the end of a farm track at Borgue to the crash site, marked by a cross, in a little over an hour. From the hill beside Borgue Loch where farm cottages have stood for decades the crash site is clearly visible. From here it is only a forty-minute walk across rough ground to the site. Furthermore, though the crash site is blocked by mountains at one side, on the other, looking east, the coast is clearly visible. However, at the time of the accident the weather, it is said, was misty; even a 'thick fog' according to some accounts. It was on the basis of the alleged poor visibility that the Sunderland came down. And it could also explain Andrew Jack's lack of success in heading more quickly towards a safe destination.

But how bad was visibility below cloud level? Andrew Jack told Nancy that he was 'surrounded by mountains'. If the mist had been as dense as some commentators have claimed, Jack would not have been able to see these mountains the nearest of which is half a mile from the Sunderland's impact point. Jack's description of his movements through the hills makes no reference to a 'dense fog' or, indeed, a mist of any kind hampering visibility. It is also hard to understand how the crash site would have been so readily found by the rescue parties had the mist been as thick as claimed. Would anglers and shepherds, witnesses to the disaster, be on the hillside in severely misty conditions? It is true that some accounts mention a 'fog', but others involved in the rescue make no mention of it. There might well have been a bit of a sea mist, but it certainly doesn't seem to have been so impenetrable as to prevent relatively long-range visibility or the passage of sound. In short, people on the hills that afternoon could see and hear each other for some considerable distance. The emphasis on poor visibility at ground level simply followed through from the explanation, rapidly circulating, that flying through thick cloud had been the cause of the pilot misjudging the plane's height above the ground.

In the aftermath of the crash Jack must have taken some minutes to re-orientate himself, although there is no way of knowing just exactly how long after the impact he came to. If he then pulled bodies from the wreckage, as his sister claimed, and, following that exertion, lain down to rest even more time must have passed. Andrew Jack had only to follow RAF instructions to crash survivors to stay on site, and within ninety minutes help would have been there. And some time before that he would surely have seen and heard the first rescue party approaching. Andrew could not be aware that that would be the outcome. But if he did everything that he described to his sister he must have seriously narrowed the gap between his leaving the site and the arrival of help. Even if Jack left the site at 2 p.m., say thirty minutes after the impact, at least six hours of daylight remained. There were also various groups of people heading in the direction of the crash even by then. But Jack, apparently, did not see or hear any of these people even though they could only have been within a mile or so of him making an audible level of noise. And no one in the rescue parties had sight of him. Jack disappeared so completely that no one had the remotest idea that he had survived. Can this be explained simply by the supposed misty conditions?

But the actual extent of the mist may in fact be irrelevant because Andrew Jack could never have been much more than a mile from the crash site for almost the whole of the time he left Eagle's Rock. When he woke the following morning even the site itself may have been visible as he tried to go for help. By this time not only had at least three rescue teams visited the site but also the remains of the Sunderland were under guard. People were swarming over the site. In that quiet countryside sound travels a great distance. Even today you can almost hear a pin drop. But Andrew Jack neither heard nor saw any of this activity. How could that be? In fact, an examination of the terrain around the crash site shows that Andrew Jack's account of his movements is seriously flawed.

Jack said he had no recollection of leaving the wreck of the Sunderland, but remembers finding himself at the foot of Eagle's Rock beside a burn. The burn leads a short distance into Berriedale Water, a river which runs towards the North Sea. This is the only river in the area and must be the one that Jack describes wading across twice before eventually settling down in some ferns to sleep. It can't be known exactly where he had reached by night-fall, several hours after the disaster, but it is clear he was no distance from the crash site even though he talked about walking for miles and miles. Had he, in fact, done this he would have reached the head of Berriedale Water and long before then come across various cottages. He would certainly have been in a different direction from Ramscraigs where he eventually emerged.

When Jack woke the following morning, Wednesday 26 August, he set off once more to find help. It was, as he himself described, glorious weather. Visibility would have been excellent. Andrew Jack again recounts walking for miles, does not see another soul all this time, before climbing a hill and finding himself on a plateau. He then continued walking and eventually saw half a mile off a cottage, at Ramscraigs. It is clear from the layout of the area that Jack would have had to have been very close to the crash site to locate a cottage at Ramscraigs. Had he wandered further south, but towards the sea coast, he would have come across a number of other cottages, none of which he mentions and, anyway, to which he would surely have gone to for help. He also makes no mention of seeing Borgue Loch, lying about a mile from the crash site, and the only loch in the immediate area. Had he climbed between Borgue Loch and a hill called Creagan Reamhar he would have noticed several dwellings lying between him and Ramscraigs. Any further south of this location and Ramscaigs would not have been visible. Incredible though it may seem, the only route that Jack could have followed to arrive at a viewpoint where only the cottage at Ramscraigs could be seen would have been to go over the ground within sight of Eagle's Rock. But if he had gone that way he would surely have seen the crash site with people around it.

So had something else happened on the mountainside? Had Andrew Jack already been found by the military personnel swarming over the site and his arrival, twenty-three hours later, set up to hide the fact? This would give time to debrief the only survivor of this disaster and explain to him why he must keep quiet about the events. While not impossible it seems unlikely. Interestingly, Jack, according to Nancy, thought he might be awarded a medal, but why expect one if all that had happened was that he had been the fortunate survivor of an otherwise fatal crash? It seems more likely that he believed that he had rendered the authorities, even the royal family, a service, one that should have been recognised in some way.

So had Jack overheard something during the flight which explained beyond doubt why the Sunderland had crashed? According to Jack's recollection of the fatal trip, after they took off the weather was reasonable as he could recall seeing the 'hills of

Ross-shire and Sutherland . . . a long way off and blue black'. The weather though rapidly worsened and 'drizzle . . . cut down visibility really to a minimum'. But visibility could not have gone completely because Jack claimed 'for nineteen minutes or so I could see the coastline below me crawling backwards like a slowly unravelling map'. There is no suggestion that the plane was heading inland. But 'then the cloud came in. We were enveloped in a grey, dark mist'. Jack then sensed that they were losing height though he noticed that the engines were on full power. However, there was no sense of urgency and Jack claimed that he 'heard a chortle on the intercom and some words about it being lousy weather'. He remembered nothing after that except waking up on the hillside. It is clear from Jack's account that the disaster was sudden and completely unexpected.

Jack speculated that Frank Goyen may have been thinking that he was still over the coast and gone down out of the cloud to take a look. Such a manoeuvre would be contrary to common sense if Goyen thought he was anywhere inland. As the title suggests Coastal Command was dedicated to defending our coasts and a Sunderland's main job was patrolling the coastal routes. Goyen was no stranger to flying a route like this perched between sea and land. So why did the plane deviate so disastrously from its intended course? One possibility is sabotage. The plane had been given a thorough going over before the flight from Oban to Invergordon as Jack described. Ample time to interfere with its controls. However, it had been taken up the Great Glen on 23 August without incident. If something was done to the plane it must have been on the evening of the twenty-fourth when it was berthed at Invergordon. There is no indication of how closely it was watched or how it was dealt with overnight. The timing of the crash with the cloud cover may have been purely coincidental. The downing in December 1988 of Pan Am flight 103 at Lockerbie was appallingly fortuitous. The plane was meant to crash into the Atlantic. The same could have been true of W4026. Maybe it was intended that the Sunderland should come down over the sea to Reykjavik where the chances of survival would have been nil and well away from prying eyes.

Jack may have heard the sound of an explosion on the aircraft, heard the reaction of the pilot and maybe even Kent to the dramatic turn of events. Perhaps he listened in those last few seconds to comments that suggested that the downing of the plane was no accident. Even guessed that they were all meant to die and that his own survival was going to be a considerable embarrassment to the authorities. So that Andrew Jack's twenty-three missing hours were not the result of a survivor wandering lost in the countryside to turn up at a hamlet only two miles from the crash site, but a deliberate attempt to hide until such time as he could gather his thoughts. Jack wanted to avoid confronting representatives of the military so he fled the crash site, and consciously hid from rescue parties, as he would have no idea who they were made up of. And only revealed himself when he arrived at a civilian cottage where he guessed he would be safe. Later, he tried to explain his disappearance by fanciful accounts of walking for mile after mile. The first doctor at the scene, John Kennedy, expressed amazement that Jack had managed to cover the two miles from the crash site unaware as to just how far the rear gunner was going to claim that he had walked. In 1961 Jack himself stated that the rescuers arrived five hours after the impact; information that was clearly untrue. But it did leave a bigger imaginary time-gap, one long enough to give Jack ample opportunity to leave the site before anyone else arrived and explain why neither he nor the rescuers ever caught sight of one another.

Sixty years on the flight of W4026 remains a mystery. And that is because pieces of the jigsaw are still missing. The British public has never been properly informed of the full extent of Soviet penetration of the British establishment and their network of agents. As late as the 1960s, according to the KGB defector Vasili Mitrokhin, at least one Soviet agent was actively reconnoitring Scotland for sabotage targets and selecting potential individuals to carry out these attacks. So what were the Soviets up to in Scotland during World War Two? Would they have been as relieved as the British government to have Kent, the international loose cannon, removed from the scene? Neither do we have the full history of the Sunderland's last ten minutes in the air. Nor the purpose of Kent's 'special mission'. And finally, we are missing a full account of the Duke of Kent's activities during the war. The royal family has never allowed an official biography of George to be written. It suggests that there is plenty still to hide.